# The Danger of Change

**This work represents a watershed in Kleinian theory. The Author beautifully integrates traditional Kleinian concepts, particularly those of the paranoid-schizoid and depressive positions, with the occurrence of infantile and childhood trauma and/or deprivations. His clinical examples are extraordinarily convincing. All mental health workers will greatly benefit from reading this book**

James S. Grotstein, MD, Clinical Professor of Psychiatry David Geffen School of Medicine, UCLA, Training and Supervising Analyst Los Angeles Psychoanalytic Society/Institute and The Psychoanalytic Center of California

Confusing clinical standoffs, loyalty to self-destruction and abrupt terminations are challenging and under-examined problems for the modern psychoanalytic practitioner. *The Danger of Change* is a timely book that addresses the so-called resistant patient so many clinicians are familiar with.

Robert Waska blends theory based on Melanie Klein's classical stance with the more contemporary Freudian/Kleinian school, to demonstrate how to understand patients that are resistant to progress. Divided into four sections, this book covers.

- Reluctant Patients and the Fight against Change: Caught between the Paranoid and Depressive World
- Greed and the Dangers of Change
- Interruptions to the Process of Change: Loss, Envy, and the Death Instinct
- Working toward Change in the Face of Overwhelming Odds

Extensive and detailed clinical material is used to bring clarity to subjects including symbolism, conflict resolution, projective identification, the depressive and paranoid positions, change and trust.

*The Danger of Change* brings hope and clarity to cases involving patients who experience progress as a threat to their emotional well-being. It will be of great interest to all practising psychoanalysts, as well as those studying psychoanalytic theory and practice.

**Robert Waska** is a Psychoanalyst and Psychoanalytic Psychotherapist in private practice in San Francisco and Marin County. He is author of several books, including *Projective Identification in the Clinical Setting* and *Real People, Real Problems, Real Solutions*.

# The Danger of Change

## The Kleinian Approach with Patients Who Experience Progress as Trauma

Robert Waska

Routledge
Taylor & Francis Group

LONDON AND NEW YORK

First published 2006 by Routledge,
27 Church Road, Hove, East Sussex, BN3 2FA

Simultaneously published in the USA and Canada
by Routledge
270 Madison Avenue, New York NY 10016

*Routledge is an imprint of the Taylor & Francis Group, an informa business*

Typeset in Times by Garfield Morgan, Rhayader, Powys, UK
Printed and bound in Great Britain by TJ International Ltd Padstow, Cornwall
Paperback cover design by Sandra Heath

This publication has been produced with paper manufactured to strict
environmental standards and with pulp derived from sustainable forests.

*British Library Cataloguing in Publication Data*
A catalogue record for this book is available from the British Library

*Library of Congress Cataloging in Publication Data*
Waska, Robert T.
   The danger of change : the Kleinian approach with patients who
experience progress as trauma / Robert Waska.
         p. cm.
   Includes bibliographical references and index.
   ISBN 0-415-38584-9 – ISBN 0-415-38585-7 (pb.)
   1. Resistance (Psychoanalysis) 2. Psychoanalysis. 3. Klein, Melanie. 4.
Change (Psychology) I. Title.

RC489.R49W37 2006
616.89'17–dc22

                                                      2005054337

ISBN13: 978-0-415-38584-8 hbk
ISBN13: 978-0-415-38585-5 pbk

ISBN10: 0-415-38584-9 hbk
ISBN10: 0-415-38585-7 pbk

# Contents

*Personal statement*     vii

*Introduction*     ix

**PART I**
**Reluctant patients and the fight against change: caught between the paranoid and depressive world**     1

1   I hear you knocking but you can't come in     3

2   Mistrust of the good object     16

3   Fighting off the good object     32

4   Problems in receiving     49

**PART II**
**Greed and the dangers of change**     65

5   Melanie Klein's theory of greed     67

6   The frightening rumble of psychic hunger     79

7   The impossible dream and the endless nightmare     91

8   Greed, idealization, and insatiability     106

9   Setting the bar too high     120

**PART III**
**Interruptions to the process of change: loss,
envy, and the death instinct** 135

10  The clinical advantage of the death instinct 137

11  Acting out and the death instinct 152

12  Borderline and psychotic patients 166

13  Oral deprivation, envy, and sadism 182

**PART IV**
**Working toward change in the face of
overwhelming odds** 193

14  A case study of borderline anxiety 195

15  Bargains, treaties, and delusions 207

16  Symbolization and the good object 224

*Summary* 238
*Bibliography* 243
*Index* 250

# Personal statement

First, I want to acknowledge the helpful suggestions, patience, and support my wife Elizabeth provides. She continues to be both the rainbow in my life and the pot of gold at the end of it.

Secondly, I wish to express gratitude to all my patients. In the work I do, I try to help them in their struggles. Often, I am successful. However, they are always able to teach me something about the depth and complexity of the human experience. The case studies in the book are all written in a manner that disguises, conceals, and distorts the true identity of these individuals. Confidentiality is maintained in all accounts.

# Introduction

There are some patients suffering from chronic and often severe symptoms who enter analytic treatment and make progress, but then come to a standstill. As time goes on and the situation is explored, it becomes evident that the standstill is more of a standoff. The patient displays a marked resistance to taking in new experiences, to making changes, and to seeing the self or the object in different ways. In Chapter 1, case material and a review of a classic paper on negative therapeutic reactions are used to show the differences between this immobilization within the depressive position (Klein 1935) and a more paranoid-schizoid (Klein 1946) standoff. While many patients are struggling with both internal situations, the case material shows how one core conflict usually predominates.

Patients who resist the progressive, integrative aspects of psychoanalysis and who appear to not want to change can be understood by many theoretical perspectives. Chapter 2 identifies these patients as still grappling with paranoid-schizoid turmoil, but also trying to navigate the choppy seas of the depressive position without yet being emotionally capable. Developmentally, these patients were forced to face the burdens of intensive depressive issues. As children, they tried to care for their objects when they, as children, really needed to be cared for. Feelings of unresolvable loss or abandonment, as well as an urgency to forgive their objects when anger was more appropriate, were part of the ego trauma created by primitive and premature experiences within the depressive realm. As a result, these individuals have problems with allowing goodness, growth, dependence, change, and reliance on the good object of the analyst. The good object ends up representing something manipulative and persecutory, rather than healthy, restoring, and soothing.

So, a particular transference standoff occurs with some patients. They have a very strong bond with or special allegiance to a bad object, a rejecting other, which leaves them feeling angry, abandoned, and persecuted. This also results in a strong alliance to the image of a bad self. Historically, as well as clinically, this comes out of a strong oral demand for an all-knowing, perfect, and completely caring parent. The search for union with a more utopian object overshadows the more available good object with its natural mix of gratifying and frustrating traits. Therefore, these patients cry out for idealized relationships and reject more available, realistic good objects. Authentic contact with the good, normal object is rejected, dismissed, and devalued. In addition, many of these patients have had a historical lack of good object experiences which would have led to a healthy counterbalance to the bad objects in their life. Instead, the lack of internalized goodness has left them all the more dismissive and disbelieving of the good object and its value.

More case material is used in Chapter 3 to show how this occurs in the analytic setting. This material illustrates the motives, phantasies, and external histories that create the need for this hungry↔rejecting, demanding↔distancing approach to relationships. The transference is grossly affected by this refusal of the good object and the good self.

These patients show a marked inability to bond with, use, or locate the good object. Variations of this problem are explored in Chapter 4. Many of these cases involve a childhood history of being controlled, manipulated, or abused by one or both parents. In analytic treatment, the patient establishes a transference which is directed at avoiding, denying, and blocking out the good object. As a consequence, the process of identification with a reasonably good, fallible, but lovable and loving object is relinquished. Theoretical understanding of this problem is addressed and linked to methods of treatment. In particular, the pathological interplay between the paranoid-schizoid position and the depressive position is examined.

Chapter 5 uses one extensive case report to illustrate the clinical benefits of Melanie Klein's theories regarding greed. Klein's concepts are utilized in the case report, but certain aspects of her ideas are also extended.

Case material in Chapter 6 demonstrates how many patients are desperately struggling with feelings of envy and greed. For some, greed is experienced as a constant hunger, a feeling of being empty and alone. Some of these patients can be aggressive or resentful in the way they feel and act. They are determined to take what they feel is rightly theirs. Other such patients are much more conflicted about their greedy phantasies. This chapter focuses on patients who are fearful and anxious about the greedy urges and strivings that shape their inner world.

In Chapter 7, case material is used to continue exploring the clinical and theoretical aspects of greed as it manifests in the psychoanalytic situation. Excessive splitting and reliance on projective identification are part of a paranoid-schizoid cycle in which the ego searches for an ideal object and an idealized self. Greed, fueled by oral aggression and envy, attacks the fragile ideal object and turns it into a retaliatory enemy. Resulting phantasies of loss, persecution, and emotional starvation are examined.

Chapter 8 takes a look at patients who try to reach an internal vision of an ideal object they can bond with and find emotional nourishment from.

The way they go about this quest is desperate and aggressive, because of underlying pathological levels of greed. This greed is bound with anxieties of loss, envy, and guilt, all experienced within the paranoid-schizoid position. These patients rely heavily on the defenses of splitting and projective identification, which are used to maintain the phantasy of an ideal object or an ideal self. Some patients wish to merge with this wonderful object. With an insatiable hunger, they empty it of all its goodness. Others turn these urges inward and strive to become perfect themselves. As Melanie Klein has pointed out, these strong cycles of greed and envy generate even greater levels of persecutory fear.

Case material is used in Chapter 9 to show how these greedy phantasies of ideal nourishment, power, and security bring on paranoid fears of rejection, loss, and attack. These patients feel they never get what they need, want, or deserve. They have unrealistic expectations of themselves, as far as how much they should achieve or receive. They also hold their objects to high demands of love, attention, and reassurance.

In Chapter 10, case material focuses on the clinical manifestations of the death instinct. The importance of the acknowledgment and subsequent analysis of the death instinct within the clinical setting is examined. The death instinct has been debated, devalued, criticized, and ignored by various analysts and analytic schools. Nevertheless, it remains a viable part of Kleinian theory. This chapter explores the advantages of the concept from both a clinical and theoretical perspective. Due to their self-destructive ways, certain patients seem to create difficult and destructive transference–countertransference patterns. Clinically, they need a period of intrapsychic and interpersonal containment, followed by analysis of the death instinct in its clinical manifestations, followed by the working through of primitive states of paranoid-schizoid loss and persecution. The death instinct can be a major factor in patients who see change as dangerous. Therefore, it becomes an important clinical focus.

With certain borderline and psychotic patients who see change as dangerous and do what they can to resist it, clinical material reveals three overlapping areas critical to the working-through process. These three transference layers are explored in Chapters 11 and 12. Acting out predominates in the first phase. Rigorous containment, support, and verbal holding is required. This is done in a psychoanalytic manner as opposed to the use of suggestion or manipulation. Many of these patients terminate prematurely. The second phase consists of the patient's defensive use of the death instinct to ward off or banish certain aspects of their mental functioning. This difficult standoff between parts of the patient's mind becomes replicated in the transference as well as acted out in other external situations and relationships. The third phase shows a bedrock problem with paranoid-schizoid fears of loss and primitive experiences of guilt. This includes fears of persecution and annihilation. Some patients abort treatment in the first or second phase and never work through their phantasies and feelings of loss. Nevertheless, much intrapsychic and interpersonal progress is possible. Given the instability and chaotic nature of these patients' object relations, the analyst must be cautiously optimistic and realize the potential to help the patient even when presented with less than optimal conditions.

The analytic situation is an intimate study of the evolving intra-psychic and interpersonal relationship between analyst and patient. Chapter 13 examines the patients who find the idea of a back-and-forth exchange fundamentally intolerable. These are patients who are enraged and pained by the concept of giving in any capacity. Careful analysis reveals phantasies of wanting to control and feed on the analyst's emotional nutrients that the patient feels the analyst has denied him. The feeling of having been locked out of the analyst/mother's resources creates resentment and desires for revenge. Envy of what the analyst has and does not provide shapes a transference reaction in which the patient is always demanding and simultaneously being careful to never be dependent or forthcoming.

Borderline patients present with particular treatment problems and require close, devoted understanding of their often chaotic and shifting intra-psychic conflicts. Many of these patients act out, making it difficult to maintain an analytic process. In fact, many terminate early on. When they do stay for longer periods, they exhibit particular constellations of defense, anxiety, and conflict. One extensive case report is used in Chapter 14 to examine the overlapping cycles of treatment with this population. Frequently, self-destructive acting out is present in the transference and extra-transference. These ways of relating to the self and the object are mobilized within the vehicle of projective identification and are best understood as primitive defenses against core phantasies of loss and persecution.

Chapter 15 examines patients who have experienced traumatic ties with their maternal object. As a result, these patients demand defensive and complex relationships with certain aspects of that object. After projecting and introjecting experiences of loss, envy, and disappointment, the ego is left with a highly unstable object relation. The ego expels this toxic situation through projective identification, splitting, and denial, yet clings to the portions of that object out of necessity, loyalty, and fear. Persecutory anxieties and depressive tensions lead the ego to strike an internal bargain with the object, or portions of it, in exchange for a fragile homeostasis. This inner negotiation is examined by redefining the concept of compromise formation, using object relations theory. A case is studied for clarification.

Chapter 16 examines patients who struggle with the acceptance of, connection to, or identification with, a good object who provides a containment-symbolization function. This is manifested as a standoff, a resistance, and a denial of the good object . Subsequently, this is also a denial of the symbolization process that is part of healthy development. This is usually due to troubled family histories and a destructive projective identification process.

The ego defensively blocks acknowledgment of any symbolizing capacity within the self and within the maternal object out of envy, fear of rejection, and dread of persecution. Destruction of symbolization and the experience of goodness within the self or in the object provides an artificial respite from the threat of annihilation yet quickly brings on even greater levels of internal chaos and anxiety. Case material is used to illustrate these points.

# Part I

# Reluctant patients and the fight against change: caught between the paranoid and depressive world

# Chapter 1

# I hear you knocking but you can't come in*

There are patients I have treated with the analytic method[1] who, at some point in the process, refuse to explore, reflect, change, or even consider new ways of relating to themselves or others.

Sooner or later, change becomes the enemy. Taking in a new, more successful or hopeful object is avoided and they cling to the view of the self as bad. Change, growth, and the creation of a more friendly or enjoyable internal world are fought off. Of course, this manifests in various external difficulties and dysfunctional relationships. In the transference, the analytic relationship begins to feel like a debate, a duel, or a dead-end. At first, this anti-growth attitude may look like the patient is simply feeling unable or too frightened to change. However, I wish to emphasize the more active refusal against life and progress. Indeed, the successful analysis of these difficult patients seems to lie in the ongoing interpretation of their active participation in this psychic standoff.

In the psychoanalytic literature, these types of patients have been studied from several vantage points. Freud (1918) felt it had to do with rebellion and later conceptualized it as part of the death instinct (1923). K. Horney (1936) emphasized issues of competition, fear of success, and the ideas of progress leading to abandonment. Melanie Klein (1957) thought envy was involved. Others, such as Olinick (1964), Valenstein (1973), Asch (1976) and

---

* This chapter was first published as 'I hear you knocking but you can't come in: two reasons to refuse the good object', in *The Psychoanalytic Review*, 25(1, 2003): 37–52.

1 Psychoanalytic therapy is characterized by the study of the patients interpersonal relationship with the therapist and other persons, their day and night dreams, and their efforts to "tell all" as a way to understand the patient's internal thoughts and feelings about himself and others. Psychoanalytic theory holds that all behavior and symptoms have deeper meanings. The patient's thoughts, feelings, and daydreams, however illogical or distorted, are carefully studied as an avenue into the unconscious mind's motivations. Just as a dream is analyzed rather than ignored, symptoms are examined rather than quickly eliminated. To the skilled physician, symptoms are clues to the deeper functioning of the human body. So too for the psychoanalyst when confronted with psychiatric symptoms.

Loewald (1972) have attributed an important role to masochism. Rosenfeld (1971; 1975) wrote that narcissism played a significant role, along with envy. Kernberg (1984) investigated the destructive feelings that were directed toward the analyst.

Many of these authors have noted how their patients tended to get worse instead of better. I believe this is only one variant of the so-called negative therapeutic reaction. The patients I am exploring do not want to improve in one respect, but they usually do not get markedly worse either. They stay the same. They make it their job to remain internally frozen. They enter treatment with severe anxiety, depression, paranoia, or other fragmented states of mind and then do not improve. Eventually, they rebel at establishing any change, as it means something devastating and terrible.

Joan Riviere (1936), in her classic paper on the negative therapeutic reaction, has described a group of patients who exhibit these negative reactions as a result of overwhelming depressive anxieties. She notes that most patients have a combination of depressive and paranoid phantasies, but that the negative therapeutic reaction is part of a more debilitating depressive phantasy. By now, it is well established that in normal development and in psychopathology, the ego struggles with these two areas of conflict simultaneously, but with one usually weighing in more heavily.

I will use Riviere's paper as a starting point to show a clinically essential distinction in understanding internal states of mind. This distinction is important in helping patients who find themselves so fastened onto a world without growth.

I will show, through two case examples, the difference between the more depressive patient's negative therapeutic reaction as discussed by Riviere and the more paranoid patient's anti-growth attitude. The more paranoid patient develops an anti-growth transference with an intolerance for taking in a new, more positive version of the self or the object. This occurs within a markedly persecutory world where the idealized object turns into an attacking and abandoning foe. This restricts and freezes the analytic treatment process in place, due to the patient's desperate struggles to prevent these paranoid-schizoid catastrophes.

In 1936, Joan Riviere wrote:

> The content of the depressive position (as Melanie Klein has shown) is the situation in which all one's loved ones within are dead and destroyed, all goodness is dispersed, lost, in fragments, wasted and scattered to the winds; nothing is left within but utter desolation. Love brings sorrow, and sorrow brings guilt; the intolerable tension mounts, there is no escape, one is utterly alone, there is no one to share or help. Love must die because love is dead. Besides, there would be no one to feed one, and no one whom one could feed, and no food in the world. And more, there would still be magic power in the undying persecutors

who can never be exterminated – the ghosts. Death would instantaneously ensue – and one would choose to die by one's own hand before such a position could be realized.

(p. 312)

Many authors after Riviere have described the depressive position in similar terms, combining the same psychological elements. I think these formulations need to be, for clinical reasons, refined. To understand and treat these difficult patients, who seem to not tolerate change or progress, the analyst must create a finer clinical distinction between the paranoid-schizoid position, the paranoid aspects of normal depressive concerns, and pathological depressive anxieties.

To my reading, and the way I approach these anti-growth situations in the consulting office, Riviere is at first describing the collapse of the depressive position into a paranoid, more psychotic landscape where, "all one's loved ones within are dead and destroyed . . . nothing is left within but utter desolation . . . one is utterly alone . . . Love must die because love is dead . . . [there is] no food in the world". This is a far more ominous inner state than the developmentally expected depressive position generally seen in the clinical situation. Riviere does bring in the concept of guilt, as an outgrowth of sorrow, and this correlates with the clinically expectable depressive reaction. In the second case example, I will highlight a man who experiences the more destructive and hopeless feelings Riviere is folding in with depressive reactions.

Again, it is clinically valuable to make a distinction between true depressive remorse, guilt, and mourning and the more primitive paranoid-schizoid experiences of loss (Waska 2002). Paranoid-schizoid states of loss are those in which the ego faces a dual threat. First, the object, in particular the idealized good object, abandons the ego by not providing it with the craved-for nourishment, security, and support. This phantasized abandonment is experienced as permanent and deliberate. This is usually the result of a greedy projective identification process in which the ego finds the object useless and disappointing. After this betrayal, "the ghosts", as Riviere puts it, or the "undying persecutors", return to hunt down the ego and destroy it. In this fragmented world, there is no rescue, no forgiveness, no hope. Instead, there is only blackness, desolation, and the eventuality of being betrayed and crushed by what was the ideal and now is the alien, the enemy.

Riviere goes on to say that the depressive patient may try anything, including a negative therapeutic reaction in order to save the analyst from harm. This is a state where there is indeed hope, because one's objects are not dead and despair is never complete because there is always the chance, even if slim, of restoration and repair of love.

The patient living within the paranoid-schizoid position feels complete loss has occurred, with no rescue possible. Riviere seems to point to the place in one's mind where there is a crossover from the depressive to paranoid phantasy state when she states, "the anxiety is so great because life hangs by a hair and at any moment the situation of full horror may be realized" (p. 313). She then goes on to describe what I view as the shift from depressive to full paranoid-schizoid anxieties if the patient believes he is unable to make amends for his aggressive ways:

> But struggle as he may and does under his unconscious guilt and anxiety to repair and restore, the patient has only a slenderest belief unconsciously in achieving anything of the kind; the slightest failure in reality, the faintest breath of criticism and his belief sinks to zero again – death or madness, his own and others', is ever before the eyes of his unconscious mind. He cannot possibly regenerate and recreate all the losses and destruction he has caused and if he cannot pay this price his own death is the only alternative.
>
> I think the patient's fear of being forced to death himself by the analysis is one of the major underlying factors in this type of case and that is why I put it first. Unless it is appreciated many interpretations will miss their mark. All his efforts to put things right never succeed enough; he can only pacify his internal persecutors for a time, fob them off, feed them with sops, "keep them going"; and so he "keeps things going", the status quo, keeps some belief that "one day" he will have done it all, and postpones the crash, the day of reckoning and judgement.
>
> (p. 313)

Finally, Riviere (1936) makes her point about the different unconscious concerns a patient has. She makes clear how she believes the depressive anxieties are more powerful and detrimental to the analytic work. Therefore, she sees the depressive phantasies as those contributing to failed or stalled treatments and a priority in what to interpret first. Here, I wish to agree with her findings but extend them as well. Some patients are indeed so trapped in depressive anxieties that they engage the analyst in a very difficult relationship that seems to become immovable at times. However, I believe there are other patients who manifest the same stuck, anti-growth transference for very different reasons. These are the patients who are immobilized within intense paranoid-schizoid anxieties of primitive loss and persecution.

In fact, I would argue that the majority of patients in private practice tend to be these more fragmented indivduals. Most of the patients I see in analytic practice, who resist the invitation of life, of change, and of pro- gress, are indeed suffering with phantasies of hurting their objects and guilt over aggressive desires. However, the more immediate, core force in these patients' psychology appears to be a paranoid vision of ultimate loss and persecutory annihilation. This is not a defense against depressive fears, but a rock bottom, core dynamic. The primary solution they see, as a temporary respite, is to avoid, spit out, and refuse any taste of the good object, the good analyst, the good mother. Instead, they demand an idealized, perfect object. At the same time, the ordinary, good, usually available object is given no entrance because it represents the shift of the ideal into the dreaded. Through projective identification, this cycle also involves a search for the ideal, perfect version of the self and a rejection of anything common, predictable, or human about the self.

Using clinical material, I will first show how Riviere's ideas are still very relevant in the clinical situation, when dealing with a patient's depressive phantasies. Then, I will present case material of a more paranoid individual to show how Riviere's ideas can be extended to understand a standoff in treatment due to very different internal experience of the paranoid-schizoid posture.

## THE DEPRESSIVE PATIENT

O was an intelligent, articulate man who prided himself in dressing nicely. He made a point of being polite to everyone he met and went out of his way to avoid conflict. He came to me for help in his late forties because he was unable to find a girlfriend. He had been without a mate for several years. "Once they get to know me, they only want to be friends", O told me. So, we began to meet twice weekly, using the analytic couch. Lack of funds and problems with scheduling prevented a more frequent contract.

Almost immediately, O developed a particular transference relationship with me. He would deliberate back and forth over why he wasn't instantly improving. He would blame himself for not working harder on his problems, then he would blame me for not curing him right away, and then he would see himself as not giving me enough to work with successfully. After only two or three months of treatment, O would say, "why am I still coming? Nothing has changed. I don't see any difference in my problems. Why haven't you fixed me yet?" This message would be repeated over and over in the course of his four-year treatment. This message of nagging hunger and discontentment was kept very split off from O's other feelings, so it was difficult to analyze how they were related to the same object relationship. This was part of a crossover between depressive and paranoid anxieties and demands that I will mention again, a bit later.

O was one of two children, with a sister two years older than he. Growing up, he had hardly any contact with his father, who was a traveling salesman and only home two days a week. From a fairly young age, O was home by himself or with his sister much of the time. His mother was a factory worker and worked the swing shift. After O came home from school, he was alone as his mother was working until the late evening and his father was away at work. Food would be ready in the refrigerator and a neighbor would look in on them occasionally.

O spent most of his days doing homework by himself or chores around the house. He ridiculed his sister for watching television or playing in the yard with friends. O tried his best to follow mother's orders, to be a good boy, and to not cause his mother any problems. When I suggested he might have been frustrated and lonely, and even angry with his parents for being so absent, O quickly denied it. He said it was no problem, he understood his parents had their own lives to lead, and it was "just the way things were".

This neutral detachment and denial of his feelings, especially any aggressive feelings toward his mother, was a major block for much of the treatment process. But, we made headway in fits and starts. In a session about a year into seeing me, O was talking about his mother. He started to feel angry with her and froze. "My heart is racing. I can't stop thinking I should be dead!" he yelled in panic. This reaction to feeling angry with mother was hard to explore as O immediately forgot what he was talking about and then switched the subject. Clearly, he had to keep the peace with this internalized object.

The two ways we were able to access these forbidden feelings were through his trouble with dating and through the nature of the transference. We could see how, when he dated, he kept this same type of mechanical distance from the other person until they felt alienated. Also, he tended to become involved with women who took advantage of him, but since he tried to keep his negative feelings at bay, these relationships would go on until he made some polite excuse to not meet anymore. By that time, he had been used. Later, he would ruminate back and forth as to whether it was his fault or the woman's. He would be furious, but unable to make sense out of the feeling or find a right place to put them.

In the transference, he was as nice and neutral as possible, except when he told me to hurry up and cure him. These more aggressive, demeaning comments were said in a way that was so detached he didn't have to take emotional responsibility for them.

An example of this occurred in the third year of treatment. O usually paid me in cash and he had recently spoken of his idea of paying me electronically, where a check would be automatically sent to me each month.

O asked me what I would prefer. I asked him for more details. O began to go back and forth about the pros and cons of each method of payment. He speculated how I might want cash on one hand, but that it might make my bookkeeping difficult and cumbersome. On the other hand, he thought the electronic checks might make my accounting easier but deprive me of the immediate cash. I said, "this is difficult because you picture hurting me one way or the other". Here, I was interpreting the depressive anxieties of harming the object. O said, "Yes. I feel I will be causing you some kind of trouble and you know how I hate conflict." O went on to discuss how he wanted to avoid any sort of ill-feeling with me or the specter of my being frustrated or angry with him. "I am starting to feel really anxious right now, my chest feels tight", he said nervously. After a few minutes of silence, O said, "I have totally forgotten what we were talking about." I interpreted that he wanted to do something for himself, making life easier via the electronic checks, and began to worry that this was selfish and hurtful. In response to my comment, he launched into another intellectual exercise about which method of payment was best, noting all the details in each camp. I commented on how he was now needing to use logic and forgetfulness to escape his anxiety about our relationship.

O replied, "I am angry with myself. This is a lifelong pattern and I haven't ever changed it. And, I am angry with you for not having gotten rid of it." I interpreted that he wanted to get rid of his problems electronically, in a distancing way where he didn't have to feel it and didn't have to deal with the dirty money and dirty feelings. O replied, "I feel guilty about being angry with you. I feel uncomfortable. Wait a minute. Wow. I suddenly started thinking about my mother. That is weird. I have always wanted mom to see me as perfect. That way, I don't run the risk of losing her love or approval." After O explored these thoughts and feelings for a while, I interpreted that he kept his mother on a pedestal to avoid facing the anger he has toward her for being imperfect and leaving him out in the cold when he needed her. O replied, "yes, I think you are right about that. But, I am quick to forgive. Even if she is imperfect, I can see why and I forgive her." I commented on how instantly he forgives, out of both desperation and omnipotence. O replied, "I am the king! I guess you are right though. If I don't make everything smooth, there would be friction between her and me. And, that doesn't feel right."

O's treatment seemed immovable for several years and this was primarily the result of the depressive anxieties Riviere spoke of. O feared exposing his mother and his analyst to the rage, disappointment, and anguish he felt. These feelings leaked out as a grandiose, biting sarcasm, as wanting to control me, and as demanding my cure. However, this would quickly be replaced with guilt, intellectualization, and repression. O believed there was a way to gain forgiveness, even though he felt this was rather magical and thin. Sometimes, it was more a facade of forgiveness in which he used pleasing, logic, or debate to wash away any conflict with his objects in order to achieve or maintain his blissful state of peace, approval, and love. While O constantly feared the loss of love, he felt it could be saved. Again, this was questionable at times and pointed to an internal teetering between the depressive and paranoid positions. However, in an overall sense, O represents the type of depressive patient Riviere wrote about.

The stalling out of O's treatment was gradually corrected as we, over and over again, explored his core fear of injuring, hurting, and disrespecting his mother and me. The more we analyzed his hidden neediness, greed, and oral deprivation the more these depressive anxieties arose. Then, it was back to working on his defenses against those. This back and forth was slow going but the treatment gradually went from being frozen and repetitive to a genuine working-through process. This took place over the course of several years, but the progress was steady and lasting.

## A PARANOID-SCHIZOID PATIENT

M was forty years old when he started his analytic treatment. He was a pleasant-looking man who seemed very suspicious and nervous, but also overly polite as if he were trying to avoid being yelled at.

M was the son of a violent alcoholic policeman who demanded the family follow his orders or else. M felt his father "was always either on the verge of being furious or in the act of being furious". M had two sisters. One has been depressed and unable to function for many years and the other, a schizophrenic, has been homeless and living on the streets for over twenty years. M's mother had a break with reality when giving birth to M and has spent her life in and out of mental hospitals. The family was very poor and isolated from the community because of M's father's reputation for violence and drinking.

M went to college, only to drop out after his father decided to no longer help him out financially. M drifted from job to job over the years. He always found work in a situation where he was doing the dirty work for a boss or company. Along the way, he made friends, but they were usually customers to whom he felt inferior. Many of his jobs were the type of jobs filled by college students on their summer break. It was difficult for M to find something he could commit to and feel fulfilled by. When I met M, he was the manager in a grocery store. As in past jobs, he worked very hard, hoping to find approval, attention, and caring. But, he ended up feeling used, ignored, and bullied by his boss, much like he felt with his father while growing up.

Very early in the treatment, M established a way of being with me, an attitude, that seemed to say, "it is hopeless, I will never get better, life is too difficult. So, what is the use?" In fact, these were his very words that he often would yell out in anger or whisper while sobbing. M had countless examples of how his boss was mean, how he didn't see the point in making friends, and how he was already an old, ugly man whom no woman would want. M told me, "no matter how hard you might try, I am beyond help".

M would tell me, "the nicer the weather is, the worse I feel. The better my life gets, the more I wish I was dead. The greater amount of good I see, the more depressed I feel." This was the way M related to me and to himself. He was refusing to take in any evidence of goodness, whether it be in me, in himself, or in the world. In fact, the more goodness he experienced, the more violent his internal reaction. At another point in the treatment, M told me, "just kill me, please. Please, kill me. Kill me, kill me! Or give me a house, a wife, lots of money, and leave me the fuck alone. I just wish someone would take me out in the woods and kill me. I would do it, but I am too chicken shit."

This type of attack on the analytic relationship and on himself was near constant throughout the treatment. Sometimes it was this active, self-attack and at other times he felt persecuted and attacked by his boss, women, and the government. M seemed to use this way of negative relating or anti-relating to prevent real, positive relating. He was a patient who fitted some of the "no-entry" criteria discussed by Williams (1997), where the ego defends against all experiences except for pathological projections that create internal chaos. Williams thinks this is part of an early infantile experience of destructive parental projections. M clearly had this type of situation in his background and I think he then fashioned it into a destructive projective identification process whereby the good object is not trusted and therefore must be neutralized. At the same time, via splitting, the good object becomes idealized in a fragile, thin way that easily shifts into a persecutory experience of abandonment and annihilation.

So, in this type of situation the analyst must make a constant assessment of what is happening to the good object and what is being done to the good object (Thorner 1952). In a successful treatment, the anxiety-producing ideal object becomes more realistic and the patient accepts its limitations. Through a process of internalization and healthy projective identification, this leads to a more realistic picture of the self and relations between the self and the object take on much more hopeful, safe, and reachable levels of expectation. With M, this was a slow and difficult path that took many years.

During one visit in the second year of his twice-weekly treatment on the analytic couch, M was telling me about his new girlfriend. The fact that he had only this one girlfriend was a major success. Throughout his life, when M felt up to dating, he refused to maintain a faithful relationship with only one woman. This had been part of a standoff in the treatment. In the transference, M envisioned me as the clever con artist, trying to convince him of the safety and importance of a white-picket-fence, traditional type of committed family unit. Once lured into my trap, M was convinced he would be victim to eternal boredom, then deprivation, and finally a terrible abandonment. He told me, "Why can't I just have sex with as many women as I want for the rest of my life. I am sure that I will be giving up excitement and fun if I settle down. I just can't bear the idea of giving up all the potential treasure around me. I would be starving and have to exist on just bread and water. And, in the end, who is to say that after thirty years of misery she would just up and leave me. I would be all alone with nothing."

As a result of our work on these types of persecutory phantasies, M was now seeing only one woman and it was making him very anxious. Prior to talking about his girlfriend, something else had happened in the session. When M first walked in the door, he had said, "I know this may be breaking the rules about what I can ask you, but I am wondering if last week you were away on vacation or business. I guess I am wondering if you had a good time somewhere, but I am not sure if I am allowed to ask. So, if it's OK to tell me, then that is good, but otherwise I will understand that it is not. I will understand. I just don't know what is alright to ask. So, if I am breaking the rules, I am sorry. I just wondered." It was clear M was now very nervous. Then, without waiting for an answer, he went on to talk about his new girlfriend.

M explained his dilemma. He thought this girlfriend was wonderful in many ways and he was enjoying spending time with her. However, he had noticed she had a bad-breath problem when he went to kiss her. M said it was troubling him because he didn't know how to bring it up with her without causing a terrible fight. He went on about this for a while, going back and forth about how this could end up in destructive results. He said, "I don't want to be a rude, judgmental boyfriend; I don't want to cause trouble. So, I don't know what to do, what the correct approach would be."

I interpreted to M, "you asked me about my vacation and then got nervous that you were causing trouble with me. You have the same feeling about talking with your girlfriend about her bad-breath problem. What seems important in both situations is how hard it is to imagine the good side of the other person. I think you are interested in my vacation because I am an important person in your life. But, you think I won't see that and I will just get angry that you are breaking the rules. Maybe it makes you anxious to imagine the reason you have these concerns in the first place. You are wanting to solve the bad-breath problem so you can kiss your girlfriend and be closer to her. You want to hear about my vacation because you missed me and think about me. It seems it is easier to think about how we will punish you rather than think about how you want to let us in and relate to us." M said, "Wow. I never thought of that angle. But, you are right. My hope is to get closer to my girlfriend and kiss her and lie next to her. And, I am interested in you and what you do. But, for some reason all I can think of is how you both will hate me."

So, I was interpreting M's difficulty with letting in the phantasy of the good object. It was easier to imagine being attacked by me than to imagine finding the union and pleasure he hungered for. This was a place where M was stuck. It was a crossroads which had come up in many other guises throughout the treatment. This paranoid anxiety is quite different from the depressive problems my other patient, O, experienced. Since this type of standoff was fundamentally different, it had to be analyzed in a different manner. With M, I needed to constantly interpret his primitive phantasies of annihilation and permanent loss.

My exploration of how and why M was so stuck was illuminated by his acting out, his dreams, and his type of "no, I won't" approach in the transference. One dream he told me of was of being with a friend and going for a hike. Now, this was in itself unusual as even in his dreams he would not link up with others in any close or committed capacity. M and this friend began walking along. Suddenly, M found himself standing on a very thin membrane of mud, with holes throughout it. "Like Swiss-cheese", M said. He started to fall through it, into a bottomless pit. His friend put his hand out and said, "hang on to me". M told me he did, but in the dream he knew that he was about to pull this other person down to death with him. When M talked about the dream, he emphasized how he was "like poison to others" and that he would only bring pain to others. Here, he seemed to be exploring more depressive anxieties. However, knowing the transference and extra-transference history, I thought this dream represented other matters as well. Also, the deadly nature of the "poison" served as a guidepost to what kind of anxieties he was dealing with. So, I said, "I think there is something else about the dream. You are convinced that if you take my hand and depend on me or anyone else, there will be dangerous consequences. It is poison. You seem to believe that to take an emotional walk with me or your girlfriend means falling into a bottomless pit. So, you usually try and do it all by yourself. It feels safer." M said, "I see what you mean. Well, it is true. I have evidence. To be committed to someone is to be courting danger."

M's response was illustrative as well. He was letting my interpretation in as a good object momentarily, but then evacuating it by saying he had evidence of danger, therefore what he feels is reality and not an internal fear that we can work on. So, his response is in itself part of the therapeutic standoff.

Over the years, M would frequently fill the hours with paranoid tirades of how everyone neglected him and how the world deprived him. I would interpret this as a wish for an ideal set of parents and an ideal analyst who would provide him with all the love and comfort he needed, but felt he never got. I also interpreted that he seemed to be demanding it, saying he would not budge until he got it. This sentiment of his came out in such statements as "I will never say a word to my boss in my review. If he doesn't automatically realize what a great job I am doing and reward me, then why the hell should I have to remind him?" Frequently, this sort of thinking and feeling would escalate and M would tell me, "I see people driving $100,000 cars, I see Jennifer Lopez living in a thirty-room mansion. Why not me? I should have a house with a thousand acres. Why shouldn't I have all that?" He would go on about how the most extreme examples of wealth and power are normal and should be a part of his life as a matter of course. He should just naturally be given a piece of that opulence. I would reply, "you want it handed to you, all the goodies. I think you feel both deprived and angry. You want parents you can look up to and count on, but instead you feel like they are unavailable and scary. To face that and try and make it on your own must feel unbearable. It seems you want me to agree that you deserve the best at all times, because without that, things feel frightening and hopeless." M replied, "if I can't have it all, why live?"

So, this was one major way M was stuck in a lifeless standoff with me. He would go on for virtually an entire session, telling me, "I am a whore for the government. All I do is work and pay taxes. Nothing else. They are killing me, screwing me in the ass. And, it is always the little guy, not the rich. Are the rich being taxed? Hell no! I am sick of my boss, my company, my co-workers. Everyone is a fool. They have been brainwashed by the system. Why is it that I am the only one that sees this? I hate where I live. Why the hell do I have to pay rent? Why don't I own my own home? Why do I have to work at all? The whole concept of work is something the government thought up to control the masses. Work is not what humans were meant to do. I want to die. If I had a gun, I would kill myself. I wish someone would kill me. Would you do me that favor, please? Please kill me. The whole system is corrupt. It is disgusting. All I ever do is work and pay taxes and work again. Over and over."

I interpreted, "all you do is work and rarely allow any room for fun or love. But you could do more. You are locked into a battle with yourself, the system inside of you. You want to convince me of how wrong things are and you won't rest until I see it. I think you want me to see how unjust things felt at home when you were growing up and now you want it made right. But, this leaves you at a standoff, with your life on hold. It looks like without the ideal world you wish for, you feel left in the gutter all alone."

M replied, "that is absolutely right. Why bother with it if it can't be done right?" I said, "you spend most of your time fighting in your mind with the world, so you are now the one that deprives yourself, like you felt at home. You often tell me you wish you could just be going for a walk on a beach. Well, you could but then I guess you would feel alone, without your fighting partner." M replied, "I don't know how to be alone. I don't want to be alone. I need you or someone to tell me what to do or I am lost in space, in blackness." I said, "if I did tell you what to do, after a while you would probably take me on as your next fighting partner". M said, "Oh boy! I never thought of it that way. Yes, I see. But, it is so hard to give that up and have nothing, nothing at all."

This type of standoff went on for years, with me offering one central interpretation: M was frightened that his turning away from constant per-secutory feelings and external fighting with his boss, friends, and analyst would result in his falling into a hopeless pit of annihilation and emptiness, alone in pieces. Essentially, he felt he had to be in a combative union with his father to avoid the terrifying fragmentation of a psychotic union with mother. There was no sense of self to provide a third option. He had to choose between these two terrible states. It was so frightening to work through this vision of nothingness that he would rather feel hunted down by his objects. My constant offering of this interpretation gradually eased his anxieties, allowed a slow integration of reality, and addressed his transference feelings.

So, bit by bit, over the years, M gave up this tug-of-war approach to life and began to invest in himself. This victory was slow going, hard won, and easily set backwards. However, he slowly climbed out of the ring with his internal fighting partners. As this progress occurred, or as a prerequisite really, we explored his fear of becoming or already being like his mother: passive, alone, lost, and doomed. Opening up to these phantasies also meant facing the sad reality of his mother's actual experiences in life. M sobbed when I asked about his mother. "She never stood a chance. She was so sweet, but so lost", he replied. I said, "I think you feel it is better to stay close to people who are like your father: mean, selfish, and ready to fight. If you move away from that, you feel you are with your mother, lost, alone, and in pieces forever. So, it seems better to stay stuck than to move ahead." M replied, "Yes. That would be death."

The two cases presented in this chapter show how patients who dig in their heels and immobilize the analytic process do so for two separate psychological reasons. The case of "O" was a patient who illustrated Joan Riviere's thinking on the negative therapeutic reaction in which depressive anxieties are central. The case of "M" was a reflection of Riviere's classic paper in some ways; however this case served to extend her ideas. By understanding how paranoid-schizoid functioning could be a part of a defiant patient's inner world, a difficult case begins to be more clinically assessable.

When the distinction between depressive and paranoid anxieties is made, the analyst is in a much better position to understand and assist these types of patients. On the outside, on a conscious level, these patients claim to want more in their lives, to better themselves, and to enrich themselves. On an unconscious level, they are extremely anxious about letting in the good object and allowing themselves to grow. The reasons for this anti-growth attitude are varied. For some patients, such as the depressive ones Riviere speaks of, they worry about harming their objects when getting better. For others, the paranoid-schizoid cases, they are sure that growth brings on the attack and abandonment of the object, with no hope of safety or reconciliation.

# Chapter 2

# Mistrust of the good object

On his way to an analytic session, Paul began thinking he would like to "share himself with me". Later, he explained that he imagined freely sharing his feelings, his thoughts, recent events, and all his latest reflections on what we had been working on. In other words, he looked forward to spontaneously free associating with me. This would have been quite different from the usual obsessive, back-and-forth, start-and-stop, defensive method he used to try not to relate to me. So, Paul was wishing for the experience of growth, union, and intimacy with me. For just a moment, he let himself enjoy the image.

Then, he told me he realized that allowing me "entrance into his life", seeing me as a good, understanding, and accepting object, would be a mistake. Paul stated, "On the outside, it looked nice. You would listen and understand. I would let you know me. But, then I bolted. It was wrong. It was a mistake. It was dangerous". He said I would be able to "spot all his flaws" and, as a consequence, I "would begin to hate him". Paul wanted to terminate treatment because he "didn't want me criticizing him that way". I interpreted that, "you imagine I won't tolerate your imperfections". He replied, "Of course you won't. I don't, so why should you!" When we explored his fear of my attacks, Paul became less paranoid and less anxious. This frightening phantasy was a transference situation that had occurred before and we were making progress. But, it was slow going. Letting in the idea of a good object↔good self and the emotions that came with that internal relationship meant acknowledging a mix of human conditions that were far from perfect. We were real. We were human. This felt dangerous and uncomfortable. Instead, Paul tried to keep it to a rigid image of a perfect self and an admiring object. This left Paul in full control, rather than vulnerable and uncertain.

Certain early life experiences between the infant/child and their caretaker can make the important transition from paranoid-schizoid to depressive position very difficult if not defective or pathological. This was the case with Paul. He maintained a standoff within the good object and the good self. It was a "no good object allowed" policy. This left him with the illusion of being on an island of control and safety, but actually resulted in lonely isolation and a constant need to be on the watch for criticizing attacks.

As a child, Paul felt very alone and forced to grow up quickly and independently. Both his parents worked at the local factory. His mother worked the late shift so his parents were either asleep or at work for much of his upbringing. The weekends, holidays, and other occasions they were around, doing their best to provide for Paul and his two younger brothers, are memories Paul has a hard time accessing. Over the years of his analytic treatment, we have discovered that he would rather not remember these good times, as they remind him too much of all the other times that felt bad, the many resentful feelings he still has, and the imperfections in his upbringing. To remember the good times and his parents as good objects means he has to accept they also have flaws. He would rather maintain them on pedestals as ideal parents.

As a child, Paul felt pushed to be a "big boy" and not burden his parents with any problems, needs, or wants. In this sense, he had to protect them from his needs because he saw them as too fragile, overwhelmed, and meager to be able to parent him properly. Besides feeling forced into the depressive perspective of thinking of others before yourself, he was also protecting himself, in a paranoid fashion. In other words, he imagined that if he tried to depend on his parents, he would be disappointed and hurt. The more he had to be the perfect little boy who could take care of himself, the more his anger and despair grew. He desperately needed good object experiences to balance this out, but there were not enough and the ones he had were clouded over by his rage and despair. So, his best solution was to convince himself he lived in an ideal family with loving and available parents whom he really didn't need because he was able to completely sustain himself. The whole and good object, a natural mix of flaws and delight, created too much anxiety and unveiled all the mixed feelings he kept locked up. So, the good object was off limits.

During the course of his analytic treatment, Paul would become convinced that I, as the good object, was going to show him how imperfect his parents were. He was so sure of this he would be ready to terminate. When we explored this panic state, he was able to describe how I stood for the acceptance of the human condition: a mixture of success and failure, joy and pain, well-intentioned as well as self-serving motives, and so on. Paul told me that when he was separate from me, away from our sessions, he could remember his parents and himself as ideal. But, when we were together, he was forced into contact with the good object of reality, instead of his idealized object. Paul said it felt like I was going to "surprise him with bad news and drag him and his family down". So, he wanted to avoid this by either terminating or keeping us apart with denial, projection, manic intellectualization, and splitting.

These emotional themes were evident in various other ways. Paul was talking about his need for others' attention and he said, "if they love me, than I am able to love myself". I interpreted that if this was the only precarious lifeline to love, it made sense he would need his objects to be ideal so he could count on the love. If they were fallible objects, a mixture of good and bad, he might feel the love was unpredictable or sporadic. His sense of self would vanish. Paul nodded in agreement and said, "I need to keep it coming. I don't want the faucet to run dry."

This fearful phantasy came to life in the transference when I was about to leave for vacation. Paul said, "I hope I make it." In exploring his sudden expression of despair and anxiety, he revealed a vision of his being so overwhelmed and abandoned that he would commit suicide. Only then would I and others realize how desperate he was. I would finally understand his great need for me. He told me that to think of losing me was similar to how he felt when imagining his family as less than perfect. "I would have nothing. I would be left alone, with nothing," he said. Paul continued, "But, if I ask for more and look needy, you will probably be disgusted and leave me forever."

Melanie Klein thought the working through of the depressive position and the internal integration of a reality-based good object were the foundation of mental health (Temperley 2001). The establishment of forgiveness, acceptance, mourning, reparation, and the ability to continue forward in the face of disappointment are the rewards of the depressive position. Of course, these internal states must be continuously cultivated to maintain healthy object relations within the depressive position. When the ego has entered the depressive realm under difficult circumstances, these healthy processes are subject to failure. This brings on regressions to the paranoid-schizoid level, but also means the depressive position can be experienced and maintained in a defective or abnormal manner. This leads to a distorted way of utilizing the advanced developmental aspects of the depressive mode. This idea has been put forth by Bicudo (1964), who notes a pre-depressive position that has elements of persecutory guilt and ego malfunction.

Patients such as Paul appear to be suffering with severe paranoid-schizoid difficulties along with many of the disadvantages of the depressive realm rather than its rewards. Another way of saying this is that the developmental advantages of the depressive position are corrupted. The cumulative results of combined paranoid and depressive problems are often an attempted retreat from both positions. However, this escape is at best temporary and eventually fails. These patients are struggling with the worst of both internal experiences and as a last-ditch effort they do what they can to fight off the good object, which represents further attacks from both realms. Much has been written from different theoretical perspectives about the reluctance to accept a good object (Symington 2004). I am developing the idea of a chronic intra-psychic standoff meant to avoid the good object because it represents the worst of both positions. The ego tries to make do on its own, but due to excessive projective identification it always feels lost, abandoned, and attacked.

These psychological situations manifest within the transference as the patient erecting a fortress which serves to defend against the dual threat of persecution and primitive loss. In the transference relationship, the patient resists growth, insight, or psychological expansion. In the countertransference, the analyst can have the experience of observing an explorer on a harsh and difficult journey, who after many trials and tribulations says, "no more", builds a fort, and refuses to go any further or come out. In addition, she or he will not allow anyone into the fort. The end result may be a moment of peace, solitude, and the illusion of safety. However, the reality is that he or she is still surrounded by the harshness and danger of the outside world and now is lonely and destined to starve, locked in the fort. And, there is the refusal to let anyone in who could help change those conditions, who could offer help, nourishment, direction, and companionship.

In the case of Paul, the vision of the analyst as a good object was a painful reminder of the lack of good objects, the frail nature of them, and his feeling of having to cater to their needs rather than depend and rely on them. So, letting the good object in just brought about self-loathing and sadness for a bond with his parents that never was. Therefore, analytic work was slow and difficult since he saw me as a good object threatening his silence, safety, and independence. Our relationship, if it became close and real, would bring out his "flaws", which to him were his need for love, the full range of his emotions, and his view of his parents as human. When we had a natural, back-and-forth mutuality, Paul considered it dangerous and unpredictable.

## CASE MATERIAL 2.1

Fran was brought up in a household where she and her father catered to mother's overbearing ways. Fran's mother had moods that dictated the tone and direction of the family. Fran's experience of it was that not only were her father and she herself intimidated by mother, but they also sensed a certain fragility that they wanted to not disturb. During Fran's second year of analytic treatment, she told me, "we had to go along with her and agree with her. I could not be a separate person and I could never disagree. In an odd way, maybe a sick way, I had to be there for her. If she falls apart, I will have nothing there for me."

My interpretive approach with Fran was guided by my clinical impression that she was forced into the depressive position before she was ready or prepared for it. It appeared that she had to be a caretaker of sorts, out of a sense of urgency and survival, both for herself and her objects. That feeling of having to give to others was grounded in paranoid phantasies regarding survival of the self, as opposed to the more depressive altruism of caring for her objects for their sake. As a child and on into adulthood, Fran was dealing with objects that were weak instead of sturdy and supportive. Growing up, she had a view of fragile parents who need parenting. So, there were these primitive paranoid-schizoid phantasies and feelings that led Fran into the depressive realm, thus tainting it and predisposing it to malfunction and perversion. She had to grow up too fast for the wrong reasons and was left dealing with life without the aid of enough good object experiences.

Technically, the analytic work with such patients has to focus on three elements, all transference-related. The seemingly confirmed, concrete, and unresolved paranoid dilemmas must be addressed, the patient's view of life through an immature version of the depressive mode must be interpreted, and the patient's attempted solution of denying connection to, desire for, and identification with the good object must be constantly explored and worked through.

So, with Fran, I would often interpret how she provided me with stories of how mother fell apart in the past or still does currently, but in an intellectualized manner. She was delivering data to me. I said, "maybe relaying it that way lets only mother fall apart and she then gets picked up. You are reluctant to fall apart with me. How will I react? Will I pick you up? Will I let you be the child for a change?" This line of interpretation, over time, led Fran to loosen up a bit and trust me enough to show her more fragile and dependent side.

Fran had only attended her analytic sessions every other week for the first two years.[1] Initially, she would only discuss this as a financial matter. Limited by a meager salary and modest insurance benefits, there was some truth to this rationale. But, I routinely brought up the emotional aspect of it as well. I interpreted that by coming to see me so infrequently, there was less chance and less threat of her falling apart with me. Fran replied, revealing her true feelings for the first time, "money is certainly a factor. But, the main reason I have put a limit on it is so I don't have to face my own desires and my own despair."

Over time, this line of exploration led to much working through. I interpreted that when Fran said she didn't want to face the desire and despair, she said it as if she would end up alone and separate, independently

---

1 I call the work with Fran psychoanalytic because of the focus on the analysis of the transference, the exploration of unconscious phantasies, and the working through of internal conflict states through the use of interpretation. The contemporary literature, as well as Freud and Melanie Klein's own work, has shown that these are the crucial elements of the psychoanalytic situation. Extrinsic elements such as frequency and use of couch are only supportive supplements to the psychoanalytic treatment environment.

dealing with it. She would be without me. I interpreted that this seemed to be both a way to protect me from her desire and despair, but also a way to protect herself from the consequences of letting me in as a good object who could help with all those troubles. I could be supportive or I could turn on her, making her regret her attempt to need me.

I repeatedly interpreted her lack of in-and-out flow between needs, wishes, and troubled feelings and her object. She had turned off the two-way flow and barricaded herself off. Due to a pathological projective identification process (Waska 2004), Fran had repeatedly taken in the object, her mother and I believe her passive father as well, and colored their image with rage, oral need, despair, and desire. When the external objects in her environment were not sufficient to counterbalance these phantasies, they were instead confirmed and further ingrained via projective identification. This continued to the point where Fran felt so overwhelmed and surrounded by failing, persecutory, and dying objects that she had to shut off access to them completely. At that point, good objects were not to be trusted. O'Shaughnessy (1964) makes the similar point that certain patients return to absent, neglectful, or abusive objects hoping the objects will finally provide the patient with a positive, loving experience. To detach from that bad object would mean being left alone with damaged and persecutory objects without the external object to ever detoxify or heal them.

In normal development, O'Shaughnessy (1964) notes that individuation from the object is a natural result of wanting to provide the object freedom and autonomy. Both the ego and the object don't want to be constantly burdened by the needs of the other. For patients such as Fran, they feel frightened to be on their own, frightened that the object can't make it on its own, and convinced there is no respite from either problem. So, the only solution is to create a no-entry policy to the good object and seal oneself off. It can't get better, but at least you can prevent it from getting worse by freezing everything in time. This is the survival phantasy of patients such as Fran.

Part of this struggle to avoid the good object for fear of its combined potential of persecution and abandonment, as well as the collapse and demise of the object, involves resistance to growth, progress, or change. Change is felt to be harmful to the object as well as dangerous to the integrity of the self. All relationships, views, and life direction must be kept at a neutral point, a balance of zero. This gives the ego a sense of control over the volatile good object and the fragile self.

Fran conveyed this when she spent one session discussing her hopes for a better job, the good feelings she had about the interview, and her plans if she should get the job. Also, she was telling me about her plans to take an art class, something purely for her own enjoyment. At that point, she paused and said, "if I go forward, I will hurt other people in a horrible way and then I will be crucified or something. I don't feel right or safe about it."

Toward the end of the session, Fran asked me if I still was driving the same car. A year earlier, she had pulled into the parking lot at the same time as I did and noticed my car. Unsure what her comment might mean, I said yes and continued to listen. Fran said, "we need to get you out of that car and into a pickup truck or something. Maybe you could wear a cowboy hat. We need to toughen you up." The session was over and I was unsure of the direction to take, so I told her we could discuss it more next time. When we met again, I deliberated about interpreting her comment. On one hand, I felt it was important to just go with it, as she was showing an ability to play with me, be intimate and interact with me as a good object without pushing me away. She was willing to make contact. And, to make an interpretation, she might begin to feel punished or persecuted.

But, I felt it was important to notice and possibly explore her move toward me. I also thought she was showing her concern for my safety. The interpretation I chose to make was, "I noticed you feel comfortable enough to sort of play with me, kid around with me. I think this shows you are more comfortable reaching out to me, making contact. At the same time, what you said about the pickup truck and cowboy hat makes me think you are trying to toughen me up to be able to survive your own progress. Telling me of your hopes, goals, and enjoyment, seemed to trigger your fear of hurting others. So, if I am tougher, I won't get hurt by you?" Fran said, "you are right. But, I wish it was that easy, just give everyone a pickup truck! I think it helps when we talk about it. Now, at least you don't seem as ready to go under." I added, "and you don't feel as dangerous or as much in danger." "Yes, both," she replied.

Stephen (1934) notes that the ego may feel it has so many bad objects inside itself, and/or is so toxic itself, that the ego will resist change or progress to prevent those bad influences from becoming unleashed. Therefore, the patient may try to protect the good object by avoiding contact with it or, in the case of Fran's pickup truck example, may try to fortify and armor the threatened good object.

## CASE MATERIAL 2.2

Betty was in her early forties when she began analytic treatment. "I cannot find a life of my own. I am trapped in my family, with no way out", was her plea in the first session. She and her younger brother had been the captive audience of her parents' constant fighting when they were children. When Betty was ten years old, her mother committed suicide. Betty's father took to drinking and became withdrawn. As a teenager, her brother became involved in drugs and dropped out of highschool. Betty felt obligated to look after him like a mother.

When Betty began her treatment, she still lived with her brother because she felt he was unable to live a "responsible" life. Over time, I came to understand that this meant Betty wanted to control him and shape him into the ideal brother she had never had. Also, she wished he could be a comforting stand-in for her dead mother. Consequently, it was very difficult for her to accept her brother as he was. His faults and differences disturbed Betty. Betty's father was in a nearby city and still lived a meager life, overshadowed by drinking. Again, Betty felt a strong need to try and change him into a better object, the more ideal father she longed for. Her efforts, externally and internally, to help, to monitor, and to transform these two men kept her focused on them and away from building her own life. So, Betty frequently felt resentful she had to care for them, angry that she had no life of her own, and despairing that she would never see that situation change.

About two years into the analytic process, we were exploring how she clings to her troubles with her brother and father, as well as troubles in other similar situations. She was insisting that it was a very practical, concrete matter, "her responsibility". I interpreted that she needed to cling to their troubles as it was the only attachment she felt she had and without it she might feel completely lost. To let go of it in order to pursue her own life must feel wrong as well as dangerous. This interpretation was based on many months of material in which Betty would tell me of how resentful she was about her family, but then become anxious and agitated when I pointed out how she seemed to avoid opportunities to separate from them, allowing her to still care for them but also care for herself. Betty replied, "it is too late for me. There is nothing out there for me." Also, she said, "I fear that without this pitiful family to fight with, I have absolutely nothing, a dark void." For reasons of confidentiality, I am focusing on her psychological struggle with brother and father and excluding the enormous emotional struggle regarding her mother's suicide. However, it usually contained the same theme of resentment, loss, and fear of nothingness.

In the transference, she had built a dynamic in which she was not only very committed, loyal, and attached to her analysis and to me, but she also felt extremely trapped by, stuck in, and agitated about it as well.

So, in the next session, Betty told me she was angry that I had "told her off for continuing to hang onto the family baggage out of fear of being alone". After chastising me for a while, Betty said, "I have to hang onto that baggage or I would have nothing." After sharing this painful insight, she turned it around and accused me of attacking her and blaming her for doing things "the wrong way" and "living a sick and twisted life". This sense of persecution continued for most of the session.

In the next session, she told me she had thought more about our conversation and began to feel a new sense of hope. Betty said, "when I thought more about what you said, and how I could maybe start to live my own life without leaving my family by the wayside, it felt new. I started to feel like I could have a beginning, a start in life." When I asked her more about this new hope and tried to explore it a bit, Betty began to lose the hope. She told me it was all a "pie in the sky hope". It "was ridiculous. It is too late for me and it is stupid to think anything will change." She went on like this for a while and I interpreted that she was attacking the hope and the new goodness she envisioned. She wanted me as a helper in making the transition out of feeling chained to her family but felt hostile when she saw herself dependent on me for the hope and help. Betty had several replies. She told me she thought it was progress that she could be angry about the whole thing, because in the past she would just accept whatever came her way and then resent it later.

Also, Betty told me, "Someone else, other than me, has to make it better before I am willing to go on and make any changes!" Betty repeated this feeling of not wanting to make any progress or allow any goodness until it was provided for her. It was a "you have to make the effort first" type of stance. Then, she discussed how angry she felt that she didn't have the nice life others appeared to enjoy. The ideal family, the nice job, the loving boyfriend, and many other pleasures in life were enjoyed by everyone but her. Here, I interpreted that she is the one who denies herself, because she is waiting for the joy to be delivered to her. Betty said, "Well, I am not proud of it, but that fits!" She went on to say more about how it doesn't feel fair that she should have to make the effort to better herself, that it was something her parents ought to have done for her as a child. I interpreted that what she says she wants or deserves is an unrealistic, idealistic state in which she has perfect parents who parent her in an ideal way. Holding out for this ideal means she has to negate the work we do, the hope that we are building. Sharing her ordinary self with me, her regular hopes and dreams, reveals the loss of her ideal wishes. So, to create an honest, intimate relationship with me in which she can examine her goodness and her flaws is out of the question.

This theme occurred in other sessions. I would point out Betty's tendency to only share her agitation, resentment, and aggravation with me. Sharing any excitement, pride, recent joy, or hopeful plans for the future were all off limits. I suggested that she felt uncomfortable or anxious about bringing me her hopes, happiness, or success. Betty told me it would be a "waste of time". She said, "I came here because my life is full of problems and misery. Why would I tell you about what goes right? I am telling you about what goes wrong so I can fix it. The good stuff doesn't need fixing." I interpreted that Betty was familiar with the misery and might be more comfortable presenting that side of herself. At first, she was angry and repeated that she just needed "to fix the problems, not hang out to be friendly and share the good times". I interpreted that perhaps being friendly and sharing the good times was a risk. After a bit of silence, Betty said, "not only does it seem like a waste of time, but I would feel selfish. It seems like there are other people out there with terrible problems and here I would be going on about my pleasures." Over the next few sessions, it came to light that Betty not only felt wrong about sharing her "pleasures" with me, but with herself as well. She told me how she would find herself thinking about relaxing after work and watching her favorite television show, an environmental program highlighting nature and animals around the world. But, then she would think of her "poor brother and pathetic father" and all the other people in the world who didn't have it as good as she did. So, she would elect to not watch television and instead do something "responsible" like clean the house, balance the checkbook, or visit with her brother.

While guilt seems to be central to this case, I felt, especially in the countertransference, that Betty was conveying a sense of anxiety about being alone and aimless. It was a measure of progress when she finally told me about her lifelong dream of being a park ranger. Her favorite television program was a nature series and when she did allow herself to read for pleasure, it was usually a book on state and national parks. But, Betty felt she would never be able to be a ranger as she would neglect her family if she pursued that career. Again, when she described this, I felt there was also a strong hint of fear of being alone, away from her family, lonely in the woods by herself. In other words, she claimed she would easily pursue the career if it wasn't for her guilt and responsibility for her family. But, I interpreted that it was also a sense of ending up all alone without the security of her family. So, when she railed against the family for "holding her back from her dream" I interpreted that she held herself back to avoid the void of being without them. Also, I pointed out that she imagined it must be one or the other. Either she catered to her family and gave up her career or pursued the career and gave up the family. This type of splitting and the projection of her feelings of persecution onto her family was a major part of what kept her from the goodness of the object and her own goodness and ability.

In the second year of her analysis, Betty began to focus on how she felt blamed by me, instead of understood and sympathized with. She told me I seemed just as "unhelpful and critical" as her family did when she was growing up. This was a difficult period as she refused to reflect on this feeling or explore it much. It was just a fact, so there was not much as-if quality to it. She told me I should be offering her "soothing messages that showed I could fathom the unfairness of her childhood instead of siding with her family". In the countertransference, this was both interesting and frustrating. My impression was that she wanted the sort of soothing words a hurt child might need, words that make it all better or at least tolerable. However, as an adult, I didn't think they would sound genuine to her. She might feel talked down to. So, I simply made my usual empathic inter-pretations but took into account that Betty was having a hard time taking in my direct comments without feeling persecuted. In other words, my interpretations were good objects that, via splitting, were categorized as either ideal or utterly failing. I conveyed all of this to her and some days it seemed to make sense to her and other days she became agitated and told me off. Along the way, I interpreted that she seemed to be craving a certain type of feeding, closeness, or dependency with me but felt the need to be in control of it for safety. And, when we got too close for her comfort or were exploring her need for dependency too directly, Betty needed to rebel and gain some distance.

Another difficult phase of the treatment was when Betty told me she would not want to get better until her family changed. She said, "it doesn't seem fair that I should have to work hard at this when my family never did anything to change. They get to skate through life. They never say they are sorry to me or try to improve themselves." I interpreted that Betty was showing me an ultimatum. She was not about to grow or change until they did and she wanted an apology before she would budge. So, she felt righteous and angry that way, but also hopelessly stuck and alone as a result. I interpreted that she wanted me to apologize for my lack of warmth and understanding before she would be willing to move ahead. At first, she replied as if this was a simple reality and stated, "Of course. What seems strange about that?" But, over time, we began discussing how and why it was so hard to accept the shortcoming of her family and analyst and why it was so hard to let herself enjoy life without feeling we had won a victory over her.

Over time, I interpreted that she had felt controlled as a child and neglected, so now she tried to control others by not thriving. My line of interpreting gradually resulted in a reduction of anxiety and a slow movement toward better relating and integration of goodness. Betty showed less of a commitment to warding off goodness or growth.

Of course, all these issues, phantasies, and relational patterns recycled throughout the treatment, sometimes modified and sometimes reaching backwards. The more stubborn and persecutory feelings of being criticized and refusing to change until I changed or apologized would reappear at times. Other moments were filled with a more depressive sadness in which Betty told me, "I am sure you are bored and irritated with me. When it is time to see me, I worry that you dread it and think of me as the nasty whiner." She also said, "I don't want to hurt you, my family, or friends by growing up, by changing or moving. I feel like I have to always be the same and never advance myself. Someone will be hurt by it. I think you will miss me when I stop being here and you will have a hard time without the income. I know it is ridiculous but that is what I think sometimes."

Another version of Betty's disturbance with talking about positive matters came up whenever we might touch on a topic such as movies, politics, current events, or music. She said it was "strange and inappropriate" to be "having normal conversations". She would say this in a defensive and accusatory way. I would eventually remind her that she had brought these topics up and then seemed troubled if I responded to them. I interpreted that this was similar to her wanting me to be understanding or soothing, but she was always critical of my attempts. I interpreted that she again wanted a close and soothing relationship with me, but became anxious that it could shift into something hurtful to one of us, so she had to extinguish it before it got off the ground. Also, we explored and discussed the way she tried to keep me as an ideal analyst/parent who was under her control, but these "normal conversations" signaled that I was human and therefore possibly full of danger and disappointment. She replied, "Why not? That was what my family proved!"

So, at times the transference took on a combative tone. Yet, it usually was mixed with a certain chummy or even romantic quality. Betty's efforts to be independent and in control were more flexible as the treatment went on, but still not without some conflict along the way. When using the analytic couch, she would put a small pillow from the sofa onto the headrest for neck support. At one point, Betty asked me if I would put the pillow there for her each time before she arrived. In the countertransference, I felt controlled, badgered, and manipulated. But, I also felt there was something intimate and cozy about it. Over the course of the session, we were able to explore the meaning of this. I interpreted that by not having to place it there herself, she could avoid the effort she made to be comfortable with me and enter our connectedness. She said, "I feel like I have to ask each time, even though I never say anything. If you get it for me, then I don't feel weird about it." I interpreted the "weirdness" as shame around her dependency and connection to me and the positive intimacy of the setting. Betty paused and said, "that may be, but one day it will be over. I will leave you and that idea bugs me. For some reason, I feel I will hurt you. I will leave you feeling sad and abandoned." I said, "maybe you worry about when we separate and that makes you feel sad and alone". Betty shot back, "well, at least I will have my prozac to keep me company. It will just be me and my little pills and we will be doing just fine!" I said, "so, you will miss me and feel alone. With the medication, you can say, 'I am fine. I don't need anyone'. But, you are imagining this whole story because you want to be independent and able to sustain yourself as well as to be attached to me. But, you worry that you have to choose one or the other." Betty said, "fuck you!" in a way that meant, "you have my number, doc". For a period of six months or so, we were able to explore many previously off-limits topics in this roughhouse manner. I interpreted that it helped Betty still feel in control and well-defended, but also let her take me in as a good object and admit and accept her need for goodness, joy, and growth in herself.

By the fourth year of her analytic treatment, Betty was in touch with quite different feelings. The old conflicts certainly continued to appear and she could still exhibit a strong reluctance to her own growth and the experience of separation and happiness. But, her analytic progress was well reflected in her statement to me, "I now see that the truth is that both my family and I have been very stuck, unwilling to grow. We all have been loyal to the muck, the bottom rung on the ladder. We want each other to be like the other, there is no room for difference. I want them to be just like me, or else. If I have to grow up, then by God they need to as well. I really got stuck in that. The saddest part of the whole story is that we are all very different people and we will never be the same. That is just the reality of it and it is all right, but tough to digest. I see now that I love them, but I don't like how they are. But, I don't have to be that way, I can be different. I think I can let them be themselves and let me be myself."

This was a real signal of Betty's successful working-through process. For her, and many similar patients who fight off goodness, growth, and the good object, differences are threatening. Differences, for Betty, stood for need, hunger, weakness, and evidence of life and joy. Separation, therefore, meant debilitating loss (Waska 2002). Betty felt a greedy desire and a fearful need to keep her objects and herself always the same. So, her awareness of this and her efforts to challenge and change it were impressive.

## CASE MATERIAL 2.3

Judy was a talented chef who worked at many different restaurants throughout her twenties and thirties. She always ended up quitting, after feeling resentful and tired of being a martyr to the business and her boss. She entered analytic treatment in her forties and, after a few months, we were able to identify a pattern in which she would ingratiate herself to the boss, coworkers, and customers in the hopes of receiving both special attention and recognition, but also to make sure she wasn't creating any conflict or dispute. Judy always worried that someone was angry with her, which was usually a projection of her anger and resentment. Over the years, there had been many opportunities for Judy to advance her career and build an independent role for herself. Invariably, she always ran away from these or sabotaged them when they started to blossom.

During the course of our work together, she quit a job she hated and left a boss she despised to become an independent chef for special events and private clients. This was a dramatic change and was at first welcomed with excitement, but quickly Judy saw it as another way she was "trapped" and "obligated to serve".

Judy grew up in a family where her father was always angry, often shouting at his wife. Judy's mother was a very self-deprecating, passive woman who tried to do what it took to not anger her husband. Judy was the third child of six who all banded together to stay out of father's way and not cause trouble. Judy told me that all the children felt they were cared for adequately, but when they reached their early teens, both parents seemed to "lose all interest". Throughout her five-year analytic work, this point would often surface as one of many ways to understand Judy's feelings of not wanting to be on her own, independent, or grown-up.

One of several themes in our work was Judy's paranoid and declarative stance of never being in debt to anyone for anything. This meant commitment was out of the question. She told me, "I will simply never ask for anything because then I am under their thumb and committed to them. No way on that one! I want my freedom!" I interpreted that she actually put herself under a thumb because the freedom she spoke of meant doing work for a client but never billing them because it was "too corporate and straightlaced. It is everyday tedium that I won't buy into." I also interpreted that after she achieves that kind of "freedom", she is resentful with nothing to show and nothing to feel satisfied with, only the bitter aftertaste of rebellion. As a result, then, she feels entitled to be given to and cared for. This was another theme in the treatment. She went between feeling and acting like a victim and feeling and acting entitled. As to Judy's hatred of commitment, I also interpreted that her loyalty and commitment to me and the analytic treatment was 100 percent. She trusted me and depended on me with one exception. Judy would only relate to me as a helpless, angry victim who should be given a better life. She would never reveal any part of herself that experienced joy, desire, striving for success, pride, or a sense of accomplishment. This independent, growth-oriented, acceptance of the good in herself and others was deliberately and strongly censored from our relationship.

Judy needed to exert control over her neediness, her desire for love, and her urges for success and independence by projecting them into her objects and then trying to save, nurture and champion those objects. She needed to maintain a level of depressive misery so as to avoid becoming demanding and arrogant. This often failed and she would rail at me about how unfair it all was and how she deserved much better. I interpreted that she spent much of her time trying to be miserable and suffering much like her mother, in order to avoid becoming arrogant and mean like her father. At the same time, keeping herself down like that made her feel angry and entitled, which in turn left her frightened that the object would retaliate. So, the ultimate solution in Judy's phantasy life was to do and be nothing. If all choices were bad, it was better to never choose. In Judy's mind, to let in the soothing good object, to allow herself to be in touch with her own goodness or to allow a commitment and relationship to a good object was, sooner or later, to bring on the return of the combined mother–father bad objects that would persecute and abandon her. It felt better to stay with the predictable misery and chronic oppression of the bad object and bad self rather than the more frightening risk of hoped-for goodness evaporating into bad and into fragmenting nothingness.

When I heard Judy telling me about something positive, usually in a veiled and subtle way, it was unsettling for her when I made note of it. She was quick to destroy it. I would comment on how she seemed happy about something or how she seemed to be pursuing some desire more than usual. She would tell me she was just fooling herself or that she was "acting like a real predator". Even though she resisted every step of the way, these types of discussions gradually led to our understanding how she felt she would become a predator if she pursued her dreams. So, she did nothing. Then, she felt safe but deprived and then furious. If someone came along and emotionally fed her it was OK or if she was given permission to act on her own behalf it was all right. But, autonomous movement forward was too risky.

Through Judy's use of projective identification, I experienced counter-transference feelings that were difficult to bear at times, but ultimately helpful in understanding Judy's internal struggles. Sometimes, I felt deprived of goodness when I was with her. I longed for some small story of pride, fun, or glory. Along the way, I interpreted this as her projection. This led to Judy talking about her family. She told me that being happy or proud "was the equivalent to becoming a target". I interpreted that she was slowly challenging and changing that image by a new way of relating to me and to herself. Also, I said, "you are still scared and careful, so you bring the goodies to me wrapped in black paper, just in case. But, you hope I realize that underneath the misery, the black paper, there is something good and that I will appreciate what you are sharing with me." This type of careful, timid unfolding of Judy's search for goodness within herself and her objects continues to build in her analytic work. Now in her fourth year of treatment, Judy has achieved a great deal and changed many of these pathological phantasies and relational patterns.

Judy and the other patients presented in this chapter create analytic standoffs in which they feel threatened by the presence of the good object and have rebelled against the emergence of goodness and autonomy in themselves. Control, rigidity, and unidimensional relating is common, often turning into sadomasochistic power struggles with the analyst if internal change begins to occur. These types of difficult patients often demand magical cures from the analyst as a way to avoid the real, painful work in which they would need to grieve the loss of their ideal vision of perfect objects taking total care of a perfect self. Therapeutically, they would need to accept the mix of good and bad within themselves and within relationships.

The desire for genuine love, of self and with another, is held hostage by the quest for idealized versions of parental figures that were unavailable in the past. For these patients, psychoanalytic working through represents the aborted hope of admiration, rescue, and soothing by a perfect object. They see a good object or a good self as a poor second choice and therefore fight off the analytic process.

A genuine working through and acceptance of mutual dependence combined with independent growth and creativity is essential, yet slow and difficult to obtain. In a successful treatment, states of fluctuating union and separation are gradually integrated to allow for tolerable levels of loss and guilt that do not inhibit growth, striving, and self-expression.

# Chapter 3

# Fighting off the good object

Fairly early in the analytic treatment, the transference with some patients is shaped into a black-and-white, all-or-nothing matrix that has little room for the middle ground that analytic work naturally strives for. Rather quickly and dramatically, the initial interest in change and growth turns into an active stance against growth. This type of patient experiences more balanced and integrated transference moments as untrustworthy, false, or dangerous. Therefore, what is usually considered progress to the analyst is viewed by the patient as a threat to the quest for an idealized object or a threat to their escape from a persecutory object.

The psychoanalytic literature has extensive theoretical contributions to help explain the dynamics of these patients. Freud (1923) paved the way with his examination of unconscious guilt and superego problems. Among the authors writing after Freud, Valenstein (1973) indicates an intractable attachment to pain is at the base of these clinical problems, with treatment being aimed at slowly helping the patient experience pleasure without anxiety. Gorney (1979) emphasizes the oppositional resistance to the supportive presence of the analyst and the need to monitor subsequent countertransference issues. Brenner (1970) makes a point that since such a negative therapeutic reaction involves so many possible variables with each separate patient, we ought to simply try to analyze the fight against the good object just as we would analyze any other transference reaction. Olinick (1970) explored the sadomasochistic aspects of this growth-resistant reaction. As mentioned in Chapter 1, Melanie Klein (1957) examined the role of envy in these individuals. Then, Limentani (1981) extended her thinking to explore the role of reparation and the reluctance to face guilt as being a main factor. Rosenfeld (1978; 1987) emphasized the external and interpersonal aspects of the patient's background and the subsequent intrapsychic fallout.

From a Kleinian perspective, I will examine two cases in which the patient had a difficult time seeing me as a good object and exhibited a certain loyalty to being connected to the bad object and the idea of a bad self. At the same time, there was an idealization of the object and often standards of what the self should be, leading to chronic disappointment and criticism. Usually, these good-object inhibited patients show contrary states of desire, fear, aggression, and confusion. With persistent analytic work, these separate and unmatched aspects of the patient's ego can be unified and integrated enough to reveal the underlying phantasies and feelings that encompass the need to fight off growth, change, and the good object.

More specifically, these patients have phantasies which concern overwhelming states of anxiety having to do with visions of great loss and the belief of irreparable damage to the object. These psychological states quickly shift into a deep sense of persecution, abandonment, and an aloneness that is impossible to bear. This internal state and the core phantasies that form it often encompass primitive, brittle, or corrupted aspects of the depressive position which overlap or intersect with more paranoid-schizoid experiences. This is referred to by Segal (1974) when she notes that the ego needs a meaningful history and contact with good objects in order to traverse the depressive position. She states:

> Where the depressive position has not been worked through sufficiently, and the belief in the ego's love and creativity and its capacity to regain good objects internally and externally has not been firmly established, development is far less favorable. The ego is dogged by constant anxiety of the total loss of good internal situations, it is impoverished and weakened, its relation to reality may be tenuous and there is a perpetual dread of and sometimes an actual threat of regression into psychosis.
>
> (p. 81)

Without the good object, the depressive position can be too difficult to bear and the ego feels it is collapsing, fragmenting, and close to a psychotic experience. I think that the psychotic experience Segal mentions is the ego's contact with a good object that is fragile, brittle, and prone to transformation to a persecutory and abandoning object. Thus, the ego is left defenseless, overwhelmed with anxiety, and fragmented. Internally, this is experienced as a psychotic breakdown.

Patients who resist change, growth, and connection with a good, yet fallible, object all have certain commonalities in their background. They have been raised in families where they were often intimidated, abused, frightened, or neglected. Even in the milder cases, they, as children, felt oppressed by unspoken messages in which they felt a need to match a parent's way of experiencing the world or face some type of threat to themselves and their object. As a result, they felt the best coping mechanism was to become sealed off, emotionally flat, and without access to the supportive, reasonable object they hoped for. Indeed, the creation of an absent object was felt to be better than the presence of a good object which merely reminded them of the unpredictable, dangerous, and inevitable collapse of the good into the bad. Better to live in despair than to get your hopes up and face despair.

So, the ego chooses to deny access to the good object rather than invite pain, loss, and persecution. And, the loss I am noting is of an unending, primitive nature (Waska 2002). Of course, to reject the good object is to bring on that very state of anxiety, abandonment, and persecution that the ego was trying to prevent. Therefore, it is a failure as a psychological solution, but one the ego is very reluctant to give up. This distancing, cutoff stance feels safer, but involves great sacrifice and primitive, self-destructive defenses that ultimately bring about far worse internal conditions.

These patients, as children, also felt both manipulated to be caretakers to their parents and forced to always be thinking of the other person. This was usually for their own sake, not out of altruistic reasons for their objects. For example, one patient had to come home from school every day and act as caretaker/parent for her alcoholic mother. Unconsciously, she resented this but also felt she would be left alone to her own overwhelming sadness and despair if she didn't prop mother up, keep her sober, and create a facade of a mother–daughter experience. Also, if she didn't help mother prepare dinner properly, clean the house just so, and keep her sober, father would come home and erupt in rage, taking it out on the entire family. So, by helping out her drunken mother, she was ultimately saving herself. From a psychological standpoint, this meant she was constantly forced into paranoid-schizoid dilemmas that accentuated primitive splitting, oral greed and aggression, abandonment fears, a sense of persecution, and an over-reliance on projective identification. At the same time, she attempted, prematurely and for corrupt reasons, to function within the parameters of the depressive position, in which concern for the object, self-sacrifice, and trying to find relational compromises are the ongoing mental tasks. Being pushed to advance developmentally under duress, with distorted motivations, brings the immature ego into a dual track of disorder with disturbances in both paranoid and depressive functions.

Steiner (1993) has pointed out a group of patients who find a so-called psychic retreat from the perils of both paranoid-schizoid and depressive functioning. They feel they gain a defensive respite from their internal struggles. The patients I am highlighting, whose signature is to fight off the good object and the good self, have not been so lucky. Indeed, rather than a psychic retreat, they seem to have erected a psychic barricade in which they take a last stand against the good object. Feeling as though they are overwhelmed by the worst of both paranoid and depressive stresses, they say "no more". They are convinced that the presence of, the acceptance of, and the union with the good object will bring about an internal collapse. So, they try to accept the fear and anxiety they have, thinking it could only get worse if they allow themselves to connect with the good object. Their phantasy of internal collapse is of complete abandonment, loss, primitive guilt, and persecution. This is all without any hope of repair, escape, or understanding. The good object is viewed as so fragile and prone to malignant transformation that it cannot be trusted. It can easily spoil and shift into the enemy. So, identification with the bad object that is already known or worship of an idealized object are both preferable options as they offer a sense of control and omnipotent, yet false, safety.

As a result, these are difficult patients who build a transference based on this psychological conviction that the best coping mechanism is to establish a barrier to goodness, which means the experience of a good self is prohibited as well. The depressive efforts inherent in the healing of the psychoanalytic process are naturally based on integrating self–object connection and dependence with freedom, change, acceptance, and difference within intimate relationships. This is considered a threat to the well-being or status quo of these patients.

For the analyst, working with these patients brings on difficult countertransference states. A projective identification process can take place in which the patient makes a dramatic demand to be treated better, to have a better life, and to experience relationships in a more fulfilling and gratifying way. Yet, they don't want to take the risk of doing the work, internally and externally, to get there. The analyst feels pressured to deliver or grant these wishes and feels frustrated and impatient with the patient for not getting well fast enough.

Alternatively, things can seem to go along well in the transference, leading the analyst to a false sense of hope and pleasure in the overall direction of the treatment. It is often at these very moments that our patients attack us for letting them down, offering nothing, or failing to provide exactly what they need.

So, the transference profile becomes one in which the good object of the analyst (not an ideal or sacred but more a fallible composite) is consistently rejected. This might be a rejection of the analyst as a person or of the analyst's interpretations. Often, it is both. Ironically, if examined closely, these troubled and troubling patients' idea of an ideal object is usually a corrupt or pathologically deceptive object. But, the patient splits off and denies those aspects, keeping only the pure.

## CASE MATERIAL 3.1

Jim was the only boy in his family, which was in itself cause for distress. He felt enormous pressure as a child to please his father and follow in his footsteps, but felt he always failed to do both. Jim's father was rarely happy and praise for his son was hard-won and short-lived. Most of the time anger, violent outbursts, and demands for excellence occurred. Jim's mother was either fighting with her husband or busy having an affair. From Jim's recollection, his father looked the other way and tolerated this infidelity. These factors were certainly part of our exploration and search for understanding during the treatment process, but the in-the-moment, transference situation was so alive and intense that we dealt with its impact most of the time.

Jim came to me to find resolution for his chronic anxiety, which manifested as a feeling of never being liked by others. As soon as I tried to explore that idea, he was quick to tell me the reason. He said it was no mystery. He was simply unlikable. It was a fact. This was followed by countless examples with ironclad evidence of why and how he was a terrible person. This began in the first session and only grew in intensity as the analytic treatment process unfolded.

There was a way Jim quickly stopped any exploration with his immediate insistence on deficiency and inferiority. However, at the same time, he was eager to find the root of his problems and look for ways to make changes in his life. He was willing to arrange his work schedule around our sessions and made a commitment to coming in on a regular basis. We started meeting four times a week, using the analytic couch.

Within the first few months, a strong transference pattern evolved that continued through the years of his analytic work. Jim would have such a negative conviction about our relationship, before I ever introduced any comment or observation, that I was shut out or distorted before I ever got off the interpretive ground. For example, Jim would come into a session and say, "I could barely bring myself to come in today. Surely, you must dread our appointment, with me just droning on and on. I feel guilty taking up your time." I would respond by asking him what he imagined he had done to me. He would describe how boring and irritating he must be and how he was sure it wouldn't be long until I threw him out. This was a fairly closed system that was very predictable. We fell into it for quite some time. Then, I began to ask Jim what he thought he was failing to do. This was difficult for him to answer. At first, he told me how he should be a good patient who provides me with interesting stories and shows progress on a regular basis. But, soon, this idea ran out of steam and Jim was left with the empty feeling of not really knowing what he could do or be like.

I interpreted that he could picture what was wrong about our relationship, but he was reluctant to acknowledge, let alone benefit from, the positive aspects of our time together. This was met with a stream of comments to the effect that I was just being nice and saying what I had to, but I obviously must despise him and dread my time with him.

So, there was a storm of negative insistence from Jim that colored our analytic work from day one. At the same time, there was a certain pattern that emerged when we examined the bigger picture. This climate engulfed our relationship from the beginning of treatment, well into the third year of analysis. When I say "we examined the bigger picture", it was more something I identified and proposed as an interpretation. Then, Jim would agree with, deny, degrade, and then use it as a weapon against himself. Thus, the interpretive process was gravely affected by the nature of Jim's phantasies and transference dynamic.

The pattern seemed to be, on a macro-level, that Jim was desperately dependent and hungry for reassurance, protection, forgiveness, guidance, and love at a very root level. This prompted pleading and near begging for more sessions, longer sessions, and phone sessions in-between regular sessions. Jim had many dreams about me, mostly with some theme of abandonment or rejection, and he found himself thinking about our prior visits or upcoming visits as he went about his day.

This driving hunger and desperate need for union with his object, the analyst, created the next layer in the pattern. Jim was sure I wanted nothing to do with him because he was so terrible. He apologized to me as he walked in the room for the "tedious, boring, nonsense" that he was about to inflict on me. At the end of the visit, he would feel remorseful about how he had wasted my time, and during the session he had a hard time thinking about much else. During these moments, I would make interpretations about his projection of hunger onto me, creating a demanding and disappointed analyst, and his conviction that I was damaged and resentful as a result. Reluctantly, he felt understood as a result and seemed to become less anxious. However, this was usually short-lived.

I also made interpretations about how his projection of this desperate burden, with subsequent apologies, served as a smoke screen for the loving pleasure he felt with me. I suggested that he felt it was dangerous to enjoy our relationship or time together, that it must pose some sort of risk. Therefore, it was better to abort the joy, color it with negativity, or simply cast doubt on it before the joy became a danger.

Jim was able to take in these interpretations and work with them, at least for a while. This was hopeful, since the usual nature of his transference was to interrupt the interpretive process and prevent the taking in of a good self↔object experience. So, at certain moments, Jim could tell me he understood what I meant and agreed with me. He said my comments helped him think and reduced his anxiety. He would refer back to these insights at various times. For example, he left a phone message the morning after an evening session. He said, "I know we got too close to something yesterday. Now, I feel I have really messed things up. I made you furious or irritated, so I don't know if I can come back in and face you. I could tell by the way you acted when I left that you were fed up with me. You can't deny it. You will say it is not true, but I know you hate me. You must. So, I am sorry for what I did, but I don't know if I can meet with you knowing that is how you feel. I guess this is the sort of thing we talked about yesterday. I think I want to push you away before you get a chance to hurt me, to fire me, to reject me. It is my way of protecting myself. (After a long pause) I still can't believe you don't realize how much I need you to help me, so I am shocked that you don't care. I guess I will see you tomorrow."

In his message, Jim shows the fragile balance between being in touch with external reality, taking in and utilizing his new insights to create different views of his object, and the old, frightening way of relating to the world that he saw as so dark and dangerous. He fluctuated between a pathological distortion of his analytic relationship in which he held a persecutory transference view of me versus the budding of a new, hopeful perspective on himself and the important objects in his life. Was I a trustworthy, good object he would allow into his life or was I to be rejected as bad and not allowed into his circle? Through projective identification, he felt this was the dilemma I put him in.

This is the type of delicate and taxing journey that is typical with patients such as Jim, all of whom have enormous difficulties creating, allowing, and integrating new, soothing object relations. In a matter of speaking, this is like an emotional feeding problem. The ego refuses to eat, or even taste, the new and different food, out of conviction that it is bad or even poison. This leaves the ego hungry, angry, and paranoid, which easily shifts into a blaming of the object for not providing better, more nourishing food.

This type of predator↔prey, rejector↔abandoned child, exacting and demanding↔persecuted and hopeless transference construct was consistent throughout Jim's analytic treatment. As with all intense transference situations, the countertransference was important to notice and utilize as part of understanding Jim's internal struggle.

During the second year of his analytic work, Jim illustrated these conflicting internal dynamics in his response and reaction to a change in our routine. His response triggered certain countertransference feelings. Due to an unexpected work meeting, he was unable to attend a midweek session. He left a phone message, stating these facts and said he would be seeing me the following day. From past experiences with Jim, I knew he was probably feeling very alone now, despairing and afraid of my disapproval. As a result, he was also probably desperately hungry for my reassurances that I understood and was OK with the schedule change. This manifested in the countertransference as feelings of wanting to rescue Jim from his plight by calling back and assuring him I was still on his side. At the same time, this countertransference rescue phantasy left me irritated and slightly pressured because I felt obligated to head off Jim's panic. Realizing this was the cycle that so often permeated the transference↔countertransference (a mix of desperation, greed, demand, panic, abandonment, and persecution), I did nothing until the next day.

When we met the following day, these variations on not being able to imagine a flexible and understanding object due to the projections of a demand for ideal feeding all came to bear, as they often did in Jim's analytic work.

*Pt*   I don't think this therapy is working. I don't see any changes. I feel as miserable as I ever did. I have been depressed and as usual I think that suicide would be way more pleasant than this day-to-day crap. What is the point? I hate myself and I hate my life. You know how unhappy I am, but you ignore me. I can't believe how insensitive you can be. With all the troubles I am having, you know how terrible I would feel not being here yesterday. You know me well enough to know how much I needed a call yesterday, but nothing. A big zero. It was like a lifeline, but you refused to offer it!

*A*    You really wish I would know just what you need, when you need it and then give it to you at the right time. So, if you want that, you are right. I let you down. It sounds like you want me to be able to care for you in a perfect way, without you ever having to ask for it. Maybe asking for what you need feels like I am not paying attention?

*Pt*   Well, of course! You should know what I want and give it to me. Why should I have to beg for that? You are being cruel to me by not calling me when you know I need a call.

*A*    You say you must beg. So, either you must beg or I must tend to you automatically. Neither one of us gets much choice. Maybe, it is hard to picture more of a back and forth, more of an asking and receiving.

*Pt*   (Jim went on for a while about how he was getting worse and how I always let him down)

*A*    I think you want us to be one, without any differences or conflicts and for me to rescue you.

*Pt*   Of course I do. Yes! (Then, Jim became very self-critical and began to apologize for being "such a horrible patient")

*A*    I see you are switching from attacking me to attacking yourself. I wonder if showing me how much you need me and how hungry you are for a perfect parent makes you feel vulnerable, so now you try and stomp out all that and get rid of the evidence before I might get angry?

*Pt*   Yes. I better cut myself off before you do. It is less painful.

*A*    But, that means you either demand I become a perfect, all-knowing parent for you, to rescue you and care for you, or you shut the door and get nothing. It is frightening and frustrating for you to let me in, an imperfect man who nevertheless wants to understand and help.

*Pt*   I don't trust that. It sounds unpredictable. But, I think I see what you mean. I just can not take that in.

The next day, at the start of our session, I invited Jim in from the waiting room. Sometimes, I say to a patient, "hello" and motion for them to come in. Other times, I say, "hello, please come in". On this day, with Jim, I said, "hello". Immediately, Jim was upset. He said he felt rejected and shunned. "Obviously, you are fed up with me. I don't even warrant a greeting. You must still be pissed about yesterday. I feel thrown away, like trash, like garbage." I interpreted the pathological projective identification process by saying, "you are full of strong feelings this morning that bring you to throw away my hello and see it as useless trash, instead of a pleasant greeting. When you do that, I think it leaves you feeling very alone and adrift."

This interpretation seemed to alleviate his panic and despair and Jim was able to explore his feelings of not wanting to accept me or my comments as good. He said, "it is odd. But, it feels safer to see it as an attack from you than to realize you are being nice to me. I guess I don't want to trust you. I don't want to let you in because then anything could happen."

During this session, we made progress in bringing together these scattered parts of his internal objects. In other words, the splitting of his inner world into rejecting or hurtful objects on one side and ideal, perfectly attuned objects in his control on the other was less necessary. The consistent transference focus helped to heal his fragmented ego and bring him more in touch with external reality. This left him more trusting and willing to let the good, but imperfect, object in to become part of his inner experience, thereby balancing out the previously persecutory storm he usually endured and fought against.

Following up on my interpretations, Jim continued, "I take the good in a person and spit it out. I quickly cover the good with the bad. I need to mess it up. I have done that with my last couple of girlfriends. I will want them to phone me, to pay attention, to show me love. When they don't, I feel disgusted with them and tear their names out of my phone book. Then, I have nothing. For some reason, that makes me think of my mother. She is cold as a tombstone. Dead to the world." I said, "dead to you, deaf to your cry for love?" Jim replied, "say no more". This opening into his troubled relationship with his mother was hopeful. We spent significant time exploring his feelings about her and the painful rejection he grew up with.

The results of this meaningful session were mixed. While it certainly represented a major working through of Jim's object relations pathology, he also had a defensive reaction to this healing shift. The next session, Jim told me that "after our last meeting I felt totally whole, completely at peace, and in balance with the world". He said, "it was wonderful. I felt handsome, full of courage, proud of myself, and more happy than I can remember in ages." This manic state of harmony, a magical union with the ideal object, was very precarious. Jim continued, "but now, it is vanishing. It feels fragile and thin. It is evaporating. Why does it have to go? I can't hold on to it."

I interpreted that he felt he had a "red carpet session" and that it seemed he needed to feel perfectly cared for in order to fend off his bad feelings. I said that he usually imagines us at such an inferior or low place together that it takes a picture-perfect session to bring us back. But, this is fleeting.

Like an addictive drug, we must maintain this state of perfection more and more or fall back into the abyss. After some talk about this, Jim free associated to his parents and how, when he grew up, both parents had a habit of parading about the house naked. They acted narcissistically self-absorbed and flaunted their bodies, leaving Jim shocked, scared, and stimulated in a confusing, uncomfortable way. He said, "they showed off like sexy and beautiful specimens". I interpreted that Jim was afraid of identifying with them, becoming arrogant and prideful. When he felt wonderful and magical about our last meeting, he felt he was prancing about in naked joy. Then, he faced the ridicule and disgust he felt for his parents, now aimed at himself. Jim responded, "I will do anything in my power to avoid being like them. It was the sin of pride. How can they act like that? They think they are king and queen, soaring on the clouds. You're right. I feel so low and crushed when I think of them being like that."

Later in the analysis, during the second year, Jim had begun one session by briefly discussing a movie he saw in which a child constantly witnessed his parents fighting and being violent with each other. He relayed a scene in which they stopped the violence long enough to apologize to their son, but then continued fighting in front of him. I referred back to this and said, "your experience of your parents' love and my care feels tainted by hate and fear. It is either always terrible or terrible for a while and then everything is better, but then it goes right back to bad. That seems to be how you feel about us today as well." Jim responded, "I was so used to things going like that at home. It was like there was this big switch that could get thrown at any moment and things would go from OK to not OK, from nice to terrible. I see what you mean. I do see us that way and I know it isn't really like that all the time, but I still feel that way. Is it real? I don't know. It feels real, but I can never trust myself."

This type of emotional situation was typical of the slow progress and the ongoing resistance to the entrance of a good object experience that made up Jim's analytic journey. The idea of a better, safer, more fulfilling object was an elusive search punctuated by Jim's attack of the good, but not perfect object, simultaneously with the gradual, ambivalent introjection of bits and pieces of a new, more loving perception of himself and others.

An example of this was in the fourth year of Jim's analytic journey. He planned to visit his ailing father for a week and told me during the last session before he left. I made several interpretations about how difficult it might be for him to leave me to go to his father and what that might mean to him. Also, I brought up the conflict he must feel about his father's frail and elderly state of health. Jim said it didn't mean much and he didn't have any feelings about it. However, his feelings broke loose when I told him that I would be away a week after his return. So, we would not meet for a week due to his trip, then we would meet for a week, and then not meet the following week. He told me he was furious with me for trying to control him and for letting him down. I brought up that he felt OK about his leaving for a while because it was in his control but he must feel abandoned by my break since he wasn't calling the shots. Jim agreed. He said, "Yes. I think it is OK if I decide. But, if you choose, it feels like an attack out of the blue. You have ripped the rug out from my feet." I said, "it sounds like you decide when you need me and if you want me and I don't deliver, then it is my fault. When you like me, all is well; when you don't like me, everything feels overwhelming and dark." Jim corrected me, "all of that is right except the like part. It isn't if I like you or not. If I need you, then you are important and valuable. If I don't need you, then I couldn't care less about you." I added, "so, if you need me I matter. If you don't want me, I am thrown aside." Jim said, "exactly!"

## CASE MATERIAL 3.2

Marti was a forty-year-old woman who came to see me in a state of frustration and despair. She had been dating a man for several years who was on occasion verbally abusive and emotionally manipulative, but mostly just neglectful and selfish. He had two affairs over the years which Marti found out about and he rationalized them by blaming her for not providing him with enough sex. She loved him and wanted to eventually marry, but could not picture a secure future with him. He had been laid off his job for drinking a year prior to Marti seeking me out, and he still had no job prospects.

Marti worked as a retail sales clerk in a dress shop and had been there for eight years. This was the type of job she had maintained since graduating college with a dual degree in Arts and in English. She, way back as a teen, had dreamed of painting and writing for a career. But, soon after graduating, did nothing to pursue that desire and fell into a receptionist job that a friend had recommended. Marti hated her current job and told me she couldn't imagine being more bored.

I saw Marti for six years, using the analytic approach. This meant frequent visits, the analytic couch, analysis of the transference, and the exploration of defenses and unconscious phantasies. During this time, many issues emerged and much was worked through. The core theme that presented itself rather immediately and remained central to our analytic journey was Marti's reluctance, fear, and outright aversion to taking in, building, or finding a bigger, stronger, more pleasurable life.

This anti-growth, pleasure-avoidant, independence-shunning stance first took the form of her censoring the negative feelings she had toward the objects that either hurt her or denied her love and pleasure. This initial struggle gave way to Marti not feeling safe to risk broadening her life and also manifested in the transference as hiding her desires and feelings from me. So, in the beginning of the treatment, Marti would tell me stories of what her day or weekend was like in a very straightforward manner, with just the facts and details.

My countertransference feelings were very important to monitor and analyze during these periods. I would listen to her stories and find myself feeling irritated, angry, or protective of her. In her stories, I heard variations of her being used, ignored, or unappreciated and then I would feel like coming to her aid. I understood this to be part of a projective identification process in which Marti would give me pieces of her experience to hold, detoxify, or champion. These were aspects of herself and feelings that she did not want to deal with. Many of the projected feelings I was encountering had to do with early, primitive states of loss (Waska 2002) that had origins in her infantile experience of neglect by her parents.

Sometimes, I would be taken over by my countertransference experiences and act out these projective identification dynamics (Waska 2004). I would listen to a story about her recent dating of a new boyfriend and end up thinking to myself, "what a selfish guy. He didn't even bother to return her calls. How rude!" Then, I might say something like, "I bet you felt like giving him a piece of your mind about that" or "what stopped you from confronting him on that?" Some of my comments sounded relatively benign on the surface. They seemed aimed at eliciting more discussion on the matter or interpreting her resistance to standing up for herself. Over time, what I noticed was that my comments were really a combination of a reaction to feeling deprived or neglected by her silence on the matters at hand, an aggressive push from me to get her to show some feeling or response to the people who seemed to victimize her (I was bullying her for not responding to the people who bullied her), and I was becoming the spokesman for all her silent protests.

Slowly, I came to better understand these components of the counterprojective identification (Grinberg 1979). As I saw this intra-psychic and interpersonal phenomenon more clearly, I could begin to interpret it for the benefit of integrating these scattered aspects of Marti's inner world. I interpreted that she seemed to have a difficult time sharing many of her more negative or angry thoughts and feelings with me. By holding back and keeping these private, she gave me an idea of how isolated she might feel sometimes. This comment prompted Marti to recall feeling very isolated and neglected when she was a child. She told me she had many angry feelings about being left alone and ignored, but she thought that voicing them would only make her parents more neglectful or even angry and abusive.

I interpreted that we sometimes were in a situation where I was like the angry parent she feared. I was essentially saying, "what is wrong with you? Why can't you stand up for yourself?" Exploring this interpersonal and intra-psychic aspect of the projective identification in the transference led to more important associations. Marti told me more about how her sister would often criticize and bully her for "not having any common sense and never doing what needed doing". Marti recalled many times during growing up in which her sister responded to Marti's timid nature by lecturing to, yelling at, or telling her what to do and when to do it. We gained a good deal of ground by discussing how this happened on occasion in our relationship.

Unconsciously, Marti wanted me to be the spokesman for her feelings and ideas. In the first few years of the analytic work, this meant I held all of what she felt to be negative, angry, and confrontive. So, my interpretations were usually aimed at exploring how and why she felt she needed to subsume those feelings into me. We worked on how she felt it was rude, unacceptable, risky, and even dangerous to own those types of urges. Marti told me that voicing "those sorts of things could make her look like a selfish bitch".

Imaging herself as selfish, aggressive, or troublesome created a fear of being shunned, ignored, or abandoned. She cried a great deal when sharing these phantasies. Given the clarity of the transference, we were more able to explore her vision of her objects. Marti felt I was someone who would only accept, tolerate, or love her if her personality were tailor-made to my likes. Her image of me was strict and demanding, wanting her to be an agreeable little girl who didn't make trouble. This, of course, made it impossible for her to embrace life, showing all of herself. Bit by bit, we worked through this victim stance in her phantasy world to the point where she could own her own refusal of the good object, the accepting analyst, because it was a risk she couldn't control. Keeping the good object at bay allowed her to know, control, and predict her world, sad and stuck as it was. Making changes in this arena was slow and choppy, but deeply rewarding and hopeful to Marti.

Later in the psychoanalytic treatment, Marti's arm's-length approach shifted from avoiding expressing what she felt to be negative or selfish to a general reluctance to let in pleasure, success, or growth. Once again, Marti used projective identification to enlist me as her spokesman, this time for the parts of her that were ready to thrive and reach out for the good object and a vision of an accepting world. As Marti's spokesman for pleasure, I found myself voicing her wishes in numerous ways. She would say something like, "on the way to work, I stopped off at this new bakery. I got myself a coffee. On the way out, I noticed they had quite a selection of freshly baked donuts, scones, and muffins." The way she said it made it obvious to me that she was really wanting to order something delicious to go with her coffee. I would be caught up in the feeling without giving it much thought and I would say something like, "I bet you wanted to take a few with you to work!" She would hesitate, but agree and maybe elaborate a bit. This was all part of a projective identification process, involving both interpersonal dynamics and intra-psychic phantasies, in which she managed to get me to hold her desires for fun, pleasure, or growth.

Over time, I came to understand this more, started interpreting more, and began acting out the projective elements less. I would say, "I think you are reluctant to acknowledge how much you want from our relationship or from life. It is hard to show me that you want more pleasure, more fun, and more fulfilling relationships with men. You get me to be your cheerleader for these things. But, I think it is important to understand why you can't voice those hopes and wishes yourself." Marti would tell me, "when I first started seeing you, I wasn't even aware that I had these feelings, these ideas for things to be better. But now, I do find myself thinking that my boyfriend could treat me nicer, my parents could be more loving, or that I deserve a raise at work. So, I now think these things but I don't tell you. I don't want to seem too selfish or pushy. It feels like I would be asking for too much." I interpreted, "so you would rather stop yourself short than to tell me and risk that I would find you selfish and greedy". Marti agreed and said, "I think it is easier to just dream of those things than to put it out there and have them backfire."

So, at that point in the analytic work, Marti no longer feared her aggressive and negative feelings, but she hid her desires for more and for better. Her view of the object and the world was essentially the same, but now more flexible. Before, the object in Marti's internal world would immediately become hostile and angry if she expressed any conflict or autonomy, due to how she disowned her own controlling, aggressive side. Now that this pathology had been worked through and was considerably reduced and more manageable, her needs and desires became evident. However, these phantasies provoked the same type of retaliatory object relations as before, due to the same type of projective mechanisms.

Therefore, I made interpretations, much in the same manner as before, that explored these areas of stagnation and resistance. I pointed out, usually in moments it was taking place in the transference, how she was enlisting me to be her spokesman for an improved life, a more enjoyable day, and a more rewarding, bountiful existence. I said, "you want me to be a good, accepting parent, willing to hear and understand your hopes and dreams. You want my support, but you are still frightened that you want too much and I will tell you so, that I will be angry, see you as greedy, and slap you down." Marti responded, "Exactly. And, if you don't put me down, you might still choose to cut me off, have nothing to do with me. Wow, I can't believe how strong those feelings are!"

Over the years, Marti changed her view of me, due to a shift in how she felt about her needs and wishes. Tied to this change was a conflict over her sense of entitlement to more love, respect, and enjoyment from her objects. The way this would manifest was in her looking to me for permission to proceed with first having the desire for more and then acting on that urge. When Marti put me in the role of spokesman, she could then feel safe and wait till I gave her permission to have those thoughts and feelings by the signal that I was thinking and talking about them. If I was talking about improving her life, then it must be OK for her to entertain those feelings as well. As a result of our work, she was more and more able to speak to these forbidden hopes, without being overcome by fear of rejection or retaliation. So, Marti became her own spokesperson. The next step of this new freedom was difficult. It became more acceptable to think about these forbidden wishes, but to actually do something to obtain them was very frightening. So, Marti now felt she needed permission to take action to achieve these goals of self-improvement, whatever they might be.

A major vehicle for this part of the transference working-through process was when Marti decided to change careers. It was a real success that she allowed herself to think about wanting a better career and realizing how unhappy she had been for so long. Brainstorming about what she would really like to do and what type of job or career seemed most exciting was a major step in not just giving herself permission to thrive, but realizing she didn't need permission in the first place. It was OK to want more and to grow. It didn't need justification.

However, when Marti had to make phone calls and go on job interviews, many of the same fears returned. She projected her own stringent, rigid phantasies into me and her potential new bosses. Was she really cut out for it, would they see right through her, would they kick her out of the interview, was she taking up too much of my time boring me about details of her job hunt, and was she just setting herself up for an embarrassing fall and failure? It wasn't that the object was deliberately attacking her, but responding to her outrageous requests. Gradually, we worked through these phantasies. Marti faced her internal demons and took actions to reach her new goals. Due to this hard work, Marti landed a new job at a company dealing with something that had always been an interest to her.

At the end of her analysis, Marti felt "like a whole person, able to own my heart and mind and actually pursue who I am and what I am about!" She was now engaged to a man who treated her with respect and love. While she still felt timid and unsure at times, Marti was proud of her new job and felt fulfilled by her work. The world seemed more accepting and giving, because Marti allowed herself to be more accepting, giving, and loving. She could now be herself without repercussions. Indeed, Marti realized that being herself actually brought about more support, interest, and devotion from her objects. She had become a good, balanced, and accepting object for herself.

## Comment

The cases of Jim and Marti show how patients who resist the positive aspects of their lives and the goodness of close relationships can be understood, theoretically and clinically. The theoretical view of this type of anti-good object transference involves a developmental deformity of psychological growth due to external and internal factors. Externally, these patients, to some degree, have all been pushed in early stages of ego development to endure overwhelming paranoid-schizoid tensions without a significant source of good object experiences. Without the aid of enough good object contact, with its containment and mitigation of anxiety, the ego is pushed to try depressive strategies of coping when paranoid options run out. Of course, this is done through the lens of the paranoid ego and as such distorts the normal depressive position into a more primitive, fragmented world. The ego is left to traverse the strains of the depressive position, such as change, loss of control, grief, dependency, competition, and abandonment, without the tools and solutions of the depressive position, such as reparation, understanding, forgiveness, hope, acceptance of imperfection, mourning, and compassion. The good object is very basic to the ego's struggle with both positions and provides the armor, the balance, and the ability to risk growth. These patients have felt the good object to be corrupt, and by identification, they feel themselves to be corrupt and a fraud. Psychic blockades are erected by the ego to fend off any experience of the good object, or the good self as a consequence.

The cases of Jim and Marti, and the similar patients I am exploring in this book, illustrate the dynamics of those individuals in whom there is an extreme difficulty making the healthy transition and subsequent fluctuations between the paranoid-schizoid and depressive states of mental life. There are pseudo-depressive attempts at relating to the self and the object, but these efforts easily fall apart, exposing more primitive and fragile ways of experiencing the world.

In the first case of Jim, his phantasies were about having hurt me, turned me off, or disgusted me. These certainly have a depressive flavor. However, this was a conviction he forced upon me in an aggressive, paranoid fashion. And, he was prone to playing out both sides of an internal drama, pushing me to the sidelines in the meantime. So, he was hungry, desperate, and pleading but would then give me no chance to respond. Instead, he would take over and reject himself for me. I interpreted that joy, love, and connection between us was dangerous, so he prevented it. This was accurate and helpful in many situations. At the same time, I struggled with this difficult case and felt confused, helpless, and unhelpful at times.

One distinct marker of progress occurred when Jim told me how he could never trust himself. This was important as it was the first time he could locate the troubles inside himself, instead of projecting it and creating a paranoid world to react to. Also, his phantasies were quite narcissistic in that he wanted me available whenever he needed me, but otherwise I was put aside. This difficulty with ongoing dependence and mutuality was part of Jim's struggle with the depressive position's separate but connected nature with objects. It was difficult for him to tolerate a constant connection to me, which could be more distant or more close at any given time, but still an ongoing presence in his life. It is a psychological achievement to learn how to tolerate your objects being present in your mind all the time, not just when it is convenient. In particular, to allow the good object mental residence was threatening. While it serves a narcissistic function to throw the good object aside when not needed, giving the ego a sense of power, safety, and independence, it also means they are suddenly gone and nowhere to be found when the need arises. So, this pseudo-independence can create a panic and feeling of abandonment as well. Fighting off the good object means inviting in the lack of meaning, safety, or love.

All of these aspects of Jim's psychology illustrated a difficulty with whole-object functioning and a very fragile hold on depressive functioning. He was not solely operating in a paranoid fashion. There was more integration than that, most of the time. However, the depressive methods he utilized were immature, corrupt, and distorted, therefore prone to breakdown and regression to paranoid and primitive states.

In the second case Marti, she strongly believed the best thing to do in life was to avoid more pain. Marti felt her current state of distress and despair was as good as she would ever have it, as good as she should ever have it, and as good as she could ever have it. In the transference, she kept to the facts rather than risk sharing her emotional truth. Expressing your needs was the same as complaining and asking for trouble. Slowly, we were able to explore these anti-growth phantasies and found out more about her feelings of being greedy. Marti was sure she always was overstaying her welcome and asking for too much. This resulted in her asking me in various ways for permission to do what felt like indulging her greed.

Again, like the first case of Jim, Marti was not purely paranoid. She exhibited many depressive qualities and tried to relate in a whole-object manner at times. However, there was something incomplete about these efforts. Trying to not offend or hurt me was part of a phantasy of me losing my grip on the shred of tolerance I had and then completely rejecting her. There was a lack of reciprocal thinking on her part. It was more of a steady monitoring of my temper and mood with her in the background.

# Chapter 4

# Problems in receiving

This chapter will continue to explore the dynamics of those patients who develop a transference highlighted by the reluctance, resistance, or even outright refusal to become connected with a better image of themselves and a less restrictive, less negative view of their objects, including the analyst. The patients in question all appear extremely cautious or controlling when it comes to letting into their minds a phantasy of trustworthy, durable, nurturing objects in mutual connection with a safe, accepting image of the self. They push back the good object and with it, the image of a good self.

They could be classified as masochistic, resistive to change, or simply impossible to treat. In a broad sense, these labels are accurate, but tend to lead to a one-size-fits-all understanding of their psychological struggle. In this chapter, I will focus on several of these difficult patients from the point of view of their phantasy life. Working with such patients, I certainly find it helpful to have broad ideas about diagnosis and theory in the background. However, I focus more on treating each patient's particular phantasies, as expressed in the transference, in the interpersonal exchanges, from the countertransference, and from the patient's free associations. Looking at how and why they perceive their object-relational world as they do, by examining how they relate in the transference, provides the most accurate understanding. Specifically, these patients have phantasies related to how they must be careful, cautious, or resistive to experiencing union with a better object, a good object, or a different object from the often abusive, restrictive, narcissistic one they unconsciously are attached to and identified with.

As previously mentioned, Steiner (1987; 1993) has identified a particular defensive method of avoiding the stresses of the paranoid and depressive position in which the ego constructs a pathological organization or psychic retreat. This provides a shield and respite from the two positions and a denial of painful psychological reality. The patients I am highlighting construct a pathological organization that fails to provide a viable psychic retreat. They have no effective shield against the fears and pains of the two positions. While a psychic retreat at least provides a temporary way to remove oneself from the destructive self-and-object phantasies that plague the ego, the patients I am exploring have only been able to close the door on the good object. The tensions and difficulties of both positions still haunt them and they cannot escape it. It is as if a bank robber has run from the police only to end up holed up in some basement. The police will still fire their guns and try and kick down the door, so the basement is not a respite, it only provides a temporary pause before predictable disaster. I use this particular analogy because these patients feel the good object is essentially like a police force ready to batter down the basement door. The other difficulty with these types of patients is that they are convinced that if they open up that basement door and let the police in, they will be killed. So, surrender is not an option. In their current condition, these patients lead restricted, isolated, and painful lives. But, to let the good object in and progress in life, they are convinced it would only spell disaster.

This produces a difficult transference *impasse*. It is a sign of great progress if a patient can even begin talking about the meaning of their standoff with the good figure of the analyst. One patient was describing how she is constantly ignored and rejected by her boyfriend, who only sees her when he is tired of his wife. My patient then associated to her times spent with her father, who was usually drunk and unavailable. Her mother worked late hours and was usually asleep or too busy to help with parenting. My patient explained how her father did not want to hear about how she felt emotionally or about her emotional needs. If she tried to express them, she was ignored and often punished.

She told a story about getting ready to go to her first ballet lesson and feeling very scared. She told her father she felt "funny" and started crying. Her father said she should go to bed if she wasn't happy. I said, "so your feelings were ignored and not going to your lesson meant you were being punished for having feelings?" My patient sobbed and nodded yes. I later pointed out how she repeats this with me and her boyfriend by presenting herself in a very flat, unemotional way and conveying most things in a very factual manner. This has the result of essentially saying, "I don't have any needs, feelings, or opinions and therefore I don't need you to pay attention to me". She keeps me, the good object, at bay in this way, saying "oh, don't bother with me. Not much going on here."

While each case is unique in its own right, all these patients have difficulty with change, progress, and the goodness of self and others. The specific hallmark for this group of patients is a phantasy about goodness. The good object, within the transference, is experienced as a warning signal to inevitable danger, persecution, and loss. The way this phantasy emerges within the transference and the degree it erases reality-testing and therapeutic potential varies among patients. However, the central theme in all cases is this conviction that the good object must be avoided as a way to prevent internal collapse and a sense of catastrophe.

Diagnostically, most of these patients could be understood as borderline or less frequently as narcissistic. Rosenfeld (1979) states:

> another essential aspect characteristic of all borderline conditions is the failure to internalize good objects which are necessary to strengthen the ego . . . the tendency of the borderline patient is to develop a transference psychosis or may lead to long lasting, repetitive acting out. This is often a desperate attempt by the patient to repair the disturbed link of mother and infant. However, the strong reparative drives are often covered by the chronic rage or despair. So, the traumatic situation is repeated in the analysis.
>
> (p. 204)

This lack of good objects is a major factor in the constant rage and despair which corrupts the reparative urges of the depressive position and leads to a pathological recycling of self–object dysfunction in place of genuine working through, unless consistently targeted within the transference work. So, these patients suffer with a fragile, impoverished hold on the depressive position as well as the unresolved conflicts of the paranoid-schizoid world. This leads to overwhelming anxieties and a standoff with the good object.

## CASE 4.1: AVOIDING A SHOWDOWN

Many patients come into psychoanalytic treatment with a history of family cruelty and abuse. In my experience, the majority of patients seen in private practice settings have grown up with one parent being abusive emotionally and often physically. The other parent was usually distant or unavailable. Alcoholism, mental illness, and environmental stress such as financial problems, single-parent families, and divorce have made it difficult for the parent(s) to provide for the children. Through projective identification and other defensive coping mechanisms, these children have typically infused their early struggles with their own anxiety, aggression, and desires, resulting in pathological object-relational phantasies.

As mentioned, the common phantasy in these troubled patients is that of having a brittle hold on a reliable, trustworthy object which then turns out to be a traitor, who shifts from safe to attacking and abandoning. These patients are unwilling to depend on the analyst or others in their life because of these anxieties and therefore they live a life of defensive independence. Another variation of this occurs when they try to be close with their objects, but perceive of rejection and disappointment along the way, which brings out a constant state of agitation and counter-attack. Usually, there is a combination of these postures, resulting in countless anti-dependent efforts but also attempts to trust others which lead to feeling either betrayed or to blame for the relationship failing.

An example of one such internal quandary was expressed by a patient who came to her appointment and thought she was five minutes late. She found my office dark and locked. She thought she must have the wrong day or time and she left immediately. I arrived a minute or two later and found a message on my telephone machine explaining all this, from her cell phone as she drove away. The next time I met with this patient, many interesting matters emerged.

First of all, I told her I had arrived at my office five minutes before our scheduled meeting time, so I wondered what could have taken place. I asked her what time her watch had. It turned out she kept her watch running ten minutes fast, so she had arrived at about seven minutes before the hour and left immediately, barely missing me when I arrived at about five minutes before the hour.

By exploring this incident, two valuable themes emerged. She kept her watch fast, so as to avoid being late anywhere. The more we talked about this, it became clear that it was part of a fear and a phantasy of being a failure to a demanding object that kept nearly impossible standards. So, coming to see me was anything but the opportunity to meet with a supportive, helpful, or nourishing object. It was a vision of inevitable criticism or rejection. This same psychological mural emerged when I asked why she had left so quickly, without staying around a few minutes to see if I would show up. She told me she imagined a potential showdown if I were to see her face-to-face when she was late. It was better to run away from the possible battle and apologize from a distance, via the phone. This patient demonstrates how fragile the good object can be in some people's minds and how the breakdown of the barely available good object into a punitive, abandoning object can taint much of everyday, moment-to-moment existence.

Waiting for permission to indulge in pleasure, waiting to see if it is OK to need or utilize the goodness of the object, and to develop one's own mind separately before the object takes the first step, are all ways of being careful and cautious to avoid the collapse of the omnipotent, dominant object into a persecutory, neglectful one. This anxious, internal phantasy leaves very little room for a good object that is not perfect, but still very loving, understanding, and constant.

## CASE 4.2: ONCE A VICTIM, ALWAYS A VICTIM?

Sue was a forty-year-old woman from South America. She had moved to the USA when she was in her late twenties, hoping to leave behind a life of fear and a constant conviction that others hated her and would ultimately hurt her. Every few years, she would either quit her job or move in order to cut ties with the coworkers, friends, and boyfriends she had made. She grew up in an alcoholic home in which both parents were often drunk and sometimes violent. Sue and her three other sisters banded together to be as nice and compliant as possible, so as to not incite either parent's temper. Every summer, she spent time with her uncle so the parents had a vacation from the children. It seems that they found a relative to farm each child out to. The uncle was not an alcoholic, but he did molest Sue. At first, this was with fondling, later with oral sex, and when she was eleven years old, it was intercourse. She had never told anyone before she revealed this to me.

Sue came to see me because she found herself overcome with anxiety at having to interact with her coworkers. They thought she was a nice person and tried to include her in the various office parties and after-work activities they all enjoyed as a group. To Sue, she felt forced to act as nice as possible and go along with these interactions, but she was convinced that sooner or later "something horrible would happen". When I interpreted that her emotional situation sounded very much like how she felt growing up, Sue shuddered and said, "I never thought of it like that, but it is like that. Sooner or later, they will find me out, realize I am a shit, a loser. Also, I am scared I will do something to offend them. I don't feel like I understand anyone's customs, expectations, or demands. It is just a matter of time before they hate me."

So, I continued over time to interpretively investigate this fear of Sue's, which turned out to be a prominent phantasy that shaped her view of the world. We met three times a week, using the analytic couch. Much of the time the transference was a combination of me barely tolerating her presence and her feeling panicked at not having enough to offer me to keep me satisfied and even-tempered.

On a Monday session, Sue had paid me for the whole week, which was not unusual but also not regular. She came in on Tuesday, looking very tense. I asked why. She said she was worried I may have forgotten that she already paid. I said, "you feel like you don't have a peace offering for the angry gods?" By now, I could say something like this and be understood without having to go into more details. This was in itself a sign of progress. We had constructed a shared language, a way of communicating that made sense to each other. This was a bridge of connection that Sue allowed. She said, "I feel like I always need to keep on top of everything or I might let something slip by which would make you angry. I don't want you to think I am delinquent or unaware of my responsibilities." I replied, "and the way you see me, I wouldn't be too forgiving if you were". Sue said, "Right! Why would you be, why should I deserve a special break? But, I appreciate that you say you would be understanding. I guess I just don't believe it." I replied, "you post a 'no trespassing' sign up when I offer understanding or when you even imagine me trying to be supportive. I think you feel in control that way and to let in the possibility of us being OK and able to talk about uncertainties feels very risky."

Here, I was interpreting the no-entry stance Sue took to a good object. It was the new phantasy of being in union with a safe, good object that triggered great anxiety. She replied, "I need that control. Even with it, I feel like everything is always just about to get me, like it is just a matter of time before this turns bad or goes away."

After a moment of silence, Sue free associated to feeling very tired because she had not been sleeping well. "I haven't been sleeping too well because I keep thinking there are beetles in the house. I get convinced a beetle has gotten in the window and is going to crawl into the bedroom and onto me." I asked her for details and she relayed a lifelong fear of beetles and how they are very ugly and impossible to kill. "They are hard, difficult to get rid of, and impossible to kill. They are disgusting. They get in your clothes and crawl all around. The worst possible thing in the world would be if they got into my mouth. It is a terrible thought I just can't get rid of."

After listening to this, I interpreted that there was an intrusive, rape-like quality to the beetle, leaving her vulnerable and very frightened. Sue felt a sense of helplessness and futility (no way to get rid of it or kill it). While I clearly thought this was linked to her early sexual abuse and the resulting helplessness and futility, I also felt it was a current phantasy with present-day objects, including myself. Therefore, I interpreted that she felt this same beetle-related dread with me and generally in her lonely, day-to-day life.

Turning away from my comment about her psychology, Sue said she wondered if there might be some sort of behavioral therapy I could conduct in which she would be forced to face the beetles, even if it meant she was left terrified and screaming. I interpreted that her wish would be a repeat of her childhood rape and her lasting sense of terror and helplessness. Sue said, "the beetles are so ugly, just gross. And, they keep coming at you regardless of what you do." I interpreted that maybe she was feeling anxious about something before she went to bed that led her to start thinking about the beetles. After a few moments of silence, Sue replied, "Well, lately I have been reflecting on what we had talked about a while back. When I was fifteen years old, I was prostituting myself. I felt really powerful. I was making money, being in charge, doing things that kids my age could only dream of. If I wanted something, I just bought it. I didn't have to rely on my parents. But, I also felt so depressed, so dirty. I wanted to die, all the time. Well, actually only when I allowed myself to slow down and think about my life, which is what I am doing now. It is a nightmare." She was shaking and crying.

When Sue came to the next session, she looked extremely tense and was silent. She was withdrawn, withholding, and reluctant to talk, even when I asked her several times to tell me what was wrong. After a while, it came out that she had spent the night restlessly thinking about our next session and how I "would force her to keep thinking and talking about all these awful things". Bit by bit, I was able to interpret the recreation of her core phantasy of being forced, raped, and controlled by her object, now within our relationship. She had become convinced that in our next meeting she would become my victim. In addition, and equally if not more important, I slowly became aware of and then interpreted the recreation of this in the therapeutic moment.

Through projective identification, my countertransference was affected and I had been somewhat interrogating her, pushing her to answer my questions. In a sense, I was relentlessly intruding on her verbally. She became quiet and withholding, I became verbal and pushy. So, momentarily, she was being raped again, helpless against her uncle. When I interpreted this transference phantasy being acted out by us interpersonally, she said, "I see what you mean. I didn't mean to do that and I don't see you that way, but I see exactly what you mean. I think this happens to me much of the time, all through my life." Sue seemed to relax a bit and become curious and open to exploring these ideas. This was part of her gradual progress in psychoanalytic treatment.


## CASE 4.3: TO BE LOVED, I MUST SUFFER

Tony was in his forties when I met him. He was twice divorced and in a very unhappy relationship with a married woman. He had been raised in a family that left him feeling tense, quick to relinquish his own needs, and a master at denying his own feelings. He had no value in his own mind, unless he could offer himself up to please others. This masochistic approach to life seemed to grow out of his close dependence on his alcoholic father and his awareness of his mother's chronic infidelity. His mother would always be away "on business" as a secretary for an international banking company. In reality, she was the boss's mistress. Tony's father would be drunk most of the time when mother was away. As the older of two children, he had to assume the role of housekeeper and peacemaker. When Tony was eight years old, his parents divorced. His younger sister went to live with mother and Tony was left to live with and take care of father. Tony plays down the many sad and frustrating years spent with his emotionally absent father. Instead, Tony focuses on the ten wonderful years when his father sobered up after Tony graduated from highschool. Unfortunately, his father died of cancer when Tony was twenty-eight.

Over the years, Tony has found himself in many relationships, with women and friendships at work, that replicate his masochistic role in his family. Notice I am using the general term masochistic. This diagnostic and theoretical term is helpful to think about Tony in a general manner, but not as useful clinically. It doesn't really capture his specific inner world and the particular way he creates relational dynamics of suffering and sacrifice. Tony is very used to establishing a bond with someone based on trying to meet their needs. If he is lucky, he will get some conditional love out of the deal. However, part of his phantasy is that he must turn a blind eye to frequent unkindness or indiscretion in the hope that things will magically right themselves. In the analytic treatment, we have explored his phantasy of being immediately abandoned should he question any hurtful moments with his lover or friend or should he ask for more love or better care. Tony says, "I would rather keep hanging onto what I have, instead of probably never getting anything or anyone else ever again." So, the transference was imprinted with this reluctance, which was almost a commitment to not offering entry to the new object, to the good and reliable object that might have a penalty or disappointment attached to it.

Tony was depressed and sad much of the time. He had suffered with sad moods and fits of crying for most of his life and had been on various medications for almost twenty years. The way his mood fluctuated depended on two factors. If he felt attached to someone who seemed willing to have him as a friend or lover, he immediately felt confident, eager, and content. This was not a manic switch from the depressed state *per se*, but a sudden sense of security and soothing. While the stereotypical excitement and giddiness of mania was absent, the emotional mania of denial was clearly present. Even if this new girlfriend or coworker seemed either somewhat questionable or a downright bad choice, Tony looked the other way.

The other way Tony was able to shift from being depressed to feeling happy was to become enmeshed in his love of books. Tony loved to read and spent many of his free hours reading books, or attending several book clubs where novels were discussed, or meeting with friends to attend book readings by authors. This was certainly a creative outlet for Tony and he was very astute and often quite brilliant at analyzing the plots, subtexts, and symbolic meanings of the books. Yet, it was also an intellectual defense.

With me, he would often tell me about the latest novel he was reading or discussing in group and share his take on it with me. In the counter-transference, I noticed two things. First, I was drawn in to his wit and personal take on the stories. I found myself intrigued and sometimes thought I might like to buy the novel after hearing Tony's wonderful review. However, something else always struck me. After Tony had gone on for twenty minutes, in depth, about a story, I noticed I had no idea how he personally felt about it. It was a brilliant review and Tony expressed excitement, critical reflection, and even wise ideas about how it could have been written differently. However, there was never any inclusion about how the story reminded him of something personal, how he identified with a character, how sad/angry/loved he felt in identification with the story, or how he realized something new about himself through the story. So, his creative outlet was also a defense in which he used intellect, wit, and detachment to talk about human emotions and intimate relationships, twice removed.

I took several interpretive directions with the transference, based on Tony's way of relating to me as the detached reviewer. I explored the ongoing tension that seemed present in his trying to both always engage me and contribute stories to bring us together, yet he had to keep himself out of the equation. It was his story and I that bonded, not he and I. In the countertransference, which I did share with him, I envisioned this as a parallel to him wishing to bond with his father, but having to be on the sidelines, watching father bond with alcohol instead. Tony, over time, told me that to bring himself into the picture felt very risky, even foolhardy. It was an invitation to being hurt, left, or criticized. And, as he had already told me, why give up what you have if you are pretty sure there will never be anything or anyone else as a replacement.

Doing my best to stay with the primary transference theme, which emerges from the core phantasy the patient is organizing their life around, I analyzed the way Tony's story telling was simultaneously a way to approach me with a gift I might enjoy, a way to keep us apart and at a safe distance, a way to impress me with what he could relay, which hid who he really was and what he really felt, and an invitation for me to hopefully see beyond the defensive intellectualization and more towards the emotional meaning of the stories and how they were a mirror of his inner life. They were his disguised way of communicating his wishes, needs, and opinions to me.

An example of this ongoing transference work on his phantasy of love and suffering came out in his discussion of a short story about a child in a foster home. The story opened with the child waiting on the doorstep to be picked up by his new adoptive mother. The little boy is left waiting and the new mother isn't showing up like she promised, or so the reader thinks. Tony went over the details of the story, emphasizing the terrible grief and betrayal in a very efficient and skillful manner. Again, it was a brilliant review of a story of sadness and abandonment. I happened to know the particular short story and pointed out that two things were happening in the room between Tony and myself. First, Tony was again keeping us safe, apart, and within a sterile, academic atmosphere. This seemed to be the best he could do to bring himself in connection to me. I then interpreted that he used the grief and abandonment that he emphasized in his review to try and secretly convey to me his fear of what might happen should he become attached and real with me.

Also, I reminded him of the ending of the story, which he had left out. The first scene of the child feeling stood up by the new mother fades into the details of his history and the foster home. At the end of the story, we are brought back to the boy, still waiting at the doorstep. Finally, she arrives and apologizes for being late and they both drive off together. The story ends with them having a very emotional talk about their difficulty relating to each other honestly and a commitment to each other to try, to trust, and to love. I told Tony that, like the child in the story, he had been hurt before and didn't want to move onto the next object of desire or try it again with the same object. Why ask for something good when you got burned before? In this case, Tony's object of desire, of connection, was his analyst. Just as he felt left behind by his mother, Tony was sure that would be the case with me if he let the goodness of our relationship, or even the potential of goodness, into his mind. This was a horrible conviction, a phantasy he lived by. He ended our story early and felt left by the doorstep because he was too frightened to keep hope alive and maybe be picked up after all. He avoided the happy ending because one bad ending was all he could take. His mother failed him and he wasn't about to let me fail him. He closed the door before the possibility of success or failure was around. Of course, this made his life sadly predictable. But, to try again to feel the excitement, the hope and the desire only to lose his object of desire all over again was too much to bear. I said all this and Tony said, "I am stunned. I can't believe I forgot the end of the story. I really see what you mean. Wow! This is heavy. This really is clear this time, it gets me in a very deep way."

The more we explored and discussed this situation, more of Tony's core phantasy came to light. Throughout the analysis, we had worked on times within the transference when Tony would do his best to keep us, me, himself, the daily events he relayed, or the characters in his reviews all on an idealistic plane. By this I mean he tried to keep everything at a zero sum, where nothing would need to be questioned, either for its deficiencies or for its benefits. We came to understand this as a way to avoid conflict and a way to not embrace the regular, normal, and sometimes painful imperfections of himself and his objects.

For Tony, bringing hope into our relationship was out of the question. To do so left me in control, put him at the mercy of circumstances, and left him anticipating abandonment and persecution. I say persecution because he was enraged at his abandoning objects, but that aggression was quickly projected onto the object, creating a sense of fear and duty to maintain the peace at any cost. This came out in not only the transference but also in his memories of growing up and needing to take the brunt of his father's drinking and help him through his binges. So, in the transference, part of Tony's anger came out as his way of capturing me or torturing me with his endless intellectual reviews. But, this was also a way of propping me up, keeping me interested, and keeping the atmosphere in the room harmonious and moving ahead without any conflict.

Over time, Tony was able to work through some of these ways of relating by facing his phantasy directly and challenging some of his core beliefs. During one session, he said, when I tell you my stories, I am on automatic pilot. Then, I can sort of look around and make sure everything is OK. It is my way of standing watch and being alert to any sign of trouble. If we start going sour, I will see it coming and be able to avoid it somehow. I interpreted his avoidance of real connection as being out of fear of his own feelings, whether need, anger, sadness, or otherwise. But, in order to neutralize any of those imagined threats, Tony also kept our relationship on ice and was not able to receive the goodness, the warmth, or the richness of our relationship. Part of my countertransference struggle with Tony was that because of the sense he was reluctant to breathe life into the stories or into our relationship, I often felt tempted to do so myself. I shared with him that this was perhaps a way he could get me to do his dirty work and watch from a safe distance. He joked with me and said, "Sure! Why would I want to take that kind of risk when I could get you to do it!"

## CASE 4.4: I WILL HURT OTHERS BY GROWING AND CHANGING

Many patients are troubled by some form of guilt. In a broad and general way, it is useful to talk about patients who struggle with different forms of guilt resulting from phantasies of harming their objects. Sometimes, this guilt, or at least what initially appear to be conflicts within the realm of guilt, leads to a therapeutic *impasse*. The very growth that analytic work promotes is experienced by some patients as an escalation of taboo acts, dangerous striving, and violations of superego bargains created to preserve the health, love, and approval of the object. In other words, analytic progress increases feelings of guilt in some patients. Etchegoyen, Lopez and Rabih (1987), Klein (1957), and the other clinicians mentioned in Chapters 1 and 3 have reviewed this phenomenon.

The patients I am highlighting appear to have similar issues, but when given closer clinical consideration, they exhibit something more primitive, more ominous, more difficult to shift. They usually show all the elements of depressive pathology but also bring in a specific aversion to connection with the good object and experience their depressive conflicts in a much more sinister and paranoid manner.

Alex was a middle-aged mechanic who originally came to see me because he believed God was "out to kill him" and on occasion was convinced a giant hand (we figured out it was the hand of God) was going to reach down and crush him. Also, the overall paranoia he lived with had made it near impossible for him to keep his job. After eight years in analytic treatment, his psychotic conflicts had been reduced and worked through to a great extent. He was now married and was a loving parent to three children. Of course, he still had many problems and having a family created ongoing anxieties. For instance, he brought up the topic of advancing in his career. He told me of an idea of going to special classes that would enable him to pursue jobs that were more managerial. Alex told me about the classes, how he planned to afford them, and how they would help him advance in his field. But, he said he had begun suffering intense bouts of anxiety when he thought about following through with the plan. The more we talked about it, it became clear that he believed his attempts to improve his life would bring about havoc to others and then to himself. This went beyond a neurotic guilt over competition, success, or oedipal victories.

Alex told me, "I am not able to sleep very well. I can't stop thinking about how I could somehow destroy other people by doing this. Nothing specific, but something like how the other guys at the shop who really need to advance would be pushed aside by my advancing. They won't be able to take care of their families anymore, they would all fall apart. And, I picture my face on a big Wanted: Dead or Alive poster because of it. I feel like there is only so much happiness to go around and if I take it all up, everyone else will suffer."

This core phantasy of there only being enough goodness for certain people was a constant struggle for Alex. He didn't believe there was enough goodness for everyone to share. In the transference, this led to power struggles, paranoid fears, and strong feelings of despair. One way this was manifested was at the start of a session in the sixth year of analysis. Alex had trouble coming into my office from the waiting room. He hesitated, almost quivering in the corner. I said, "you look really scared to come in and be with me. How come?" Alex timidly replied, "I am sorry, but I don't have anything to offer you today. I have nothing to give you." After he reluctantly entered my office, we were able to explore this panic. Based on his transference history with me, I made several interpretations. I said, "you paid me yesterday, so maybe you feel you don't have a peace offering for the angry Gods today." He said, "no, I don't. So, I don't know where we stand or how you feel toward me." After discussing this for a while, I said, "when you say you don't have anything for me, I wonder if you also mean you don't feel that who you are, or what you think, or what you want to talk about, is good enough for me. There is some kind of expectation I have and if you are going to really show yourself to me today, it won't be what I want or what I approve of." Alex said, "Boy, that sounds a lot like dear old Mom to me. Yes. I think you are right. I feel inadequate and I feel like if I just go for it and be myself, you could be disappointed. Plus, I can't figure out what I could say or do to please you anyway, so I feel screwed either way." I said, "it is hard for you to believe I just want you to be yourself". He replied, "Definitely. It is hard to believe or trust that."

When Alex mentioned his mother, this was in reference to the kind of relationship with his mother that he grew up with. As a child, he always felt his mother was asking him to follow her ideas, goals, and beliefs. He recalls his mother showing irritation, disapproval, anger, and a scary fragility whenever he would try to do something he wanted that was different from his mother's choices. In his analytic treatment, Alex conveyed his fears as a child that if he were to be himself and follow his inner direction, it would harm, anger, or repel his mother. Thus, he ended up feeling he was a constant threat to his mother and her well-being. He thought that if he went too far, he might end up on the Wanted: Dead or Alive poster.

## Comments

The patients described in this chapter experienced depressive pain, guilt, loss, and grief. However, those states were experienced as overwhelming and without solution. The consequences felt fatal and unworkable. To accept that the self or the object is not ideal, that it is a mix of good and bad, brings on such fragmentation and anxiety that it must be avoided. So, a stalemate in treatment, a stalling out of progress, or a resistance to growth or change are all reasonable responses. In the transference, the patient's primary phantasy is of the analyst forcing goodness upon them. This goodness is experienced as a lie, a manipulation, and an invitation to danger. Slipping back and forth in the normal transition from paranoid functioning to depressive functioning is certainly expected. But, the difficulties these patients have is with a more violent fragmentation of both positions at the same time Some of this is the result of a fragile effort to prop up the object in an idealized way, an artificial edifice. Sooner or later, this crumbles. Often, it can be the analyst's interpretation that reveals the facade and the patient will react defensively because the experience of the object becoming real brings the patient in touch with massive feelings of betrayal, loss, anger, and a complete lack of control. The fall of the object drags down the ego and all seems lost.

The patients described seem unable to bond with, utilize, or locate the good object. The goodness in this good object would include flaws and faults, but overall represent a solid, dependable, and healing object that, unlike an idealized or a demonized object, is realistic, available, and supportive. Pathological projective identification, destructive greed, entitlement, masochism, and domination through obsessive mechanisms are some of the elements these patients can exhibit. However, the primary unconscious phantasy the patient holds regarding the good object and how that emerges within the transference is the key to understanding each case.

The first case in this chapter displayed a more distinctly paranoid view of her objects, in which a barely available good object easily transformed into a betraying, critical, or even dangerous one. My patient's core phantasies revolved around the idea that it is best to always keep one step ahead of the object, should disaster occur. And, for her, she believed it was inevitable that something would eventually sour the relationship. The period of treatment I highlighted with this patient was evidence of primarily paranoid-schizoid functioning. It was only later in the analytic work that she began integrating healthier views of herself and her objects and gradually letting go of these more paranoid ways.

The second case of Sue also involved intense paranoid dynamics. "It is only a matter of time before they hate me" was a vivid description of this frightening way of seeing her objects. Yet, she was able to explore her need to keep the goodness of the analyst at bay as a way to establish control. This ability to reflect on her methods of relating showed some integration and acknowledgment of self-involvement, rather than feeling completely victimized.

The third case of Tony was more of a depressive problem that was colored by paranoid fears. He believed he needed to please others at all times in order to be loved. Also, he made sure to not contaminate that fragile bond with his own needs or opinions. Tony wanted a happy ending, a bond with his good object, but he would keep himself away from that with intellect and wit. In his mind, this defensive posture prevented a relational collapse: better to serve me than to lose me. Avoiding conflict was important, but Tony went about it in a much more integrated and complex way than the first two cases did.

The fourth case of Alex involved depressive phantasies of harming others as a result of creative, autonomous growth. The flourishing of the self could harm others. When this took on a more primitive quality, Alex had a phantasy of revenge, retribution, and persecution that took the form of the Dead or Alive Poster image.

Change and progress is deeply connected to the good object. In normal development, the good object is not only necessary for optimal growth, but the ego envisions the good object as encouraging and supporting growth. For Alex and other patients who struggle and fight against the good object, they are convinced it is a matter of time before the good object turns into a persecutory object (Waska 2005). Often, change and progress is seen as the trigger to that catastrophe. This shift into a bad object is believed to happen through the changing, autonomous self hurting and betraying the good object which then, via projective identification, becomes retaliatory and abandoning (Waska 2004).

Part of why these patients are so difficult to work with is that they feel it is safer to keep the bad object–bad self relationship intact because it is under their control. The ego feels independent and fortified this way, compared to feeling dependent and vulnerable by making contact with the good object. To move toward the more whole-object status of the depressive position proper is to accept that one is both dependent on the good object and at risk for hurting it or losing it. But, this threat is particularly harsh for these patients as it also means the collapse of the good and the return of evil and despair without shelter. In other words, the hope and stability of the depressive position is lacking. Normally, there is faith that trouble can be rectified, the hurt object healed, and the loss tolerated and worked through. The good still exists side-by-side with the bad. I am highlighting patients who get halfway into the depressive mode of experiencing life, but fail to achieve, maintain, or regain the restorative aspects of it.

As Steiner (1987) notes, when these types of patients do make a move into the depressive position, it is very important to comment on and interpret these progressive moments. Doing so allows the patient a chance to reflect and explore the anxieties that come with that change as well as the urge to start fighting off the good self–good object experience. At the same time, and this is a bit different from the dynamics Steiner is discussing, the depressive-position world these patients are navigating is a corrupt one which they entered prematurely, often feeling forced to take up the hazards of it in order to placate their objects or to find a way to avoid the retaliations of the angry bad object.

Therefore, unresolved, toxic and potent paranoid-schizoid dynamics filter into the ego's immature and premature introduction to the depressive position. This results in the worst of both developmental experiences, pushing the ego to try and escape both, refusing to engage the very thing needed for healing and rescue: the good object. So, in the transference–countertransference matrix, the analyst often sees a patient who dramatically shifts back and forth between more advanced and then more primitive ways of relating, but also exhibits a sort of handicapped version of mature depressive relating. At the same time, this back and forth is frequently punctuated by a brakes-on, full-stop, psychological standoff, wherein they refuse to allow contact with the good object analyst. The patient is convinced it is better to hole up, stall out, and seal themselves off from union with the good object. Even though this brings out the chronic depression, despair, and resentment that these patients are noted for, it seems better to them than the dangerous movement toward the good object, with whom they have no sense of control or trust. If you feel stuck in a minefield, it may be a terrible place to live, but it seems better to stay there than to try and venture out to the safer areas where no mines exist, because that journey to the better land could be fatal.

The variations on this reluctance to connect to the good object are many. The central themes of the patients' phantasies involve loss, grief, and the avoidance of the persecutory anxiety that is unleashed when allowing the separateness, the aspirations, the back and forth, the natural conflict, and the anguish of normal imperfections that exist in the good object and the good self.

# Part II

# Greed and the dangers of change

# Chapter 5

# Melanie Klein's theory of greed

Melanie Klein proposed certain ideas about infant development as well as later adult life that clarify the origins and manifestations of greed. She made observations about infants who seem very greedy in their approach to feeding, and she thought there was a parallel in their greedy approach to their object relations. Klein (1952a) felt these infants used people around them as vessels for attention and gratification, without much acknowledgment for the person as an individual. She also noted how these infants were prone to feeling abandoned without the constant presence of the other, indicating a lack of internalization of a secure, soothing object. She thought these infants continued to have these problems as adults.

In my analytic practice, some patients enter treatment suffering from patterns of greed, abandonment, and oral aggression. The transference and extra-transference become charged with greed as well as the defenses against greed. I will use one case study to investigate this idea and to show how greed acts as a block to healthy change.

Klein believed that some patients begin life with innate levels of aggression and greed that go beyond the essential levels of love and hate that Freud felt all children to have. She also believed that, with proper internalization of good objects, this aggression and greed could be partially mitigated. While I think this is accurate, the nature of greed generally discounts and destroys the good object, leaving the ego barren and always hungry for more.

While Klein was a real pioneer in discovering the internal world of the infant and later adult, she also was very much aware of the interaction between internal and external. She felt innate aggression was heightened by unfavorable circumstances in the family environment. At the same time, love and caring from the family help to balance out innate aggressive feelings. Klein (1959) pointed out how some infants have great resentment when faced with disappointment or deprivation and express this by refusing to take in subsequent opportunities for gratification. Klein felt these infants were dealing with stronger levels of greed, which were possibly genetic.

These abnormal dynamics could be better integrated within the early family environment or made worse.

Klein was describing a destructive cycle that many patients bring into treatment and into the transference relationship. These patients are greedy to the point of both destroying the gratification they do receive and refusing to take in good experiences. Subsequently, they feel denied the gratification they craved, but don't see the role they play in that deprivation. The original external trauma is replicated and fortified in the patient's internal world.

## CASE MATERIAL

Paul came to see me when he was thirty-five. He told me in a desperate yet demanding tone, "you are my last resort. I have tried to change for many years, but it is all a lost cause. I haven't been able to find somebody to love, I don't enjoy my career, and I feel hopeless about my future. I am fat and feel ugly, but I can't stop overeating. Even though I know I am smart, I feel stupid and I am sure no one would ever listen to me if they realized who I really am and what kind of person I really am."

I told Paul it must be difficult to start seeing me, since he was already revealing who he really is and therefore was already faced with whether I would be able to accept and understand him. He said, "you are absolutely right. But, I have to take that gamble. It is my last chance." In the countertransference, I experienced this way of relating to me as greedy. I felt that I had better begin working hard to save and satisfy Paul. Since it was his "last chance", I felt pressured to perform well and feed him properly.

Growing up, Paul felt scared, intimidated, and revolted by his father's angry outbursts. His father was prone to dramatic mood swings, becoming aloof and cold but often angry and loud. This left Paul fearful and alienated. The brunt of his father's verbal and sometimes physical abuse fell on Paul's mother, but Paul certainly was victim to it as well. It wasn't until his father was an old man and Paul was middle-aged that Paul felt he could "access", as he called it, his father's safety. By this, he meant that his father was more of a passive man who now wanted Paul's companionship. The lack of his violent attitude and his new interest in Paul gave Paul a confusing yet hopeful sense of security. Paul's lack of a safe or reliable father combined with his experience of his mother as more of a fellow victim than a source of nourishment or security and left Paul a very insecure, lonely little boy.

From an early age, Paul turned to intellectual pursuits and solitary hobbies as a way of not thinking about his life. This pattern continued into his adult life. Today, he feels his parents did their best, but he has a great deal of conflict over his hostile and resentful feelings toward them.

Over the next few years of analytic treatment, seeing him twice a week on the couch, certain patterns emerged. The theme of greed cast its shadow on the treatment in many ways. From the beginning, Paul's relationship to himself and to his analyst revealed this critical demand and hunger. In the transference, there was a reluctance to give, in the form of being distant or aloof. This combined with a wish for more intimacy and soothing from me and his objects. This urgent desire was projected into external areas of focus such as his weight problems and dating difficulties.

From the start, Paul could not tolerate imperfection. For the most part, this came out as a grueling demand on himself. He would cite countless examples of how he had fallen behind others, let himself down, and failed to maintain what he felt were normal standards of living. This included his job performance, how he treated his friends, and even his attitude toward strangers on the street. Paul thought he should be more compassionate, more hard-working, and faster to learn. This was far from a self-reflective assessment of himself. Rather, it was a "I have to have it better immediately" kind of approach in which all that he had was bad and all that is good should have been delivered yesterday.

All this self-incrimination was also directed outwards, in that he secretly was judgmental and demanding of others. However, this was something that I had to interpret by pointing out to Paul how he was far more comfortable blaming himself than others. Regardless of how nice he tried to be on a conscious level, he kept people at a distance and had an underlying current of control and rigidity.

Naturally, Paul also maintained distance in the transference, for a sense of control and safety. He was very reluctant to see us as having any sort of relationship other than what he called a "professional working partnership". This businesslike and often mechanical approach left us in an odd place. I pointed out that while he had come to me to learn how to have better relationships, he was in fact demonstrating how he had problems in relationships. After a quick nod to this idea, he said, "well, tell me how I should be relating to you, so I can start altering myself and make that change!" This urge to power-through any emotional discomfort was part of Paul's underlying greed. He wanted to get better and he wanted it now. My countertransference was a feeling of being rushed and being asked to deliver the goods immediately. I felt like a cog in his machine.

This projective identification process also came alive for a while in the guise of a request for medication. He wondered if all his problems were "just a chemical imbalance". So, he wanted the latest wonder drug immediately. While he spoke about it intellectually, the affect was clearly demanding and bossy. I interpreted this as a combination of self-blame (having a biological defect) and greed to be all better immediately without having to endure any pain. Also, I said he saw me as his dispensing machine rather than someone to explore these issues with. He responded with, "well, what is wrong with that, Doc?" This shift from a sad, hopeless perspective to a sharper, narcissistic attitude was part of the more aggressive and greedy side of Paul's personality.

On the surface, this seemed to be a back-and-forth swing from the splitting and greedy projections of the paranoid-schizoid position to reparative attempts found in the depressive position. For paranoid patients, the world is a black-and-white place of attacking and attacked objects. Forgiveness is nowhere to be found and annihilation is always around the corner. For Klein's depressive patient, one is always trying to ease the pain of others, avoid the discomfort of difference, and defending against the tragedy of rejection and loss. However, reparation and repair of hurt feelings and conflicted relations are usually possible for the depressive.

Klein (1959) points out how greed is destructive to social relations and how the greedy person, in wanting more and more, stops being considerate or attuned to the normal sharing in a two-person system. Paul went from trying to be nice and blaming himself to wanting what he wanted immediately. Then, he seemed to recognize how he may have hurt me and tried to undo it by apologizing. I think this was accurate, but the motives were more self-serving than altruistic. Thus, Paul related to me and to himself from aspects of both paranoid and depressive anxieties. However, his greedy phantasies pulled him into more core paranoid and primitive object relations.

Steiner (1985) has described this oscillation between the paranoid and depressive states as a sort of protective way-station between the two intrapsychic states. Paul sometimes seemed to fit Steiner's criteria, but again it seemed the aggressive and self-defeating nature of his greed destabilized the internal way-station. Paul's internal emphasis on greed and all the feelings of being deprived prevented him from truly accessing a more stable whole-object relationship for any length of time.

After much work on these types of transference issues and internal phantasies, Paul shifted his focus onto his weight problem in the second year of treatment. Paul's weight issue continued to reveal his unconscious greedy desires. He had been overweight his whole life. His family and friends were always supportive in his chronic dieting battle. It was easy to feel sorry for Paul and give him advice on how to eat better and to exercise. However, I noticed something about most of the situations where he would overeat. Whether it was around other people or by himself, Paul would begin to feel that he was destined to be all alone, "a lonely loser" as he called it. It was at that point that he would devour as much food as possible, seemingly without much thought about the consequences. However, the more I investigated, I found he did think about what he was doing, but he didn't care about his actions. So what looked like a passive, victim role revealed a more active participation in something more aggressive. When we explored what went into his eating patterns, the following emerged.

Paul would start to think about all the security, confidence, love, and fulfillment his friends seemed to have. Then, he would feel like he was so far away from ever having that level of happiness that he felt hopeless. He became full of despair and anger. This fueled his aggressive feelings of oral greed and he would overeat. It took some time for us to see how Paul was bluntly saying to himself, "I don't care, I will take as much as I please!" This was frightening and humiliating for him to admit and explore.

This avoidance was also present in the transference and became clearer during the third and fourth year of analytic work. Paul or I would bring up different topics in which there was some type of significant strain, anger, or distress in relation to someone. This could be with a friend, a coworker, a family member, or with me. From the way Paul went about discussing the problems, it was obvious he felt significant, if not severe, emotional pain. However, he split off these feelings by remaining detached, intellectual, and sterile. He quickly put his anxiety and outrage into me via intra-psychic and interpersonal forms of projective identification.

When phantasies and feelings are intense, projective identification spills over from unconscious to interpersonal levels and often affects the analyst in the countertransference. So, I would find myself feeling outraged or in wonderment at the situations Paul described. He essentially said, via his detached way of relating to me, "I see this as no big deal, I don't have any problem with it, and I am above anything that could be so distressing." I was left to deal with his feelings, which usually comprised strong urges to disagree, to have more, and to receive attention instead of feeling held back, rejected, or ignored. This put me in the position of being the spokesperson for Paul's feelings and phantasies.

Because of this dynamic, I made two types of interpretations. First, I told Paul that he must be frightened of needing so much and feeling so hungry. To this, Paul would reply that it felt as though he didn't want to "rock the boat" and that the other person "wouldn't be able to deal with the conflict". When we explored this, we found that Paul was sure that in unleashing his greed, need, and desires he would destroy the relationship. This was a critical revelation in the analysis because it showed Paul's lack of belief in understanding, reparation, and healing when conflict emerged in his object relations.

The second interpretation I offered was to suggest that he was protecting his objects from his greed. I followed up on the results of my first interpretation, but emphasized his sense of being dangerous to the object. This was based on my impression that Paul's anxiety had to do with depressive concerns, along with his primary paranoid-schizoid fears. When we pursued this idea, the result was illuminating. Paul clarified and corrected my hypothesis. On one hand, Paul did feel he would be a terrible burden on his objects and could easily overwhelm them with greed and dependence. However, this attempt to protect the object really served another more primitive fear. When Paul felt greedy, he feared he would be both abandoned and annihilated. So, protecting the object was ultimately a way of protecting himself. This was helpful from a diagnostic perspective. Paul was describing the more primitive phantasy of destroying the very thing that kept him alive. The object was important, but only as a way to prevent pain and suffering.

Many patients face this type of psychological strain. They appear to be operating at a depressive level, but much of that activity is actually geared toward preventing more paranoid-schizoid conflicts and fears. Paul said it this way: "I want to keep the other person propped up, alive, and happy. I don't want to hurt them and knock them off their place. If I do hurt them, then they would be gone and I would be left to the wolves. I feel like that, like a baby left in the forest and I start to hear the wolves approaching."

At times, Paul spelled out his phantasies very plainly. More than once, he told me, "I feel like someone who hasn't eaten in far too long. When I smell food I go crazy. And, when I finally have food in front of me, I don't care about my manners, I become a cannibal. I want to eat everything as fast as I can." I added, "and you don't want to share". He said, "of course not! They have had plenty all along while I go starving. It is my turn now!" This was the greed and oral aggression that left Paul feeling so conflicted. We could both see how strongly Paul's internal world of oral greed shaped and formed his external symptoms.

I made my interpretations in the context of all three aspects of Paul's psychological experience. I pointed out how his greed and subsequent fear and rage, manifested in his external world, in his internal world, and in the transference. At times, Paul resisted my comments. Increasingly, however, my interpretations seemed to offer him a respite from his chronic anxiety and feelings of deprivation.

At the same time, this was tricky. Because of his tendency to compliance and accommodation, he would agree with me when he privately felt otherwise. So, I had to be watchful and not be taken in by this false sense of alignment. It was a slow, uncomfortable process for both of us to notice this secretive, manipulative dynamic that was representative of the more aggressive, greedy, and stubborn side of him.

Paul had a very difficult time dating. This had been a lifelong problem that only improved toward the end of his treatment. Wanting a girlfriend brought on a constant sense of failure and hopelessness. He was convinced he would never find anyone who would love him. He thought women would find him flawed. In investigating these fears, I found that, at the core, Paul felt he was too needy and selfish and that these qualities would repel anyone who started to know him. When I explored these feelings and was persistent in looking into any examples he had of this actually occurring, one thing stood out. Paul was afraid his craving for a special union with one special person would destroy his chances of ever finding this treasure. He phantasised that his greed would destroy the idealized object and it would return as a rejecting and attacking enemy. Paul was so troubled by these aggressive, needy urges, and the fallout he imagined would come from them, that he did his best to act the opposite. He became very passive, hoping the object would be reassured.

At one point, Paul summed it up this way, "it is better to stay really quiet and hope for the best". When I asked him to elaborate, he said, "otherwise, it could get really noisy and things could go very badly. I guess I settle for what I've got, even though it is not enough. I think I will never get what I want even if I try for it." The act of "trying for it" meant he would unleash his greedy phantasies which would impact on his object, beginning a cycle of disappointment and destruction.

I aimed my interpretations at all three areas of Paul's psychology: his developmental history (internal and external), his current life experiences, and the transference. So, when he said it is best to be quiet and hope for the best, I not only explored the meaning of this in the transference and extra-transference, but in its genetic roots as well. It was easy to see, and fairly easy for Paul to remember, how the playing-possum approach to life was linked to his intimidating father. Paul was able to discuss how he felt scared of his father and tried hard to not make any fast moves in the hopes of reducing any tension between him and his father or between his father and mother. We also explored this strategy as an identification with his helpless and ineffectual mother. Without her as a reliable, nurturing, and protective internal object, Paul felt fragile, endangered, and hungry.

Midway in the treatment, the transference took on a more intense push–pull dynamic. This was part of a difficult working-through period that was followed by deeper genetic work on his family experiences as a child. At that point, Paul was able to take a more honest and painful look at his upbringing and begin to integrate those feelings and fantasies. This deeper work led to an exploration of his transference love and his ambivalence to trust me as a reliable, supportive object.

To be able to explore his memories and feelings about his family was a sign of progress. In the fourth year of treatment, Paul was better integrated and therefore he felt safer, stronger, and more able to face the painful and confusing feelings he lived with.

Paul's demanding nature and exacting qualities, and his disdain for failure, left him with a constant feeling of anger and negativity. In the beginning of treatment, I would interpret this aggression as it occurred in the transference or extra-transference. This often worked, but also led to quite a few standoff situations in which Paul felt attacked and judged.

Therefore, over time, my strategy shifted a bit. Eventually, I found it best to first interpret the lack of control and fear of abandonment, rejection, and persecution that lay behind the aggression. Then, I addressed the greed and demanding hunger. This approach seemed best suited to Paul's fear of being judged as inferior to me and to others. He was slowly able to take in my comments and use them to work through his anxieties and hopelessness.

Overall, at this point in the analysis, I think Paul had a better psychological integration, yet still a fragile one. What I saw in Paul was a psychic brittleness that left him always creeping, shifting, and oscillating from more stable psychological functioning to more primitive states of mind, and then back and forth. These shifts gave him the experience of being at the mercy of his own mind.

During one session in the latter part of treatment, Paul was caught in an obsessive struggle about how he viewed me. Paul said, "I am trying to think of what you are to me. I was just taking a walk and thinking about therapy and I tried to find a term to describe what you are to me. At first I tried the word 'best-friend', but no, that is not it. Care-provider? Maybe. You are somewhat like family, but that is not it either. The term care-provider seems somewhat sterile but it still conveys how you do care. At the same time, it is like saying you are a nurse, or a short-term friend. But, it is more than that. I am struggling. Maybe, because it is a one-way street with us, it is hard to find a term that incorporates that and everything else. I don't know."

I was struck by several things in listening to Paul. First, he made our relationship sound mechanical and he used the word "it" instead of the personal term "us". And, it was interesting that he never considered what his feelings toward me were. I think that is why he couldn't define me, since he ignored his feelings about me which would naturally define who I was to him. He also was wishing for more from me, when he mentioned it not being a two-way street.

I replied, "it seems uncomfortable for you to face your feelings for me. You are thinking of the closeness we have and your gratitude for my caring. But, then you try and make it more manageable by taking your feelings out of it. So, we become not too hot, not too cold, not too sterile, not too cozy. In the end, you feel confused and lose the thing you like by trying to control it and protect yourself." Paul said, "I know what you mean. All I am left with is a headache and confusion."

It seemed that talking about his defensive struggling and listening to me interpret his anxieties reduced his discomfort enough to go on. Paul now turned to exploring his feelings of greed, guilt, and loss more directly. At least, it appeared that way.

Paul explained a series of troubling thoughts he had begun to have in the last week. He had begun to obsess and ruminate over the possibility that if he wanted to start "hanging out with the guys" more often, his girlfriend might not approve. He feared she would become angry. He felt guilty and scared that she might "blow her top".

I asked Paul to elaborate. He said that if he hurt his girlfriend's feelings, she might get furious and leave him for good. "If I ignore her needs and leave her to suffer, she would get really mad." He paused and added, "it is that god-damned loss thing again! I feel I would end up all alone and helpless. I wouldn't make it without her." He swallowed hard to stop the tears.

There was one important factor to consider about Paul's worries. At this point in his life, Paul did not have a girlfriend and actually enjoyed spending time alone rather than going out with the guys. I pointed out how he had created these future worries in which he had what he wanted (a girlfriend) but then he wanted more (time with the guys). This path of thought led to a fear of rejection. So, his phantasies of greed and the awful results had created a distortion of reality. This seemed to be a displacement and a defensive spillover from his more direct exploration of transference feelings and conflicts.

This inner violence destroys the ideal object and leaves the ego with a persecutory object in its place. I conveyed this to Paul by saying, "you seem to be feeling like this: 'I am worried about how I impact other people, how they see me. If I cause problems, I could drive that person away or make them want to retaliate.' You have felt that way with me in the past and today you are explaining how that fear colors your imagination about the future." Paul said, "it is my past, my present, and my future. It is my dread!"

I want to emphasize the psychological experience that Paul struggled with so much. While he clearly had pseudo-depressive concerns regarding the health of his objects and how he treated them, there was a specific twist. His objects were easily destroyed and easily driven to dangerous levels of retaliation, leading him to anxiety about annihilation. I believe Paul expressed a particular aspect of paranoid-schizoid functioning. This pseudo-depressive fear is perhaps a precursor to more whole-object relating, but when unbalanced by greed and oral destructiveness, the more primitive, paranoid, and persecutory concerns rule the day.

Klein (1955) thought that greed, envy, and hatred were the primary motivating affects in aggressive phantasies. I made my interpretations to Paul based on this belief. In his case, he imagined his greed would bring on the object's aggressive attack since he was projecting his hostility into the object. Klein (1959) also thought that "the greedy person wants more and more, even at the expense of everybody else. He is not really capable of consideration and generosity toward others" (p. 261). In this regard, Paul was able to intellectually consider others, but emotionally and in phantasy he went ahead and did what he had to in order to have more. Paul expressed this thirst for total love, acceptance, and power when he said, "I want everyone to prove their love for me. If I have to show love first, it does not count and I still feel empty."

## THEORETICAL CONSIDERATIONS

Paul illustrates my thinking on pathological forms of greed and I believe he is representative of many other patients. Greed corrodes and destroys the capacity for healthy object relations and blocks the potential for creativity, free thought, and achievement. The feelings and phantasies that encompass greed color the transference and extra-transference.

Melanie Klein has illuminated the ways early greedy phantasies toward the mother occur in conjunction with splitting and projective identification. These conflicts regarding oral hunger and primitive aggression continue to shape the adult's world and his or her ability to shift into depressive functioning.

Klein (1959) thought these individuals are never satisfied because greed always demands more than what is available. Nothing holds the person's attention for long, as greed quickly empties the object of its goodness. This cycle of fading and depleting objects creates more anxiety of loss and abandonment, which makes for more greed. My view is that the ego, when anxious and hungry in this way, projects its oral aggression and greed into the object. Therefore, the ego's experience of loss and abandonment is followed by phantasies of persecution and dread.

Klein (1952b) thought there was a natural balance between libido and aggression. This balance could be effected by experiences of deprivation, whether external or internal, resulting in greed. Greed brings with it frustration, oral aggression, and a sensitivity to feelings of persecution. Klein (1952d) thought the ego's capacity to tolerate anxiety was regulated in part by its innate ability to love, the level of greed, and the ego's defenses against that level of greed.

With some patients, the balance Klein discussed is tipped very early in life, so that the predominant feelings and phantasies involve greed. By its very nature, greed brings on excessive splitting, idealization, projective identification, and envy, all of which in turn generate more greed. Greedy phantasies bring on persecutory guilt, in which hurt and drained objects become retaliatory. Former idols turn into enemies, seeking revenge. The ego faces phantasies of permanent loss and subsequent annihilation.

The psychic crossroads between the paranoid-schizoid and depressive positions is marked by several variables. Whether or not the ego becomes more integrated or continues to vacillate back and forth in more regressive ways seems to rely on at least three factors. To what degree is the ego steered by greed? To what degree does the ego have a resource of positive internal and external objects that can counterbalance oral aggression, deprivation, and greed? And, are healthy projective identification dynamics available to create positive cycles of internalization?

Gratitude, reparation, forgiveness, and the desire to give are usually all products of the depressive position. When greed has colored the ego's structure, these elements still exist, yet are perverted. Instead of a true concern for the object, patients like Paul tend to use reparation and other depressive defenses as a shield to ward off the object's rejection and attack. In other words, the reparative actions are taken not out of care for the object but for self-survival. This can create a pattern of always trying to be polite and nice to avoid trouble. This type of masochism is a paranoid-schizoid prevention strategy.

When Paul felt deprived and empty, it was difficult for him to listen to or take in my interpretations. There were never enough of them and each one was never good enough. He was too anxious and his desire to have something to fill him up immediately and make it all better now made my comments seem inadequate and weak. So, this was a projective identification cycle in which the hoped-for ideal object/interpretation was destroyed and Paul felt abandoned and lost. At that point he would either attack me as useless or he would attack himself for "never getting it". With greed, the desire to have all makes it never possible to have any.

Klein (1957) clarified this in saying, "greed is mainly bound up in introjection" (p. 181). Therefore, the ego is so busy trying to fill up with ideal amounts of ideal love that there is little room for the regular love of regular people.

Clinically, one is struck by how some patients struggle with feelings of greed. This seems to pervade their relationships and eventually the transference as well. Paul was one patient who seemed to be affected by this internal struggle in a marked way that colored most of his life and most of his analytic treatment.

When Paul began treatment, he was plagued by various symptoms and anxieties. These persisted for quite some time, but gradually eased. He lost weight and his eating habits became less of a daily battleground. At his job, Paul felt more content since he demanded less perfection, accepted mistakes, and could see how the ups and downs of his job all added up to a fairly rewarding career. Paul's initial symptoms were external manifestations of his intra-psychic world and were conflicts around his greedy, aggressive desires and the phantasies concerning the impact they had on his objects and, in turn, on himself.

While difficult and lurching, Paul's progress was steady. After five years of analytic work, he had changed quite a bit. His mind was better integrated and his external life reflected this increased inner calm. Caper (1992) has defined the healing of psychoanalysis as the successful integration of former split-off and projected parts of the mind. I think this is a useful guide for the analyst, as long as he realizes no patient will ever achieve a full integration of their former divided self. Accordingly, Paul was still susceptible to his old feelings and fantasies. However, they were less severe and didn't last as long since he could notice them and make his own internal clarifications, confrontations, and interpretations. In other words, he was more able to explore, learn about, mourn, and accept previously split-off aspects of himself.

In a session during the fifth year, Paul expressed evidence of these changes as well as the remaining remnants of his internal turmoil. Paul was thinking about how far he had come in analysis and when he might see the day of termination. The more he talked about ending and how he felt healthier and more ready to end, the more defensive he got. This tug-of-war conflict took on a persecutory feel. He said he worried I would never let him go, trapping him for his money. He felt he wouldn't have a say in when he was better. Paul went on like this for a while, saying I would not want to let go of him and lose the control, regularity, and money I was used to. I interpreted that he was projecting his fear of loss onto me. He thought about it a moment and replied that he could see how he does that in many of his relationships. "I end up feeling trapped or suffocated in my friendships and at work too. I think they need me and won't let go, but I think you are right. It is me that has the need and is scared to let go", Paul added.

After pausing for a while, Paul started to reflect on his progress in analysis. He said, "I can see things more realistically, not so twisted around. I don't feel on the verge of some kind of catastrophe all the time now. That fear of loss or being excommunicated and left to die like some kind of Frankenstein on an iceberg isn't so present now. Instead of living in a constant vicious cycle, I feel my life is more of an enriching cycle." I added, "and that gives you hope, which helps you keep going". Paul said, "yes, I don't fall down as much. And, when I do, I can get up and keep going."

Working analytically with paranoid-schizoid patients is usually a difficult and stormy process. But, when greed is the core dynamic, as was the case with Paul, these treatment encounters become even more grueling and confusing. The analyst needs to remain humble, flexible, and open to being a less than ideal object in the patient's phantasies. These types of analytic treatments are often terminated before goals are met. A mix of old and new internal dynamics is often the best hoped-for end result. However, operating from a Kleinian perspective enables the analyst to better cope with the complexities of greed as it colors the transference. Utilizing the Kleinian point of view helps the analyst with the inevitable countertransference difficulties these greedy, needy patients evoke. Then, the analyst can choose the best clinical technique to assist these struggling individuals who need so much but experience so little because of their craving.

# Chapter 6

# The frightening rumble of psychic hunger*

Hinshelwood (1994) examined the introjective processes involved in greed and their underlying aggressive components. He thought greed's oral hostility is so strong that the object, in phantasy, is destroyed. Then, the object returns as a persecutory demon.

Melanie Klein (1957) thought excessive envy in the infantile ego brought about a persecutory form of guilt over having injured the object. She believed this object then, via projective identification, became an attacking object in phantasy and the ego was unable to cope with the combined anxieties of the depressive and paranoid positions.

While I agree with Klein and Hinshelwood regarding the persecutory phantasies that envy and greed create, I think excessive or pathological greed brings about another form of phantasy and defensive dynamics. This excessive greed can be a mixture of constitutional, intra-psychic, and environmental factors.

Being an introjective phenomenon, greed is about being filled up with idealized aspects of the object. When greed and envy result in the destruction of the object, there is a profound sense of loss. This loss is catastrophic, leaving the ego barren, isolated, and collapsing upon itself. Loss of self is the resulting fear: no more object equals no more self. Therefore, the greedy ego usually faces a dual threat of primitive loss and annihilation anxiety.

Problems with greed bring on complex and destructive internal object relations. Rosenfeld (1971) examined the death instinct as it operated in narcissistic patients. I believe excessive greed and the resulting anxieties over loss and persecution bring out destructive narcissism. Claiming supreme independence and disdain for the object are ways of fending off the ego's insatiable craving for idealized nourishment and fulfillment.

* This chapter was first published as 'Greed and the frightening rumble of psychic hunger', in *The American Journal of Psychoanalysis*, 64(3, 2004): 253–266.

Greed is a combination of constitutional endowment, environmental/developmental impact, and the outgrowth of complex phantasy relations between the self and important internal objects. Spillius (1993) states that if a person's envious feelings stop when the object of envy becomes available, then it was not true envy. I would extend that idea to issues with greed. If a person reaches the goal they demanded, receives the attention they crave, or obtains the security they want and still immediately desires more, then this is genuine greed. Ironically, the way these patients quickly turn back to look for more dramatically erases the gains or rewards they just received.

Brenman (1982) has discussed the difficulties some patients have with separation and separateness. Greed, by definition, creates an ongoing threat of separation from the ideal, all-fulfilling object. Greed is a constant phantasy, present regardless of external factors. Therefore, even when the analytic relationship seems to be proceeding well, the patient may be suffering from the threat of separation, loss, and persecution from the idealized analyst. Of course, external factors such as vacation breaks, awareness of other patients, and the analyst's own needs can complicate the unconscious anxieties already present.

Greedy visions of desire and deprivation promote ever-changing layers of defense. Manic, narcissistic defenses are common. So are masochistic strategies. These are all mechanisms that omnipotently eradicate any knowledge of separation, loss, or vulnerability to damage from the threatening object.

Masochism is a form of magical defense against greed in which the ego says, "I have been so hurt before, so starved by my ruthless objects, that I give up. I no longer need anything. I will not try to take in anything, anymore. I don't deserve anything and I don't want anything. If I am to be starved, abandoned, and destroyed, then I will do it myself."

So, this is a masochistic-narcissistic victory, via manic and magical thinking and self-imposed suffering. Some patients seem to emphasize the narcissistic, grandiose aspects of this defense while others are more hopeless and self-critical. In regard to the countertransference, these patients evoke an image of a desperate child, acting defiantly in the face of overwhelming tragedy.

Another way masochism appears alongside of problems with greed is in a quest for perfectionism. Here, the ego is foaming at the mouth for nourishment, love, and attention from an ideal object but is scared to focus that on the object. Such greed is felt to be a threat to the object, easily destroying it and causing it to retaliate in devastating ways. Therefore, the ego takes the strategy of holding itself up to the exacting standards it really has for the object. This translates into patients who are always giving people the benefit of the doubt but exacting perfection out of themselves. This approach usually sets them up to be used by others, and then they blame themselves instead of the abuser.

## CASE MATERIAL 6.1

Christy was a young woman in her twenties. Raised in a very religious family, she was told that it is sinful to want. This was combined with a strict schedule of studying and chores. Staying out late with friends or going to parties was forbidden. Even if Christy were to have wanted more, it was not there to be had. Her family was poor, so she had little in the way of material goods or educational advantages. Emotionally, she remembers her parents as preoccupied and uninterested in her needs. So, over the years Christy stopped wanting from others and turned her angry, starved needs onto herself. Her unmet emotional needs became demands to excel. She became an A+ student and excelled in gymnastics. In college, she was on the Dean's list and won several grants.

Christy expected perfection from herself and would accept nothing less. When I interpreted that she wished she had love and attention from her family and felt hostile about it, but was taking that out on herself now, she would agree. Next, she began to feel enraged about their neglect. Suddenly, she would turn the anger on herself and say, "but I should have learned to deal with that by now!" This stimulated countertransference greed in the form of my wanting her to continue expressing her anger and other feelings to really get at the root of things. But, when she shifted away to self-attack, I felt abruptly frustrated and as if a roadblock had been put up in our journey. I wanted more. I wanted continued progress and now felt slightly deprived. These were all feelings and phantasies I gradually understood as part of my patient's projective identification process in which I now felt some of her ongoing struggles.

In the transference, she felt she should have fixed her problems by now and that she was furious at what a "slow learner" she was. She apologized for taking too much time. I interpreted that, by seeing herself that way, she didn't have to deal with depending on me, learning about herself, and possibly being disappointed in the process. I said she must feel it would be a set-up for getting let down. She responded, "you must think I am very stupid. I know I feel that way. I am convinced of it." So, much of the transference struggle and therefore many of my interpretations had to do with her wanting to have us be this ideal, perfect pair without any difficulties or needs.

Christy's ego-ideal pushed her in many cruel and destructive ways. She would often work overtime till midnight and start back to work the next day at 5 a.m.. Making mistakes or falling behind her self-imposed deadlines was intolerable. Her body had to be just so as well. Christy took laxatives every day to expel the small amounts of food she did allow herself. She felt men would not find her attractive unless she conformed to her own idealized vision of beauty.

In the transference, she called herself "dumb and lame" for not immediately learning from our time together and quickly changing her life. At other times, she was able to relax into her need for my support. She was able to say, "I am so glad to be here. It seems like it's been forever since we talked last." When I announced my upcoming vacation, she told me, "thanks a lot. Now, I am really going to be in a tailspin." Here, we were able to talk about her need for my help and the strong wish for my company in her difficult daily struggles. However, as soon as she began to reveal how much she relied on me, she would start to dismantle it. "Well, I am starting to sound like a real loser. I can't even live my own life without therapy!" Then, we talked about this sudden attack on what felt like a more needy, greedy, or hungry self. In my countertransference, these shifting alliances left me feeling happily on track one day, pushed away the next, then guilty that I wasn't providing a big enough or fast enough cure, and then back again.

I also interpreted Christy's anorexia and her use of laxatives as an effort to be rid of the dangerous feelings and thoughts she felt too full of. She tried to expel the dangerous greed and oral rage in a concrete way, to save herself from the object's rejection and attack. When I made such comments, she would agree and there was often a short period of more normal eating. During these times, it felt like we were more of a team, both feeling filled up and satisfied with the pace of our work together. These brief victories then changed back to her critical, demanding vision of her body and the need to starve and empty herself.

In the second year of treatment, Christy started to talk more openly about her desire for more. She began working through some of her disturbing feelings of greed and the phantasies that came with them. She wanted a boyfriend that respected her and loved her, she wanted a job where she would be considered knowledgeable and talented, she wanted nice clothes that were fashionable, and she wanted friends who were reliable and honest. Christy was furious that others seemed to have these things and she did not. While it was a positive change that she could now admit to what formerly felt like dirty secrets, she also now felt she glimpsed a land of opportunity that would never become hers. She felt excluded and unwanted.

I gradually interpreted this as her reaction to unconscious greed and a sense of painful deprivation. She felt a tremendous hunger to be filled with all these things that she had never had. But, she felt she was undeserving and if she complained too much she would be in trouble. It was easier to feel excluded and rage about that than to deal with the fear of being abandoned and persecuted if she pursued the objects of desire. She responded to these interpretations by saying she was worried she would fail if she was granted these opportunities in life. They were too big a challenge and if she couldn't keep up with them, she would be outraged with herself. I interpreted that when she let herself feel OK about wanting more, her fear and guilt created a new greedy demand. Now, she would need to prove worthy of all she desired and if she failed, she would be the one that would reject and attack herself. This was too dangerous. The pressure felt so great that she was more comfortable staying at her current station in life and complaining about it.

As we approach the third year of treatment, some of these issues remain. However, Christy is more able to share her phantasies about all she wants from her objects, including her analyst. We are working on understanding the nature of her hunger for idealistic gratifications and how that has distorted her normal desires for a better life. We continue to examine her greedy, exacting way of relating to herself and others. In part, we do this by analyzing her defenses against greed. The nature of the transference continues to help in this understanding.

Klein (1959) thinks the greedy person is very ambitious, to the point of being forceful. At the same time, some patients react in a desperate manner against these parts of their personality. To be too ambitious, competitive, or pushy means hurting or destroying the object and possibly facing an intra-psychic catastrophe. Therefore, these patients often act humble, meek, and self-effacing instead.

One such patient would often start off the session by asking me what I would like to talk about. Or she would say, "it is your choice, what topic would you like me to discuss today?" When I pointed this out, she said she didn't want to be "taking up all the space by diving right in". Later, it came out that she was worried about me not liking her. She didn't want to "rock the boat" and hoped that we could stay "friendly" and not "have problems".

It can be difficult to see the difference between patients full of greed, yet trying to deny it, and patients who are masochistic. Indeed, they often overlap. However, I am exploring patients who use masochism and other ways of relating as a method of eradicating, disguising, and atoning for the greedy phantasies they feel possessed by.

## CASE MATERIAL 6.2

Ann was a social worker in her thirties when she came for help with depression. She said she was ready to start dealing with her past, because she knew it was destroying her chances of having a fulfilling life. Along with this positive eagerness, Ann also was timid and unsure of me. She said, "I have never trusted anyone. I always get burned. So, it is hard to be here and think about staying for very long without feeling threatened."

Ann's upbringing was traumatic to say the least. She was close to her uncle, but felt betrayed when he tried to fondle her when she was sixteen. Her father was an alcoholic who also took drugs. He shared his speed, hashish, and cocaine with Ann when she was in her early teens. Ann's mother stood by and did nothing, scared of her husband's violent temper and the risk of being left. While Ann remembers some positive times with her father, what made the deepest emotional impact was his violent and erratic nature. When he was drunk or high on drugs, he could turn from laughing and fun-loving to cruel and intimidating. He would shout at Ann and beat her with a belt. This experience of her father turning from a puppy dog to a pit-bull overshadowed most of her childhood years and shaped her adult psychology.

As an adult, Ann's relationships with men were strongly influenced by her early traumas and the phantasies she constructed around them. Her boyfriends were always men with problems, including financial, alcoholic, mental, and criminal. Ann would quickly take on their problems by bailing them out of jail, lending them money, or letting them move into her home. I interpreted this as a way of controlling her objects, in order to prevent them from turning into attacking, bad objects. I also interpreted that she identified with how needy and emotionally hungry they were but didn't feel worthy or safe expressing it directly. Once she established these self-sacrificing romances, she started to feel unappreciated and taxed. These men sometimes beat her, frequently disrespected her, and often used her for their financial and emotional gain.

In exploring these abusive relationship patterns, Ann shared her phantasy about the true nature of relationships and the essence of her own internal experience. Ann told me, "I cannot be alone, I fall to pieces. I need somebody there. It does not matter who it is, as long as I am not alone. I don't want to be seen as a bitch, somebody that needs too much, so I try and be really nice and give them what they want. That way I am sure of having them. I think weakness is attractive to men, so I make sure I don't look like I want much and don't get too pushy. I try and be good and not do anything to make the other person mad, because I can't bear to be alone."

Over time, we were able to pull apart the feeling and ideas behind this stark outlook. Ann felt she needed everything from her object, twenty-four hours a day. She told me, "I need constant attention and reassurance, or I feel lost!" But, she felt the demand would surely alienate any man. So, she did her best to hide her hunger to possess the entire object and instead tried to please the object by appearing weak and caring. I think her greedy desire to take in all of the object was a way of preventing herself from "going to pieces", combined with her fear of her object turning sour and mean. In fact, I think she felt her greed and need might be exactly what turned the object into a rejecting and attacking monster.

Ann's more blatant feelings of greed for the object would come out in remarks like, "I get so afraid of being alone, I cannot stand it. What I need is someone to be with every day and I don't really care who it is. I just have to have somebody all the time!" In my countertransference, I not only pictured Ann as an emotional vampire when she said this, but I felt she was experiencing some type of horrible panic, an inner collapse. So, I told her she must feel very anxious and in a complete crisis at those times, as if something terrible is going to happen. She replied, "Yes, like I will be destroyed, something catastrophic!"

Inside Ann struggled with these greedy hunger pains for an omnipotent, always reassuring object to protect her from a cruel and abandoning object. But, she was convinced her desire to capture and own such a security blanket would result in her being all alone, so she dressed up her desire with a disguise. She would present herself as an all-giving and nurturing object to men who seemed needy, as a way of getting them to be with her.

In the transference, Ann's fear of her own needs, desire, and greed came to bear. She had two powerful feelings. First, she felt I would never be able to provide her with all the answers, never fully help her, or ever stop her pain. And, she felt I would not be able to ever deliver these goods as quickly as she felt she needed them. I thought it was progress, and interpreted it as such, that she could risk telling me these things at all.

Indeed, the second feeling she struggled with was the fear that by revealing herself to me, she would be rejected by me. More specifically, Ann worried that her having some sense of self, an identity, would make me reluctant to care for her. She felt that if she was weak and formless, I would remain interested and not abandon her.

These two transference phantasies were linked. The more she wanted from me, the more she feared I would fail her. This left her anxious, desperate, and more needy. The more needy or greedy she felt, the more she was convinced I would turn away and/or retaliate.

This dual phantasy colored the transference relationship in many other ways. Ann used her insurance benefits to help pay for her treatment. At one point, there was a complicated mix-up in which the insurance company began requesting more and more paperwork and rejecting my reimbursement claims. This was a frustrating burden on me and Ann saw my reaction as scary and dangerous.

One day, Ann told me she had decided to stop treatment because it was "just too much trouble". For a while, she sounded fed up with our work and sick of the accompanying insurance problems. However, once I started exploring her feelings and thoughts more deeply, something quite different emerged. Ann was actually fearful of my potential rage. She pictured me becoming fed up and angry with her for causing so much trouble. She said, "I don't want to cause you so much hassle and grief. Eventually, you will just want to throw me out on my ass. So, I think it is better to quit. I don't want to send you over the edge." I interpreted that she pictured me in the same light as her father, on the edge of becoming mean. We talked about how she felt we couldn't find any common ground and how she strained to avoid that type of crisis and loss.

Some patients have phantasies of being too aggressive and competitive. This tends to trigger guilt over hurting the object. Feeling guilty, they try to make some sort of amends, such as a failure to undo the competitive feelings. Obsessive worries over how to please the object and make it all better start to take over. This is very different from Ann's vision of a more global loss and total persecutory rejection. For her, there was no restitution.

So, for Ann and other patients with similar internal dynamics, hope is not a viable commodity. It is the goal of analytic work to create hope in these cases. The way to do this is the ongoing working through of the anxious fearful phantasies of loss and persecution that usually emerge together.

Greed, while having a negative connotation, is part of normal growth. It can be found as part of everyone's personality mix in the optimal growth cycle. Within a loving and functional family, a child's natural greedy expressions are gradually modified with understanding containment. Positive cycles of projective identification and a nurturing external environment create hope. The ego develops a creative belief in a fallible yet strong and sturdy object that can feed the ego in a way that is fulfilling enough. This integrative development generates healthy symbolism, sublimation, and frustration tolerance. Forgiveness, tolerance, and understanding of self and other are the psychological rewards. Many patients, such as Ann, have not been so fortunate.

After I returned from a brief vacation, Ann started off by asking how my vacation went. I was unsure what her question meant, so, after saying I enjoyed my vacation, I was quiet. To myself, I wondered if she was trying to find out if I had been glad to escape her company, if she was worried about me when I was away and wanted to know if everything was OK, or if she wanted to find out more about me as a person outside of the office. I also wondered how my vacation had been for her. In other words, what sort of reaction did she have to our separation.

I let her continue talking. After a while, she was discussing work-related matters and said she would always rather talk about others than talk about herself. I suggested she may have asked me about my vacation as a distraction from having to focus on herself. Ann said, "if I don't use a distraction like that, I will let you in. I will end up letting you in and trusting you. Then, the trust will be broken; it could be sooner or it could be later, but I am sure it will be. I will be alone then. Once I let you in, you have information about me. When you break the trust, I will be alone and you will use the information against me."

I told Ann she feared getting close to me because she pictured me using her need for care against her. She said, "absolutely!" I suggested she felt this way because of how intense the desire for trust and closeness was. I said she felt greedy when she noticed her desire for trust and closeness and that she imagined she would be triggering a disaster by letting that all out. Ann said, "Yes. When you see how selfish and needy I am, you will be disgusted and throw me out. Or, you might pretend you still like me but it would be fake, a professional courtesy." I replied, "I would betray you, behind your back." "Yes. And, that might be even more painful", Ann responded.

Here, Ann was exploring a core phantasy of being abandoned and attacked as the result of trust. However, this unconscious phantasy was about trust being part of a greedy or selfish effort on her part and the object's retaliation against that perceived aggression.

About six months into the treatment, Ann told me how she could be mean to certain people as a way of not showing her true self. She felt it was safer to push others away and hope they understood it as a friendly act than to risk showing herself and face some kind of internal danger. Ann told me, "Sometimes, I act shitty toward people so they don't get to know the real me. Also, I hide my opinions. If I have some kind of identity, I will be attacked and I do not believe I will be able to survive that attack." I said, "you have some opinions here with me. Maybe that is why you say you are so nervous when you get here." "I believe that is true," Ann responded. "At the same time, do you think I have taken my mask off all the way with you?" she asked. I said, "No, of course not. Given what you have told me, you believe the risk is too great. You are too scared. It may change, but right now you worry that showing me your opinions, identity, and needs will make me not like you." Ann agreed. These sorts of interpretive exchanges seemed to bring us closer and build a level of comfort and security around Ann.

About a year into treatment, Ann discussed her feelings of being greedy, her defenses against it, and some genetic links. I was exploring her masochistic way of relating to a boyfriend. He was clearly taking advantage of her emotionally and financially. It was clear through what Ann said that she was angry about this relationship and wanted something better for herself. When I said this, she told me she felt very selfish to think that way. She said, "I feel like I am asking for way too much. I feel selfish. What I have always done is to try and be understanding of the people that hurt me. I did that growing up too. When my parents finally divorced, I felt compelled to take care of them. I don't exist in my relationships. The other person gets top billing. When I told my mother about the sexual abuse, she said, 'how can you do this to me? Why are you bringing such shame to me?' She got mad at me. It became all about her. I feel ashamed of wanting to be important to somebody, like it is asking for way too much."

As we worked together, this clarity and progress continued. Ann slowly shifted from more chaotic states of mind to more stable, integrated moments. This progress went forwards and backwards. Bit by bit, she seemed to find a meager foothold in her mind and in the phantasy of a safe and fulfilling relationship with the object, but also a fragile one that could quickly fall apart. This was a psychic place best described as a primitive beginning or primitive form of the depressive position, described by Quinodoz (1996) and Grinberg (1990).

Ann demonstrated a confusing tangle of primitive guilt, desire, projected greed, and persecutory phantasies when she came to a session dressed in gym clothes rather than her ordinary office clothes. Ann said, "I apologize for looking so sloppy. I don't want to offend you and you deserve to be treated with respect. I feel guilty making the decision to come from the gym to your office rather than cut my time at the gym short, run home to change, and then run back here." The more we discussed it, it became apparent that Ann was worried I had the potential to react like a judging and demanding father who was greedily demanding things be his way or else.

While she agreed with what I had to say and actually was the one to suggest most of these ideas, she also was responding in somewhat of a dismissive manner. For example, some of her comments on her own insights or on my interpretations of them were of the "yes, but so what" or "don't you have something more substantial to offer?" variety. So, I said, "now, you seem to skip over any sign of vulnerability, dependence on my ideas, or knowledge about yourself and start to act like a demanding father. At first, you felt I was a demanding, judging father about your clothes. I wonder if you are demonstrating how there is actually a part of you that is very demanding." Ann said, "unfortunately, I think you have hit the bull's-eye. When I stop being the nice girl, I think there is a lazy, angry, monster underneath. When that leaks out, I feel terrible. I hate myself for being such a greedy, angry bitch. Most of the time, I am able to keep that part of me under control, but you are pointing it out to me now and that hurts. It is embarrassing. When I stop serving others, I feel so guilty. But, when I stop serving others, I end up feeling so hungry. I want more. But, then I feel selfish and guilty and terrible. That is when I started cutting myself last time."

Indeed, Ann had a history of cutting her arms or burning them with a cigarette every few months. We had been able to trace this to feeling very guilty at wanting total care and love from all her objects all of the time, but then fearing retaliation for that greed. So, she punished herself first, an atonement to the good object turned bad object and its potential rage or rejection.

So, for patients like Ann, loss, separation, and the phantasized consequences of greed shaped their internal and external lives. When splitting and idealization of self or object fail, the experience of separation, loss, and persecution occurs, leading to cycles of feeling abandoned, rejected, and attacked by a lost and vengeful object. Being separate brings on envy and insatiable greed, leading to cycles of destructive phantasies fueled by projective identification and pathological splitting.

Envy is the hatred of difference and a phantasy of the object as more and the self as less. Destruction of the self or object is envy's solution, a manifestation of the death instinct. While envy leads to a wish of the object's demise and involves pathological independence from the object, greed leads to a wish of possessing all the object has to the point of aggressive dependence. Envy says, "I will destroy what you have, so you are no longer better than I." Greed says, "I will take you over and absorb you until you are gone and only I remain." So, competition and control play a part in envy while loss, domination, and oral incorporation play a part in greed.

## CASE MATERIAL 6.3

Patients often present with both issues: greed and envy. One patient, Ed, expressed his envy when talking about his highschool reunion. He said, "I am going back there with a vengeance! I will go back with a nice tan, tight muscles from working out, and a good job to brag about. I hope they are all lazy, pasty, losers with dead-end jobs so I can laugh at them. I can put them down and say, 'see, look at me! I am the king!'" I commented on what I thought was his hidden self-doubt that fueled this hatred of difference. In other words, his hatred of difference and wanting to be the best was based on him feeling he was in fact very inferior or even the worst. I said, "maybe, you are worried they don't think much of you, so you have to prove yourself". Ed replied, "I am a piece of shit and come from a shitty family. So, I have to do extra to just break even. If I can put them down, I can at least feel adequate."

Later, when Ed was talking about relationships, his greedy struggles surfaced. He said he can never picture being in a lasting, committed relationship because he likes the freedom to have sex with as many women as he pleases. I said, "you sound like you feel pressured to be a certain way and are not going to take it. You are not going to be boxed in." Ed said, "yeah, and I don't want to have to be trapped with one person and never be able to do as I please. The funny thing is I want the other person to be totally committed to me, dedicated even. But, I can never be that way to them, it feels too suffocating." I said, "I wonder if you want the other person to be so needy and dependent because it is hard for you to own that side of you?" Here, I was interpreting his projection of greed into the object because it felt too dangerous to have it within himself.

Ed replied, "I want to have total love, but I feel like it would turn out to be a joke, a disappointment, a disaster." I said, "you have told me how you look forward to being here, wanting to make the most of every minute. You say you want to be here. You are committed to this relationship. How does that feel?" Ed replied, "well, today I didn't want to come in. I am worried you will be disappointed in me, tell me I have made a setback." "Why?" I asked. "Because I went to a prostitute this weekend, used more drugs again, and had unsafe sex", he said. I replied, "so, when you think of being in a committed relationship with me, you worry I want everything from you including good behavior. Instead of us trying to understand what you did, you imagine I am upset and disappointed in you. You worry that what I want is more important than what you need." Ed said, "yes, that is right. I am afraid I will get punished for wanting it all and that you are angry for me not doing it your way."

So, Ed seemed to have a needy and greedy side to him that he projected onto others. He enjoyed having the attention and devotion of others but also noticed a cruel side of himself that belittled and rejected his needy girlfriends. When I interpreted these two aspects of his personality, he was able to reflect on them. He became aware of his own greedy desires for "total love" and his fear of this dependent wish turning sour. He also could see how he put me in the role of a demanding or exacting object that wanted him to be a certain way, or else. He pictured me as greedy, wanting my objects to conform to my wishes or I would banish them.

My countertransference was helpful in this case. Ed's picture of me as exacting and greedily demanding of "good behavior" made me feel pushed to be extra nice to him. To counteract his persecutory vision of me, I felt an urge to show him how accepting I was. But, then I felt pressure to figure out just the right type of way to be nice and exactly the right time or situation, so he would be convinced of my good intentions. Gradually, I saw that my feelings were a parallel, the result of projective identification, to his nervous worry about me.

When overcome by phantasies of greed, the ego becomes incapable of forgiveness, understanding, and restitution. Therefore, due to projection, Ed was worried I could not set aside judgment in order to try and understand his self-destructive behaviors over the weekend. With the ego's insatiable oral needs that comprise greed, the demand for love creates the phantasy of a withholding object. Through projective identification, the ego feels persecuted by an object cruelly withholding what feels like essential life-supplies. This brings on more demanding, hostile feelings from the ego and then, via projective identification, the object becomes more exacting, demanding, and cruel as well. All these pathological cycles create the need for the ego to protect the object from both the ego's vengeance and the urge for self-protection from the enraged, cruel object. Thus, there is no safety, no fulfillment, no completion. Loss is constant and danger is always looming.

# Chapter 7

# The impossible dream and the endless nightmare*

It is interesting that a search of twenty major psychoanalytic journals, from the years 1920 to 1997, elicits only one article with the word greed in the title. I believe this shows that greed is so fundamental to the human experience that either it is easily overlooked or it is spoken about from other vantage points. This is partly due to how elusive the clinical phenomenon of greed can be. Greed can be disguised and defended against with countless other ways of relating and it can be easily confused with other experiences such as competition, envy, and aggression. In addition, I think many analysts are uncomfortable with the concept and feel it easier to label greed as something else.

## THEORETICAL ISSUES

The greedy ego eats up the good object so the ego always needs more. It plunders its own food supply, bringing on feelings of abandonment, loss, rage, and persecutory guilt. In contrast, envy involves an ego that feels deprived of the object's wealth, strength, and love. Then, it resorts to spoiling the object's treasures so no one can enjoy them. With greed, the ego is never satisfied with what it has. It devalues the quantity and quality of what it already owns. By contrast, the envious ego feels left out and denied so it defaces the source of deprivation. As a defense, the ego then feels falsely content at having dominated the object. This is often part of a narcissistic transference presentation. So, while envy involves destructiveness followed by narcissistic superiority and eventually more envy and rage, greed fuels obsession with ownership and amassing greater amounts of the object. Idealistic demands create cycles of expectation directed at the self and the object. This brings about internal experiences of endless hunger,

* This chapter was first published as 'The impossible dream and the endless nightmare: clinical manifestations of greed', in *Canadian Journal of Psychoanalysis*, 11(2, 2003): 379–397.

lack of fulfillment, and great hopelessness. Self-induced emotional starvation is the result, even when surrounded by adequate or ample degrees of love, success, and knowledge.

So, greed is an unrelenting and unstable internal experience. It produces constant unrest and an endless hungry search for more. Schneider (1988) has clarified how the infantile ego, under the sway of the death instinct and the overuse of aggressive projective identification dynamics, feels there is an inadequate object and therefore experiences emotional starvation. This generates even more states of greed and builds a persecutory phantasy of a greedy ego desperately trying to feed on a withholding, empty, angry breast.

As a defense, envious and narcissistic patients phantasize about successfully conquering and controlling their objects. The envious ego destroys any evidence of feelings or thought to the contrary. For the greedy ego, the battle is never over and never won. Always seeking to own and feed on the ideal object, the greedy ego is never secure. Greed strips the ideal object of its goodness so the ego feels angry and vengeful. Via projective identification, the ego is now faced with a good object turned bad, a nourishing oasis turned into poison. This leads the greedy ego into a cycle of craving, searching, loss, persecution, and savage guilt.

Klein (1955) pointed out the important link between projective identification and greed. The multiple functions of projective identification include defense, creativity, reparation, and communication. For patients coping with demanding and greedy ego ideals, the function of projective identification is usually more defensive, competitive, and evacuative. Therefore, phantasies are not so much about elaborative and reciprocal object relations. Due to a great deal of projection, these patients feel the world is populated by dangerous, demanding, and unforgiving objects. In response to this harsh world view, they adopt a siege mentality and refuse to let much in. Introjection is a threat. Such patients live in a narrow niche where they are constantly on the alert for trouble. Technically, this makes for a difficult analytic process. When these greedy and fearful patients receive interpretations, they hear them as persecutory demands and judgments. So, they try to avoid them or evacuate them. Many of these patients abort treatment after a few weeks or months, convinced the analyst is another disappointing, unstable person who betrayed them.

When the paranoid-schizoid ego is primarily functioning under the sway of oral aggression and greed, and has insatiable demands for ideal love, power, and knowledge from the self and the object, there is a breakdown of object relatedness. With projective identification, the ego feels persecuted by a withholding and exacting object. At the same time, the ego must find a way to protect the object from the ego's own violent greed and thirst for ideal control. This all leads to severe difficulties in intimacy and trust. Belief in negotiation, forgiveness, and understanding is difficult if not impossible.

With excessive projective identification and strong greedy phantasies, normal splitting processes break down and the painful reality of separation, difference, and distance assaults a fragile ego. In the paranoid-schizoid world, this leads to phantasies of abandoned, rejected, lost, and attacked parts of the self and parts of the object. Indeed, part of the problem is the confusion between self and object.

Being separated by greed from the ideal object or ideal self creates even more insatiable need, leading to a cycle of destructive phantasies. The greedy patient avoids, denies, and hates any sign of difference between self and object and between the actual self/object and the idealized self/ object. All evidence of the life instinct, which would include need, hunger, yearning, loss, and healthy greed, brings on feelings of loss, primitive guilt, persecution, loss, and more need. Therefore, the death instinct is prominent in these patients' psychic struggles. They want to keep themselves and their objects as one, the same. If the ego owns the object than there is nothing it needs from that object. Maintenance of status quo is important and keeping everything looking normal and smooth is a daily task. In this world, separation leads to loss, persecution, and primitive guilt. This is based on paranoid-schizoid phantasies of very fragile object relations between aggressive, greedy parts and overwhelmed→destroyed→vengeful parts of the self and of the object. Separation occurs through distance but also through difference. Difference makes two things separate and apart. For the greedy patient, difference not only signifies loss and danger, but brings on the feelings of another object that has what the ego so desperately wants.

Trying to sort out why certain patients' internal world is so shaped by greed, one is struck by the combination of early, external stress or trauma and the ongoing inner search for an ideal object. It would be easy to say that the lack of adequate early parenting causes such reactions. However, many other patients have suffered similar environmental strain without following the same psychological pathway. I think the infant may process these early states of trauma and neglect in particular ways that led to complex anxieties and conflicts, sometimes typified by greed. In other words, phantasies about the neglectful or unavailable object are formed and the external world is colored and complicated by the internal.

Critics of Melanie Klein claim she devalued the impact of the child's actual early experiences in the family. This is not the case. In her writings, Klein (1940; 1945; 1946; 1948; 1952d) emphasized the important relationship between the external and internal world. She wrote about the impact of the real mother on the child and how the child would mentally translate that experience using his or her own feelings, ideas, and phantasies. I think this great respect of how powerful both the environmental and the emotional worlds are in shaping the individual's psychological perception, separately and in combination, is Klein's theoretical strength.

When working with patients, I have yet to see someone who doesn't eventually report some degree of early neglect, abuse, or marked relational difficulty in their family unit. The combination of these traumatic or confusing bonds with loved parents and authorities with the developing ego's unique management of those relational atmospheres creates patterns of neurotic, borderline, or psychotic process we see via the transference. So, I always think of greed as being the result of real-life situations as translated by the mind's unique method of relating to these threatening, unavailable, yet beloved objects.

## CASE MATERIAL

M's childhood was marred by chaos, abuse, and uncertainty. Her father was an alcoholic and her mother would scream and shout at her husband until they came to physical blows. When M was five years old, her parents left their native country to avoid political persecution. They were unable to take M and her two sisters with them. The children remained with grandparents for five years. M's parents would come back to visit every six months or so. They also wrote letters and sent packages.

M remembered her grandmother favoring her sisters and criticizing M for being small, slow, and plain. Much of the time, a neighbor babysat M. He molested her for several years, making her perform oral sex. She cried when telling me, saying she didn't know why she never told someone. I asked how she felt when he used her this way over the years. M sobbed and said, "terrified!"

When I met M, she was thirty years old and still living with her family. Her sisters were married. M told me of all the ways her sisters irritated her and how her parents seemed to ignore their faults and emphasize their achievements. I interpreted M's hidden desire for her parents to take care of her and pay her more attention. M sheepishly agreed and said, "I can't drive a car, cook a meal, or have my own place. I don't think it is because I am unable to do these things. I think I am smart enough to do these things, so I don't see why I am so helpless." I said, "perhaps you simply refuse to care for yourself and inside you are demanding your parents to finally take care of you the way you wanted as a little girl. You are angry and want them to make it right." This interpretation was based on the many passive–aggressive, masochistic comments she had made about her family, all indicating a sense of righteousness and a feeling of "they owe me". M replied, "Yes. I know I need to grow up, but I don't want to sometimes."

I believe M was referring to a general feeling of resentment in which she wanted to be given to, to have everything made better, and to have her parents be servants rather than caretakers. Ultimately, this global desire for an ideal object that she could control and possess left M unable to find direction in her own life. Klein (1957) spoke to this when she said, greed is an important factor in indiscriminate identifications for the need to get the best from everywhere interferes with the capacity for selection and discrimination. This incapacity is bound up with the confusion between good and bad that arises in relation to the primal object.

(p. 126)

In other words, M was so intent on being emotionally filled from her objects that she was unable to focus on developing her own identity. Indeed, she was confused about the goodness and badness in herself, as well as in her objects.

M's demand to be cared for cast its shadow on the transference. M said she often felt suicidal and was constantly crying. One week, she had felt very abandoned when she felt a close friend had said all was fine between them, but acted aloof and cold. M felt betrayed and wondered if the friend was secretly dumping her for another friend. She became so upset over this that she ran into the bathroom, locked the door, and started cutting herself with a razor. The way M told the story left me feeling worried and controlled. As M turned to another subject, I was left still thinking about how volatile she was. I felt as if she was making a veiled threat of "if you don't take proper care of me that is what will happen". I believe, through projective identification, M had put her desperation, fear of betrayal, and sense of persecution into me. I now wondered and worried if M would hurt herself and when she might do this. I felt helpless to prevent it. When I tried to engage her in exploring her dark mood, she breezed over it as if it had been a passing fancy, not important enough to waste time talking about. She had used me as a refuse container to discharge these feelings and now she seemed to want to ignore the scene of the crime.

This projective identification dynamic, inducing my countertransference, was part of M's evacuative character structure. Grinberg (1990) has explored the need for more primitive patients to evacuate their phantasies of persecution, loss, and primitive guilt. Unable to process these states of mind in more elaborative form, these patients rely on projective mechanisms for psychic equilibrium. Therefore, I was put in a position to contain and detoxify M's aggressive and overwhelming feelings. As Steiner (2000) has noted, this is a difficult situation because the patient does not want to re-own these feelings and phantasies and resists the analyst's interpretations of this projective cycle. So, when I pointed out to M that she needed to have me feel the threatening feelings she was having as well as the sense of loss and lack of control, she told me "of course I didn't want to feel that way", and didn't wish to explore it.

Sometimes, M was quite masochistic with her friends and family as well as in the transference. Sometimes, I felt sorry for her. However, the more we explored the situations where she felt victimized, it often turned out she was projecting her greed into others and then felt bullied by their selfishness and demands. At other times, M appeared narcissistic. She wanted others to serve her and did not want to acknowledge the differences between herself and others.

Later in the analysis, M explored her feelings and fears of loss and persecution enough to understand them in another way. I pointed out how, when she engaged me with her disputes and arguments, she seemed to be asking me to become angry and set her straight. It was as if she wanted to be with me when I was being a more dominating, angry parental figure. When I made this interpretation, M immediately said, "well, that is how my grandfather always was when he was drunk. Come to think of it, I always view men as sort of weak or normal and boring, unless they are kind of abusive. If a man seems smart and able to control me, to take care of me in a strong way, I feel safe and warm. But, if they seem weak, I feel like I could easily hurt them or take advantage of them. I hold myself back as a way of protecting them. My last therapist seemed unable to handle me when I got out of hand. I wanted him to get tough and set me straight. When he didn't, I felt like I won. I often felt like I could just run right over him with my strong feelings. Look out, I am going to get what is mine and if you're not strong enough, you're going to get plowed under! Of course, I mostly keep these feelings to myself and end up looking like the weak one, but you have had a taste of the real me and you passed the test, Doc! You seem strong and smart. I admire that."

During one session in the first year of treatment, M clearly displayed her phantasies of fear, greed, and emotional hunger in the transference. After she talked about several relationships, including ours, in which she was worried about being too rude or arrogant, I interpreted her constant vigilance over the fragile nature of peace turning to war. I suggested that, at a moment's notice, she pictured us becoming very adversarial and that she consequently felt threatened. Trusting me might prove dangerous. M replied, "that is my life story! I have spent my life walking on glass, trying hard to never make noise or rattle any feathers. I am in charge of damage control, always avoiding the bloody blowup. That is my life!"

For the rest of the session, we explored the consequences of this way of relating to the world. I brought up how much M must feel on the outside of our relationship, maintaining a level of control and safety, but never getting closer or feeling protected. In other words, I started to point out the motivation and consequences of her internal bargain with her objects. So far, we were dealing with the side of her that tried to deflect or deny any sense of greed or desire.

At the end of the forty-five-minutes session, M said, "I notice we only meet for forty-five minutes. I wonder what you use the other fifteen minutes for. Maybe it gives you a chance to unwind from all my bullshit. You probably think, 'thank god that ass is gone!' Maybe it takes fifteen minutes to recover from the mindless complaining and endless crap I dish out. I am sorry I do that. I really am. Thank you for seeing me today, Doctor." Then, M paused and I said, "maybe there are other feelings you have. Maybe you wish we could have spent a few more minutes together?" M said, "actually, I wonder if you are going to be able to help me. I don't want to be disrespectful, but I don't understand why I can't have my fifteen minutes. The sessions are sixty minutes, an hour, right? I don't know why you cut them short. You must have a reason. I am paying for it, right! I don't want to sound too harsh, but why are we stopping?"

I explained to M that each session was forty-five minutes long. Then I said, "first you put the anger and the neediness onto me, that I needed the time and that I was angry at you. Now, I think you are taking the risk to tell me what you feel. You are angry for not getting everything you need and want." M agreed and said she felt terrible and didn't want to seem ungrateful. I pointed out that again she was starting to apologize, which may be more comfortable than addressing her desires and disappointments. Here, I was addressing M's hunger for me, her fear of my intolerance of that need, and her resulting anger and increased hunger.

It is common to see this defensive layer of masochism hiding the more core affect of greed. Again, I want to emphasize the word greed as an expression of a particular type of ego hunger, rather than a negative judgment of personality. Greed, like aggression and sexuality, is part of the human condition and an element of health as well as pathology. M's eagerness for more time with me was contaminated with excessive splitting, severe guilt, phantasies of retaliation, and the need to hurt herself before I could attack or reject her. Rather than healthy greed or eagerness for fulfillment and giving, it was a shameful, dangerous yearning for an unobtainable ideal. It was an unmanageable hunger.[1]

1 A common critique of Klein's ideas, typically from the self-psychology perspective, is that they don't pay attention to the real deprivation the patient has suffered in childhood and continues to feel unconsciously. This is a basic misunderstanding of Klein's theoretical views as well as the contemporary Kleinian approach to clinical material.

My patient, M, is a helpful example to clarify this. I am taking what I consider a Freudian–Kleinian approach to conceptualizing, understanding, and treating this patient. In doing so, I see her as having been psychologically marked by early neglect, abuse, and environmental unpredictability. At the same time, M received this early experience through the filter of her own innate temperament, emotional disposition, and very particular sets of self–object relational phantasies. These phantasies were shaped by her ego strength and the availability of good, supportive objects, both internal and external, that could serve as resources and provide a balance and protection from the conflicts with her primary objects, both internal and external.

I think, following Klein's theory of the mind, that M colored her early deprivation and confusion with her own projections, splitting, and other mental distortions. These reshaped experiences mixed with the external environment to produce new mental landscapes. These internal histories continued to evolve over time and affect her daily functioning.

This type of greed→fear→masochistic-surrender cycle arose in other transference situations. M would spend weeks on end telling me about her "learning disability", her low intelligence, and her conviction that she was retarded. She gave me countless examples of how stupid she was, unable to negotiate the simplest of everyday tasks. This was a frustrating time for me, as I felt, no matter what I said, she would try and prove she was too stupid to get better. I finally said as much and added that I believed she was worried about how our relationship would be if she weren't stupid. In other words, she had to control us in a narrow way: I was the smart doctor and she was the incurably stupid patient. If she were just as smart as I was, then what? If I didn't wield the power and dominate her, then what? I suggested she was worried about how having a brain and an identity meant she also had strong desires: sexual, emotional, and otherwise. I said she might be unsure of how our relationship would weather that. M said, "wow! If I had my way? Boy, I just don't know! That is overwhelming to think about. I guess I see that as a recipe for disaster, so I just don't go there!"

M's masochistic profile shielded her from her overwhelming greed that was laced with persecutory and guilty feelings. In other words, she could pay her penance ahead of time just in case. The other way that M avoided these pangs of emotional hunger and greed was to use obsessional defenses. Because M operated more in the paranoid-schizoid position than in the depressive position, these obsessional mechanisms were severe and of a primitive nature (Grinberg 1990).

M was working for a computer software company when I first started seeing her. She had been bouncing from job to job from the time she left highschool, quitting about every six months. M said, "I don't know what I want to do, so how am I supposed to know what job to look for?" She would feel bored, unhappy, and angry at each job. Her coworkers seemed idiotic and her job duties felt pointless. M hated what she did but did not know what to do instead. She was full of panic and desperation. She was caught in a frenzy of anxiety, anger, and confusion, literally yelling at herself to figure it out and pick a career path. Obviously, the more she

So, I think the best psychoanalytic approach, be it Kleinian or otherwise, is one that attempts to treat both aspects of the patient's makeup: the historical and the psychological. However, Kleinian technique, and certainly the way I practice it, emphasizes the benefit of seeing both aspects as constantly intertwining and influencing one another. Of course, this is the universal nature of what we term the transference and extra-transference phenomena. The patient takes in our interpretations and our way of relating interpersonally (external reality) and filters or modifies that experience with their own phantasies and historical perceptions and relates to us accordingly. Our job is to gradually make sense of that process and convey our understanding to the patient, so we can help the patient to master it and make it a more helpful and hopeful part of their identity and character. Pathological projection becomes a healthy and healing introjective process.

railed at herself, the less she was able to focus on what she might want to explore. M was too demanding and too on guard to be curious. In fact, she would get angry with me over the idea of exploring anything, since she felt she was running out of time and needed to find out the answers immediately. I pointed out how she now felt I was as frustrating as her career search. In her greedy quest to quench her thirst for more, M felt I was denying her the mental health she wanted so badly. And, she felt life was somehow cheating her out of finding a perfect career.

I believe M's career problem mirrored her other struggles. She had built an impossible ideal for herself. She wanted it all. She literally wanted to know, immediately, the exact, right career that would satisfy her for years to come. This was supposed to suddenly appear without her efforts. Actually, she felt unable to think for herself, so she wanted it to come from somewhere else. This instant career had to make lots of money, be creative, give her emotional satisfaction, and require virtually no training. Whenever M thought of careers that required a college degree or some amount of extra study or training, she dismissed them. She said, "I am not sure that is the right career so why waste time training for it?" Naturally, this created a cycle of self-defeat.

At times, I was enlisted, via projective identification, into this cycle. By projecting her frustration and idealism into me, she was still the victim, but no longer the tyrant. I found myself slightly pressing her with suggestions on possible classes to take and career paths to consider. Fortunately, I caught myself and was able to point out how we both were now involved in this taskmaster dynamic of having to find the perfect thing, immediately. The more we discussed this, it became clear how greedy and demanding M could be. She would not settle for less than the best and if there was uncertainty involved, that meant failure or disappointment and was unacceptable.

This greedy expectation for perfection spilled over into many areas of M's life. As I said, she felt her coworkers at every job were fools. M saw them as immature, irresponsible, and consistently failing at their appointed tasks. This was part of her need for impossible excellence, the quest for an ideal object. If she was surrounded by less than ideal objects, then she felt less than perfect too.

The same feelings emerged around her workout schedule. M wanted to practice aerobics every day. If she couldn't complete a rigorous ninety-minute regime every day, she felt deflated and cheated. Even when she managed these near-impossible schedules, M would become upset at not having done some small part of the workout perfectly. She felt weak and stupid.

In the transference, I was often a disappointing workout as well. "This just isn't working" would be her lament. Here, her greed and anger spilled out and were without the masochistic disguise. M felt analysis took too long, didn't work, and never gave her any answers. When I made an interpretation, she would say something to the effect of "so?" Or she would avoid having to digest the interpretation and avoid thinking about it by immediately throwing it back at me, saying, "OK, so how do I fix that?" Indeed, we spent many hours debating, fighting, and struggling with her one-foot-in and one-foot-out approach to our relationship. She felt so hopeless that she saw no point in continuing, threatened to leave, and even set various termination dates. This distancing and rejecting also occurred in the moment-to-moment aspects of each session. My interpretations were things that were not good enough to consider, too confusing to understand, and too unsettling to take in. So, for the first year of treatment, M often questioned why she was in treatment and seemed to be like a baby who was hungry but also proved to be a very finicky eater.

Needy, anxious, and greedy patients show this inability to settle into the analytic relationship. They cautiously circle, refusing to land. M lamented what she felt to be the overwhelmingly unsatisfying and negative feel of analysis. I believe she and other similar patients protest like this for several reasons. M felt, in phantasy, a lack of proper and continuous feeding. If I was not spoon-feeding her, she would have to grow up and learn to feed herself and even be willing to feed and care for her objects. So, analysis represented a struggle with autonomy, control, and sacrifice.

I believe the strongest underlying factor in M's protest was her attempt to not harm me. This was a phantasy of destroying me with greed and desire, which would in turn engender my rage and attack. So, she felt rejection, loss, and abandonment could occur at any moment. This was a phantasy of a barren, poisonous breast that left her alone, in painful loneliness (Klein 1963). This is in contrast to a more healthy and tolerable state of solitude (Quinodoz 1996) that emerges through integration of the depressive position.

One day, in the second year of treatment, M announced her "find". She had found a reference to one of my published papers on the internet, tracked the paper down, and read it with excitement. What caught her attention the most was the description of a patient who had brought me a gift. M was intrigued at what she called the "special intimacy" the gift conveyed and how full of feelings my and my patient's discussion about the gift had been. She was fascinated at how emotionally charged the relationship seemed. M talked about all this with a sense of bewilderment, as if she had noticed something completely alien to our relationship. She said, "I was really struck by how much closeness you had with this patient. It didn't seem like anything we ever have. My treatment is so sterile and dry."

After two years of associations and dreams that conveyed similar ideas, her complaint was no surprise. I said, "you really noticed my special relationship with that patient. I think you are hungry to have that with me. At the same time, by wanting it you are denying the fact that we already have it. We share many intimate moments together, but it is difficult for you to admit that because you risk depending on me, losing me, or giving me the upper hand. So, you deny our specialness and then end up feeling ripped off and empty." M replied, "you are right. I want it so bad, but I can't admit it. It feels weak and stupid. But, I want to have it all, now! At the same time, I don't want to be accountable to anyone!" Here, I was confronting M's anxiety of being without an object to fulfill her oral needs (Klein 1948). By using denial, followed by projection into the relationship in my article, she avoided this internal tragedy.

M's overall transference and this particular phantasy of owning a special closeness without having to contribute to it is a mental state of greed and envy, and a fear of loss and persecution. With such patients, there is a greedy push to create and to possess an ideal union with an ideal object. This demanding need dominates the personality. It can exist in extreme form and be a hallmark of the paranoid-schizoid position. This was the case with M. It can also manifest in more neurotic, oedipal forms, characteristic of the depressive position. I think paranoid-schizoid greed is tied to phantasies of not only loss and persecution, but also feelings of sadistic guilt. This is a primitive guilt that is centered around relentless ego demands and fears of retaliatory danger. Boris (1986) points out that greed brings on envy, spite, and revenge. Greed creates countless layers of pathological defenses and psychic bargains between self and object. I think greed easily generates pathological cycles of projective identification in which the ideal object is not only wished for and pined for, but hunted down and held captive, until in phantasy it retaliates and exacts revenge.

When the infantile ego is overloaded with aggressive, greedy, and envious phantasies and the external environment is traumatic, a template of pathological object relations is formed and reinforced. M's early family experiences were severe and they pushed her to focus on phantasies of persecutory and betraying objects, objects she could never reach or trust for the love and nourishment she craved.

Even when patients like M begin to make progress, they easily slip back into phantasies of dangerous and abandoning objects. When they feel they are finally getting the love, care, or success they desire, it is as if they go on a feeding frenzy. So, again, the ideal object is torn apart and lost, leaving a vengeful bad object in its place.

Three or four years into her treatment, M experienced this type of backward slide in a set of dreams and in the transference. They followed a week of positively expressing her feelings toward me and experiencing what she termed her "dependency, neediness, and greed" in a more positive light. She had also felt more confident at work and with friends that week. Over the course of one night, she had the following three dreams.

In the first dream, M was a football star. She was always clear for the quarterback's pass and caught the ball with grace. Touchdowns were easy and she rarely was tackled. The quarterback could see her and he successfully passed to her every game. M said that even though she scored more than other players, it didn't feel overly competitive and it all seemed fair. After the game, she signed a few autographs. M said this also felt balanced and wasn't a matter of needing to be important. In fact, she felt particularly caring toward several children who came seeking autographs and she spent extra time talking to them.

In the second dream, M felt very conflicted. She and her friend decided to go to lunch together. M's friend said she wanted to go to her favorite restaurant. M thought this was somewhat inconsiderate and wanted to go to another restaurant instead. In this dream, the two women were disagreeing, each wanting to have it their way. There was tension in the air. Both parties had firm ideas about what they wanted and they didn't want to concede or compromise.

In the third dream, M was a child again and in her parent's home. She looked around and saw that she didn't have her own room. All the family members had their own room, except M. M went to her mother and asked for a room. This led to an argument. Having been awoken by the shouting, M's father stormed in screaming. He beat M's mother bloody and then took a knife and killed M and her mother.

M was very disturbed by the last dream and said she wished she could go back to the first dream, but it seemed so short-lived. When I asked for associations, M said she never gets what she wants and it feels as though other people always get their way. Here, I felt M was emphasizing her masochistic experience of being dominated and having to suffer. I told M I felt she was not so passive in her thoughts and feelings. I said she in fact wants to be active and partaking of life, but feels there are bad consequences to being greedy.

In the first dream, M tried to create a special balance between being special and not harming others or being attacked for her attempts at being unique. She was the star, her teammates were OK, and no one was envious of her. This magical harmony seemed too much to maintain for very long and the next dream showed more conflict. The first dream seemed elaborative (Grinberg 1990) and the last two were more evacuative (Grinberg 1990). In other words, M's ego seemed to be working with various elements of conflict in the first dream and somewhat in the second dream, but merely projecting and ejecting raw, persecutory material in the third dream.

In the second dream, M felt aware of the tug-of-war competition she and her friend had over where to have lunch. They were unwilling to negotiate or share. This shift into a more every-person-for-themselves stance seemed to trigger a cycle of greed and persecution that culminated in the third dream. Here, the situation was raw. M had no sense of identity, acceptance, or belonging in her family. Wanting union with a good self-room and the good object-family brought on phantasies of being denied access to that ideal. Why would one follow the other? I believe the combination of her actual life history of similar deprivation and abuse and her own greed to possess her objects in a totalistic way brought on phantasies of violence and revenge. This was a blending of her own aggressive greed being projected into the object and her fear of the hoped-for ideal object being turned into a crazed, violent, bad object.

I pointed out how these same dynamics colored the transference. M tried to maintain a self-sufficient, aloof, and independent stance. I felt she did this to deny her own needy desperation and also to ward off what she felt to be a greedy, intrusive object. By projecting her greed into myself and others, M ended up feeling surrounded by demanding objects. This projective identification process became an interpersonal dynamic as well as an intra-psychic phantasy. M would say things in a vague, dismissive, and aloof manner. This left me feeling curious and in a lurch, so I would ask clarifying questions. She would become defensive and more vague, so then I would have to ask more questions. Eventually, M would break down sobbing and say I was interrogating her and making her feel "hassled and harassed".

Another example of this interpersonally laden projective identification process came about when M began to diagnose and treat herself. She started telling me how she had read a few books on depression and had ordered a set of self-help tapes on anxiety disorders. She told me she suffered from anxiety disorders and that it was caused by negative thought patterns. The tapes told her to avoid negative thinking. Every session would be marked by some reference to these tapes and how she agreed with them and was applying the recommended solutions. In the countertransference, I felt curiously left out, slightly competitive, and I found myself wanting to win her back to the analytic solution. In other words, she had projected her feelings of greed, loss, abandonment, and hunger into me. I decided to address these elements from the idea of her fear of engaging me and needing me. I said, "I know how much you are listening and learning from the tapes. You seem to avoid using me as another resource." M replied, "well, I always try and do everything myself. When I depend on people, trouble happens. I get hurt or disappointed. They misunderstand and we have conflict. I see what you mean by how I kind of ignore you. It is kind of silly, you are right here and obviously know about these sorts of things, but I don't see you as being accessible like the tapes." I interpreted that she feels safer controlling and owning the help from the tapes, whereas I am more of an unknown and a potential risk to depend on. She agreed and said, "People are uncertain. Things, like tapes, don't bite."

Over time, I focused on M's fear of disturbing me with her needs and desires for care and attention. I analyzed her greed and her phantasies about those feelings. We explored her fear of what I would be like if she directed those feelings at me. At the beginning of most sessions, especially in the first year of treatment, she would thank me for seeing her and act as if I was doing her a big favor. She was worried she had interrupted my valuable time. In a similar vein, she would ask permission to use "my" bathroom even though there was a sign indicating the public restroom off the waiting room. At the end of many sessions, M would apologize for having been "a bitch" or a complainer. She hoped that my next patient was in a better mood. M worried about getting my analytic couch dirty with her shoes and felt she was taking up space that I could easily fill with a higher-paying and more cheerful patient. I interpreted all these ways of relating as her fear of not only being too greedy and selfish, but also picturing me unable to endure or understand her hunger for help and care.

Patients such as M, who are constantly struggling with feelings and phantasies colored by greed, persecution, loss, and envy, oscillate in how they relate to the analyst. Sometimes, they are eagerly trying to gobble up all the love, strength, or power the analyst represents. As the result of pro-jective identification and counter-identification, the analyst may then feel overwhelmed, harassed, or confused. At some point, the patient will begin to fear that their aggressive thirst has made the analyst furious. They phantasize that their greed has awoken a sleeping giant, who now will attack them. This leads to paranoid standoffs in the treatment. Many patients will try their best to avoid this frightening shift of good food turning to poison by denying, reversing, or projecting their greedy feeling. M tried many different ways to escape this sense of loss and persecution.

She was apologetic when she needed to sit up and use a tissue for her tears. In making occasional requests for a schedule change, she always brought them up as if she was going to get hit or yelled at. By and large, M did whatever it took to not rock the boat and create conflict. At the same time, what she talked about, the way she talked at people, and the over-arching way she related to me all spoke of an enormous hunger to possess, own, and take in the objects in her vicinity.

M and patients like her are operating within the paranoid-schizoid position and see the world as a place dominated by threatening, retaliating, and abandoning objects. Forgiveness and understanding are not reachable, or if they are, they crumble quickly under the aggression of greed and envy. The hoped for idealized object, the warm mother, turns into a cold monster.

While some behaviors and transference phenomena may seem designed to deal with worries of hurting the analyst, the situations I am highlighting are not depressive-position, reparative concerns. Hurting the analyst, for these patients, is equivalent to inviting annihilation. So, the focus of most acting out and transference material is on self-survival.

This dynamic works both ways. M tried to be polite and nice to avoid making me angry. Instead of expressing her greedy hunger, she emotionally starved herself to avoid abandonment and attack. However, via projective identification, I sometimes felt attacked when M's greed broke loose. At the same time, M would try and protect her objects from her aggressive phantasies of greed and control. She explained how she stays her distance from men she likes because she is afraid of "going ballistic if they don't give me 100 percent attention".

M continues to be in treatment, now in its fourth year. She lives in her own apartment and has kept the same job for over a year. She is better able to see herself and her objects in a realistic manner. While still uncomfortable with the idea, she can accept her own limitations. This is in large part due to an integration of her expectations of herself and others. In other words, her ideal has shifted from such a greedy and demanding place to a more forgiving and accepting stance. Less greed and aggressive hunger have led to more balanced expectations, which in turn have led to her achieving more and feeling more successful.

M feels safer in wanting my care and attention because she is not ready to devour me. Therefore, she feels able to make a connection with me that results in her feeling gratified and grateful. She feels emotionally full. Overall, M's ego ideal has been modified and the greedy, aggressive phantasies that came out of that ideal have been tamed and integrated into more creative, manageable, and sublimated phantasies and feelings. Thus, via projective identification, M is able to imagine her objects as more friendly and giving. Therefore, she is more willing to take these new objects and thus build even more stable inner object relations. A more positive and affirming cycle has begun.

# Chapter 8

# Greed, idealization, and insatiability*

Many of the patients we encounter in private practice express a general feeling of never being satisfied with themselves, with their lives, or with the people close to them. Even in the face of external success, this lack of emotional gratification remains. As shown in the previous chapters, some of these patients are experiencing life within the paranoid-schizoid position while others have one foot in the paranoid-schizoid position and one foot in the depressive position. In both cases, these patients feel like life is happening to them with no sense of self-involvement. This is because they constantly raise the bar of expectation, for themselves or their objects, until it becomes an impossible demand. "I never get what I really want; I can never get enough to feel full and secure; I can't find a way to please people; I am never good enough" are central strands of unhappiness that echo through their inner worlds.

Some of these patients have difficulty entering treatment and staying for very long. Needing help is in itself a sign of failure in their constant reach for perfection. They quickly perceive the analyst as a judgmental person, someone there to fix damaged and defective people. Therefore, interpretations are taken as an accusation of imperfection and a verbal attack rather than an understanding observation.

Most of these patients have suffered chronic trauma or disappointment in childhood. Their own normal levels of constitutional aggression, greed, and desire for control converge with both the environment and the dynamics of projective identification to produce a cycle of excessive and pathological greed, guilt, loss, and persecution. All these internal phantasies and feelings prevent any lasting contentment or fulfillment with the self and one's important objects. Any good and satisfaction are destroyed by greed and turned into loss. Everything is sacrificed for the sole goal of finding a perfect self or object, leading to self-destruction along the way.

* This chapter was first published as 'Greed, idealization, and the paranoid-schizoid experience of insatiability', in *Scandinavian Journal of Psychoanalysis*, 26(2003): 41–50.

## CASE MATERIAL

Nina came to see me when she was forty years old.[1] Nina had been on various antidepressant medications and migraine treatments for years, but this was the first time she was seeking psychological services.

We began a journey that was to last for over three years. Three times a week, on the analytic couch, Nina slowly shared her internal conflicts with me. From a Freudian–Kleinian perspective, I helped her explore her unconscious phantasies as a way to better understand and master her self–object struggles. Acting out was a factor in this case, including both acting out within the treatment relationship as well as outside of it. The transference was a repeat of the interpersonal and intra-psychic system that ruled her life. Much progress was made, yet integration of her borderline patterns was only partial. However, Nina worked hard at improving herself and used the psychoanalytic relationship with me in a way that greatly benefited her.

In the first several visits, I could not get a word in. Nina chattered nonstop, mechanically informing me about all her symptoms, her history, her financial troubles, and her anger at her current boyfriend for never acting "like a man". By this, she meant he was never helpful and seemed pathetically slow and unmotivated in life. Compared to Nina, he was a real slug. She said he seemed so wonderful and dynamic when they met, but now he was worthless, spent all her money, and was verbally abusive.

I was amazed and slightly overwhelmed by how much stress Nina felt, how many activities she tried to pack in her day, and how exacting she was with everyone in her life, including her boyfriend. Thinking of how she might be projecting her own vicious demands on others, I said, "you expect so much, I am surprised you can keep up with it all and find a way to ever please yourself". Nina mumbled something about "that is just life" and went full-speed ahead to other topics. It wasn't until after several sessions that she told me my comment had made her "think a bit about things".

In her matter-of-fact, nuts-and-bolts way, Nina told me about her childhood. Both her parents were alcoholics who fought all the time. Her father would come home at night and get drunk. Her mother started drinking in the mornings and was drunk by noon. Naturally, Nina felt confused,

---

1 I have disguised this case as I have all cases in this book, using numerous ways to protect the confidentiality of all my patients. In agreement with Gabbard (1997), I think the critically important issue of maintaining our patients' confidentiality can be accomplished by disguising the unique personal details, while keeping the essential psychological dynamics intact for the reader. Therefore, my case material shows the actual transference, phantasy states, and interpersonal situations that made the case useful to study, but still disguises the personal elements of the patient's personality and lifestyle enough to guard his or her confidentiality.

anxious, and frightened by the chaos. When she grew older, she started to despise her parents for being "so weak". I interpreted this contempt and devaluation to be a mask for her hurt, pain, and helplessness.

When she was ten years old, a family friend molested her. Nina kept it a secret, thinking her mother would minimize it if she knew. In her early thirties, Nina's only sibling, an older sister, was struck by a car and became comatose. Nina still visits her in a state hospital, where she remains in a coma. Again, these terrible events were presented as more of a shopping list than a traumatic experience.

Drawing attention to her mechanical way of communicating, I said, "you tell me all these facts about yourself in such a logical, mechanical way. Maybe that is easier than showing me the pain." Nina replied, "I just keep moving, you have to. That is life." I said, "You are not very compassionate with yourself." She said, "I guess I see that as being weak. That is what I tell my boyfriend. He seems weak for always wanting hugs and affection. I expect him to pull his weight around the house and he never does, so I don't respect him." I said, "maybe you are trying to pull your own weight here by making sure I know all the details and information about you, like a report that is due. Maybe you are worried that if you slow down and just tell me what you feel and think in the moment you will look weak." Nina replied, "Well, yes. I feel I need to cover all the facts, like filling in the information sheet in the doctor's waiting room. I never thought I could just say what I feel. That seems like a waste of time."

Nina worked in sales at a real-estate company. She had a supervisor who constantly demanded better numbers at the end of each quarter. Everyone in Nina's department resented this supervisor, but managed to ignore him and didn't let him get to them. Nina, on the other hand, found a perfect vehicle for her own slave-driver mentality. She put the demanding and exacting aspects of herself into her supervisor and then felt hounded and harassed. She felt overwhelmed by his expectations. Over many months, I interpreted this as the lesser of two evils. She felt better when being persecuted by him than she did when being attacked by her own expectations because she could blame him for being unfair. Her own self-assassination over not doing enough and not being enough was severe. It felt like a relentless attack to Nina, from which there was no escape. Therefore, her supervisor's attacks were less painful and more manageable.

I noticed the same fluctuations between self-attack and projection of demand with Nina's migraines and depression. Sometimes, she would blame the doctors for not prescribing the right medications and her family and job for creating too much stress in her life. Other times, she saw herself as culpable. Nina felt she was "weak and stupid" for not always being mentally confident and physically strong. She felt she was a "slowpoke" for not achieving everything she wanted, not being in perfect health, and not producing everything her supervisor asked for.

Naturally, these internal phantasies colored our relationship: the transference. In the transference, Nina was careful to be on time, pay her bill, and follow the rule of free association. Her general approach to being with me was colored by caution and timidity. The more I explored this, the more Nina was able to uncover her phantasies of not wanting to be a burden and to be as independent as possible to avoid making me angry.

It took a long time before we could see the other side of this. She envied the people she felt were able to express themselves and consequently could show need and have their needs met. This envy of those who dared to be greedy and seek out what they wanted was too much to tolerate. She tried to erase and destroy those thoughts and feelings. As she became more anxious about these forbidden and dangerous phantasies, she literally chanted, "I have enough, I don't need any more. Why am I so selfish?" She hoped this would shut up the hungry and savage side of herself that wanted at least as much as everyone else, and often more. I brought this up in terms of the transference and I also pointed out how I imagined she resented mother's ability to be nursed and loved at Nina's expense. I also said she might wish to be more casual with me, but kept a strict and proper relationship with me just in case. At this point in the treatment, she was able to take in my interpretation. However, this was still a tricky area.

As Nina felt closer to me in the transference, she felt dependent. This made her feel imperfect and distrustful. Nina worried that I seduced patients into dependence and made them into my "zombies". As my zombie, she would have no thoughts of her own and be helpless and weak. At times, this phantasy made her furious and she contemplated stopping treatment. It was hard for Nina to see that she thought and related in this dictator-like manner, even though it was in disguised and subtle ways.

After six months, Nina was impatient with me. Her analysis was taking too long. She wished I would just tell her what to do so she could move on and be a success. Less frequently, she thought I must be frustrated with her for repeating topics and not quickly changing. I told her, "you don't picture me as too patient or understanding. Maybe you figure I am just as impatient as you are." This interpretation relieved her anxiety and helped her reflect on how she related to herself. She said, "you mean this is not a race? That is a wild idea. I can just take my time!"

Nina focused on the concrete externals and avoided noticing any feelings she had toward me or the analysis. I interpreted that she was worried over just about every part of our relationship except our actual relationship. She treated me like a car mechanic whom she hired to fix her poorly functioning engine. I interpreted her need to be in control of our relationship that way and to remain dominant and safe by appearing neutral or indifferent. Over time, we slowly understood this as a bargain between herself and her internal objects. If she couldn't have an ideal, perfect union with an all-nourishing breast that she controlled, then she established a perfectly neutral stance where she was independent and withholding. Based on her associations, I interpreted this first as a fear of being rejected, a fear of loss. Next, she was scared the loss and isolation would somehow bring on outright rejection, betrayal, or attack as well. If she trusted me, I could leave her and return as the enemy. To protect herself, she turned the tables and tried to take her love away from me and instead control me and attack me with indifference.

As I came to know Nina, I noticed how much persecutory guilt (Grinberg 1964))and greed played a part in her internal world. She felt scared that her greedy wishes would push everyone away and leave her alone and lost. So, Nina tried to pretend she didn't have any needs and was totally independent. The more she denied her own needs, the more she felt hopeless to find success or love. More specifically, the more she denied her greed for an ideal object to fill her wish for endless love, the more she felt hopeless and helpless, left with a decaying self and no reachable safe object. This was because she tried to destroy her emotional hunger by keeping herself on a very short emotional leash and instead projected her demands into her objects.

If Nina felt greedy and angry, she would then be overcome with a sadistic guilt and imagined rejection and severe punishment. Next, she would double her efforts to be grateful for what she had and to be nice to others. It was not until sometime into the analysis that she was able to "admit" to wanting more sessions, but then quickly took it back. She felt selfish, greedy, and way too needy. Nina insisted she was fine and didn't need any "hand-holding". "If I can't handle these things after coming here for years, then something is very wrong," she said. Later, she was able to talk about the intolerable disgust she felt at being needy and wanting "extra" from me. I interpreted that she was retaliating first before I could attack her for being so greedy. This type of interpretation slowly paved the way for a gradual working through of some of these entrenched phantasies.

In the countertransference, I was called upon to be the spokesperson for Nina's greed and aggressive outrage (Steiner 2000). She tried to protect her fragile idealized object and ward off its possible retaliation by projecting her outrage into me and others she felt close to. Therefore, I was often the one who brought up the subject of her desire and resentment. Nina would tell me some story about her work or her love life in which she obviously felt slighted or betrayed. These were situations in which she wanted much more than she was being offered. However, at that point in the story, she would start discussing how she felt selfish and how she deserved whatever she got because she was rude and greedy. While she went on to elaborate her sins, I would begin to feel irritated and righteous against the people she was describing. I felt like saying, "They are selfish and mean. You have the right to demand as much as you want! If they don't deliver, you should get rid of them! You don't need that sort of person in your life, and you can do better!"

After much reflection, I began to interpret to Nina that she was having me hold her feelings of greed and outrage. Also, I interpreted her splitting of the greedy outrage and the helpless loss. I told her it was hard for her to imagine needing more from me or others in a moderate, fair-handed way. She thought of it as black or white. My countertransference was one side of the splitting. After some self-analysis on this, I was able to see more of the whole than just the pieces. Therefore, I geared my interpretations toward integrating the split-off parts and helping Nina to create a more realistic whole object. This was difficult for her to hear and internalize. She took my observations and hypotheses as attacks, a blaming of her character. It was difficult for her to take in as it meant she would have to reclaim and own her projected feelings of insatiable need and desire. Also, she would have to endure the painful loss of her ideal self and her idealized object. It was only after a few years in analysis that Nina could really acknowledge and explore these phantasies and feelings. Overall, my analysis of the countertransference, transference, and extra-transference material led to a shift from her only being able to acknowledge herself as a victim to our uncovering journey.

In general, over the course of Nina's treatment, my countertransference emerged in two parts, both concordant (Racker 1968). I felt sorry for Nina. No matter what I said, she was determined to stay the course. Nina had to have what she imagined men could give her and would not give up her idealist quest. I felt my sense of hopelessness and sadness in working with her was a replication of her childhood depression, in which she felt hopeless of ever finding a caring, loving, or nourishing parent. She had told me these sad facts about her upbringing before, but now they came alive in me through projective identification. I interpreted this both genetically and in the here-and-now transference. I interpreted that she felt so hopeless about being loved and fed that she tried to change a flawed and unavailable object into her ideal. But, this quickly failed and she felt angry and lost. I also interpreted that it was painful for Nina to share her sadness with me so she became cold and mechanical, leaving me to deal with the feelings.

My second countertransference feeling was a lonely frustration at being unable to get through to Nina. She fought my interpretations and turned away from what felt so obvious to me. This "don't you see!" feeling helped me understand what she went through while growing up and still felt in her adult life. She had described all these childhood feelings and situations before, but now I could really understand the emotions behind them. I interpreted that she was showing me how hard it is to get through to someone and how confusing it must be to feel on the outside and not able to get to the thing she wants and needs so badly. I interpreted that she resisted my comments in order to not face the sadness and rage of possibly ending up with an object who was unavailable and who betrayed her. I also said I thought she kept me at a distance so as to not risk that happening again and again. She listened tentatively, and seemed to be less anxious.

Internally, Nina battled with feelings of inferiority and abandonment as well as rage and greed. Interpersonally, she was both submissive and masochistic, as well as aggressive and arrogant.

Nina always had an ad in the newspaper's dating section. For years, she ran a profile of what kind of man she wanted. It had a cold and controlling tone to it. She wrote, "Picky woman with class seeking sexy, fun-loving man who has passion and is ready for a serious relationship. Not ready to settle for less!" Nina included a personal description of herself and signed it, "Ready when you are!" Sadly and predictably, she met many men who fitted the same mold and the relationship went in the same direction each time. Initially, Nina felt that "something clicked" and her hopes soared. She had "crazy sex", went out to dinner all the time, and felt swept up in the new man's potential. This potential was the ideal she built and held up as the standard she needed and had to have no matter what.

Within several weeks or months, she would ask the man to move in with her. Soon enough, Nina would spend a great deal of money buying the man clothes, gifts, and showing him a good time. This was the interpersonal, external aspect of her intrapsychic goal to build and maintain an ideal object that she could then feed from. Slowly, the reality-based part of Nina would begin to have doubts about the man's loyalty and love. She noticed red flags. The man might be a drinker, a gambler, a womanizer, or verbally abusive. He might start controlling her emotionally, manipulating her financially, or pulling her away from friends and family. As soon as Nina noticed these warning signals and problems, she tried hard to rationalize them away. She denied them, blamed herself, or made excuses for any evidence of him being less-than-perfect. Since she stayed with these men for longer than she would have if she had paid attention to their faults, she often wound up in trouble.

Nina had been engaged three times and was left financially bankrupt by another relationship. It was only when Nina was deeply committed to these men that she began to doubt them and resent them. She still didn't pay too much attention to their gross faults and abusive ways. Instead, she noted things like how they didn't take out the garbage after she cleaned the whole house, how they forgot to fill up her gas tank after she loaned them her car, or how they didn't give her a birthday card after she spent thousands to take them on a vacation. In other words, she developed masochistic feelings of being under-appreciated for all her hard work. Concentrating on how she was never rewarded for all her suffering made it easy to ignore how her ideal object had abandoned her and abused her. It was also a way to avoid seeing how she contributed to this problem. She wanted a perfect man and basically tried to buy one through the personal ads. This was a cycle of greed, idealism, and disappointment, followed by feelings of anger, loss, and persecution.

In exploring these patterns with Nina, I was slowly able to have a clearer understanding of her unconscious phantasies, feelings, and desires. Her relentless craving for an ideal object who could provide her with endless and perfect love drove her to seek out men who came on strong with false love. She took the bait and became ecstatic, wanting more and more. These greedy urges to possess the ideal object made her reliant on the dynamics of splitting. When she saw a flaw in her ideal picture, she projected it out of her mind and kept the good portion of the object. In Klein's view, greed is an unrealistic demand that exceeds what the object can possibly provide (Kaplan 1991). The greedy ego does not care what is realistically available and rushes in for more. The ego is so urgent and aggressive that this desperate feeding happens regardless of the consequences to the ego or to its objects. Nina put unrealistic, greedy demands on her objects and then tried to force it to happen. Consequently, she was the victim of her own impossible demands. Over and over, she sadly created the very loss and persecutory abandonment she feared.

This view of the object as only a breast to feed at and control, without compassion for the effects of one's feelings on another person, is characteristic of the paranoid-schizoid position. The object is felt to belong to the ego and is an extension of one's self. Through projective identification, the reverse is true as well, leading to paranoid feelings of being controlled and used by the object.

Consciously, Nina felt used. She resented her boyfriends for not appreciating her. She felt sad that she wasn't loved in return for loving them. Nina believed that if she showed love and kindness, she should automatically be loved by the person she picked. So, on the surface she appeared to feel victimized and hurt. Underneath, and much harder to analyze, she was angry that the breast she chose at random didn't instantly flow with pure love. A masochistic presentation covered the more greedy, predatory nature of her ego.

This predatory greed made it hard to interpret these dynamics. Whether I tried to interpret the greed or the persecutory loss that Nina also defended against, she was quite resistant to letting my ideas in. When I made these sorts of interpretations, Nina would tell me it was normal to want to be loved and that no one can pick the right boyfriend every time. She told me, "I know the perfect person is out there. I just have to find him. Someone who will love me and appreciate me. I know you think I set myself up to be with losers, but I don't think there is any way to know how a relationship will turn out until you live with the man and see." Other times, Nina would become more swept up in her romantic phantasies of possessing the ideal object. This magical feeling served as a shield as well. She told me, "I think this guy is 'the one'! I will finally have the perfect family I always wanted, just like the families you see on television."

Over the years, things changed. On one hand, Nina continued to turn away from my interpretations and tried to be in control of our relationship. She still greedily pursued love in ways that were self-destructive as well as callous to the object's separate and unique identity. On the other hand, Nina spent less time in these vicious cycles. There was slow progress.

Nina made progress and gradual change, but her core internal conflicts and phantasies were never fully resolved. This may be typical when dealing with pathological greed and the underlying problems of primitive loss.

I consistently interpreted Nina's greed as well as her angry and desperate efforts to possess an ideal object. I also brought her attention to her masochistic way of doing anything to get to the ideal object and an ideal self-image even if it were self-defeating. These interpretations made a difference. While she would still pursue these ill-fated relationships, she put herself at less risk for being hurt by not giving everything to each new man in the hopes for love. So, Nina was less reliant on her masochistic bargains of being a doormat in exchange for security. Also, when she did end up in these chaotic situations, she would end it much quicker. Since she left the abusive relationships sooner, she was hurt less. This progress was significant and hard-won.

At the same time, Nina's greed persisted. In fact, the less she used her masochistic defenses, the more she felt entitled, enraged, and determined to possess not only the ideal object, but an image of herself as perfect. Now, when she dated men who answered her newspaper ad, she was more and more demanding. She felt she had the right to openly demand whatever she wanted. During the first date, she would basically interrogate the men to find out if she could expect to get her wishes filled. Nina would ask questions like, "are you ready to get married?" and "are you willing to provide me with the kind of lifestyle I want?" This approach created two results. First, most of the men never called her back. But, some of the men saw Nina's arrogance as evidence of her vulnerability. They promised her the stars and then took advantage of her. Without the masochistic defense, the phantasies and feelings of loss and annihilation grew stronger. Therefore, Nina escalated her aggressive and greedy demands for the promise of a reliable and perfectly attentive object.

Nina's greed and all-or-nothing attitude colored the transference and somewhat offset her gradual integration. She wanted to keep the mental comfort of her phantasies rather than accept the realities and possibilities of my interpretations and have to face the scary phantasies of loss and attack. She told me, "when I go out on another date, things are going to be different. I am setting limits so I won't get hurt. But, I have the right to be loved and I am going to make that happen!" So, on one hand she was determined to stay the course no matter what. At the same time, she was dependent on me but would never speak to that level of vulnerability. What she said was, "I don't need anyone, I am fine making my own decisions." But, her behavior with me and other men was a clinging attachment. She was punctual with all her appointments, alerted me to schedule problems six months in advance, and always paid on time. I felt these actions were a combination of being in control and in charge of our relationship as well as protecting me from her destructive and greedy side. It was a magical charm that protected her from loss. When I tried to explore any of these clues to her inner life, Nina would quickly retreat. Nevertheless, she slowly made progress and felt happier and more secure in her daily affairs.

After several years in analysis, Nina was able to reflect on and work with some of her core phantasies and feelings. She said, "I felt so ignored by my parents, so unimportant. That was worse than the beatings. I wanted their love so much, it was hard to bear. I waited and waited for them to notice me and love me but it never happened. Now, I think I just look for anyone to fill that void. I don't care who it is, I just want it and I want it now! Without it, I feel lost, so lost." With this kind of insight, Nina was able to work through and challenge some of her core phantasies and begin to create a new world of less pathological internal objects.

Unfortunately, this growth was stunted by Nina's greed. She met another man who promised her the world. He persuaded her to buy a home in Europe and to put his name on the deed. I felt helpless to intervene as Nina would have nothing to do with anything that interfered with her fairytale romance. She told me how it was obviously love at first sight and told me about all the evidence that it was a perfect match. The fact that they liked the same color, enjoyed similar foods, and liked similar music was not a simple indication of two people with a possibility of getting along, but "hard evidence" of "something very, very special".

However, after a few months, Nina saw that he was manipulating her for money and ended the relationship. But, it was too late. She now had to pay for a house he legally owned. Nina could barely afford this and had to pay a lawyer to contest the matter. She had to move to Europe to fight this legal battle and try and untangle the web she had created. This failure to reach an ideal object, the betrayal by a false ideal, and the sight of herself as so much less than perfect was devastating. She said she was giving up on herself, on analysis, and on the hopes of ever finding someone to be with. She said, "my chances to find love are gone, my life is now just a daily grind for survival". I felt sad to see her go and felt this was a missed opportunity. In the transference, I was one more failed relationship and a loss of an idealized object she wished to merge with. However, I think she was very close to breaking that internal and interpersonal pattern.

If we could have continued our work together, Nina may have been able to use this feeling of total collapse as a way to begin mourning her lost ideal. I believe that would have helped her face countless childhood disappointments as well as her current feelings of rage, greed, and pain. I received a letter months later from Nina. She was dating a bit, but mostly felt empty and depressed. Her connection to me was a small new piece of security she carried with her in her jungle of self-failure and never-ending hunger for the ideal, all-nourishing object.

Patients such as Nina cannot tolerate their needy, greedy feelings. Initially, Nina expressed her wish to not burden or hurt the object. The more we explored this seeming depressive concern, she revealed a more paranoid fear. To want too much would hurt the object in a way that would turn the object from a hopeful lover to a menacing rejector. This is partly the result of having no hope of making reparation or restoration if conflict occurs. The ego's hatred and greed overrides and corrupts the urge to make peace. These feelings of greed and aggression are projected into the object and the ego feels threatened and persecuted. So, these patients are difficult to analyze. Via projective identification, they quickly deny ownership of the core greed that creates these persecutory and primitive loss phantasies. They feel that to admit these feelings and thoughts is the same as action. To share these desires and urges is to bring about abandonment and annihilation. Therefore, interpretations about these matters either bounce off a shield of denial or create a storm of paranoid protest.

These patients are difficult to treat and evoke many countertransference struggles. Their constant focus on creating and possessing an ideal self and an ideal object often overrides any interest in change. To change would be to admit to failure as a person, to feel lost without an object, and to be attacked by one's own relentless, sadistic demands for perfection. These patients think the analyst is saying they must give up their quest for what seems necessary for survival. Therapeutic progress is intolerable as it feels like forced starvation. Therefore, the analyst becomes, in phantasy, another obstacle in reaching their goal of perfection.

At the same time, greed destroys any insight and intimacy made in analysis. The hunger for more combined with the oral aggression that fuels greed makes introjection and the maintenance of good objects, including the analyst, very difficult.

This oral greed perverts the normal developmental cycle of splitting much in the way Klein (1957) felt that envy corrupts the normal splitting process. Therefore, good objects are attacked and devalued as much as bad objects, leaving the ego with precious little to cling to.

Looking back on my countertransference struggles with Nina, I can see some areas that I wish I had handled differently. Perhaps, if I had, the treatment outcome may have been different. Specially, I think I was caught up, at times, in the same quest for an ideal self or object as Nina was. Through projective identification, I often felt I needed to be interpreting more accurately and successfully and that Nina should have taken in my helpful comments more readily. I think this mutual pressure for success and respite from persecutory inferiority hindered the treatment. In other words, the projective identification and projective counter-identification was never fully analyzed or resolved. I think it would have been helpful to the treatment to have interpreted some of this mutual impotence and helplessness as an aspect of the chronic trouble with greed that Nina was communicating to me.

Nina is representative of a group of individuals who have experienced a lack of sufficient good external objects in their early childhood. The majority, if not all, of these patients have grown up surrounded by various forms and degrees of trauma. These early experiences include divorce, alcoholism, sexual abuse, neglect, controlling and dominating parents, different forms of emotional blackmail, and pathological family triangulations. In normal development, an adequate amount of good external objects help to balance out the normal degree of internal bad objects that arise from infantile aggressive phantasies. This balance has been upset in these patients' internal and external worlds.

Segal (1974) points out, "the importance of the environmental factor can only be correctly evaluated in relation to what it means in terms of the infant's own instincts and phantasies" (p. 15). She goes on to explore how, when the ego is in the grip of angry or greedy phantasies, it needs as many good objects to counterbalance these internal conflicts. If instead the infant's actual external experiences are negative, they serve to confirm and fortify the ego's hostility and trauma. Segal goes on to elaborate on how the early ego becomes convinced that both the internal and external worlds are to be feared and fought.

My patient Nina, and other patients with similar dynamics, vary in diagnosis from borderline to psychotic, but can all be categorized as narcissistic. To Klein (1952c), narcissism was about the omnipotent union with and control of the object, rather than an objectless state. Klein (1946) and Rosenfeld (1964) examined the way in which the omnipotence of narcissism creates a blurring or destruction of boundaries between self and object. Segal (1983) points out that narcissism is often a defense against feelings of envy, and as such is related to the death instinct. In other words, the ego realizes the source of goodness is external and often out of reach. The ego turns its back on the good object out of rage and pretends it is self-sufficient. Better to refuse life than to have to ask for it. For the paranoid-schizoid ego, the feeling is, if one can't be in control of the game, why play.

I believe this applies to greed as well, with one distinction. Greedy patients are usually not able to fully contain, disguise, or deny their greedy feelings and, instead, they alternate between narcissistic withdrawal and angry, emotional grabbing and demanding. The worse the blurring of self and object, the more this is evident. Unfortunately, this usually becomes a vicious cycle of greed, loss, persecution, rage, and primitive guilt.

For example, Nina wanted a man who could give her love, security, and attention. She wanted this so much that it became a quest to find anyone, immediately, rather than somebody who was a good match and whom she could gradually like and love. When she realized there was no instant and perfect love, she couldn't bear being denied. So, she took possession of the object, via projective identification, and held on no matter what. This was out of greed, terror of loss and abandonment, and fear of attack. It was also out of revenge, for having gone too long without someone to love and be loved by. Nina's greed became narcissistic in that it was no longer about finding a compatible mate who had their own personality, but a fevered search to own someone who met her specifications. The level of greed pushed her into acting out these violent and desperate phantasies in her interpersonal life. Her phantasy of loss and persecutory abandonment was severe and, as such, reinforced her feelings of greed and need for control of the object.

Suffering from a primitive sense of greed, loss, and guilt, these patients avoid making contact or conflicting with the object with a strategy of idealization. As a result, they find themselves always failing to reach their own unrealistic expectation. They keep setting the bar of desire higher and higher to protect the object from destruction and protect themselves from the object's sadistic retaliation. In this primitive phantasy of persecutory guilt and loss, the ego kills off the ideal but fragile object with its greed and aggression, only to be hunted down by the resurrected rage of the now hostile object. Consequently, these patients feel they are never good enough and will disappoint and hurt others by failing to meet their requirements. In turn, they fear rejection and criticism and will often attack themselves first to avoid an unpredictable attack from the outside.

While being a subject which has received modest inquiry, greed has seen some interest in the psychoanalytic literature. Recently, Boris (1986), Spillius (Frankiel, Harris and Spillius 2001), Hinshelwood (1994), Moser-Ha (2001), Feldman (2000), and Segal (1997) have all looked at the place greed takes in clinical work and in psychoanalytic theory.

Most of these authors believe, as I do, that greed is often mixed with other aggressive and conflictual emotions and phantasy states. They also agree that greed is part of a normal psychological experience unless magnified, distorted, or complicated in some way by external and/or internal factors.

In optimal development, the intra-psychic storms of greed, envy, and hate are modified by plentiful external objects and internal/external experiences that are internalized. These new internalized good objects serve to balance, contain, manage, and modify the greed, hate, and fear the ego struggles with. The patients I am exploring did not have this helpful psychological environment in childhood and they, as adults, continue to see the world through the lens of greed, disappointment, and persecutory loss. Due to unmodified, runaway projective identifications fueling the greed, they demand it all, from both self and object. In this sense, the boundaries are blurred between good, bad, self, and other.

This cycle of greed replaces the good object experiences with demands for an even better object. This also destroys the working-through process in psychoanalytic treatment. Interpretations are brushed aside as unimportant or not good enough. Then, the patient will say they are disappointed with treatment and feel they never "get any feedback" from the analyst. In this way, they put the analyst in the same no-win situation that they feel. This is the interpersonal aspect of a pathological projective identification dynamic: a demanding, hungry object and a pressured, against-the-wall, can't-ever-do-enough self. In some cases, this seems to be an exact replica of what the patient remembers from their childhood and in other cases it seems to be more a product of the patient's own hostility and greed. Often, it seems to be both. The presence of the containing and interpreting analyst normally mitigates and transforms harsh and hostile internal dynamics. Greed erases, erodes, and destroys this transmuting experience.

Therefore, successful treatment requires the analyst to be patient, persistent, and able to accept what the patient fights so strongly against: disappointment, loss, and the mixed-bag nature of the real world. This includes ongoing self-analysis and monitoring of countertransference problems. Realistic and resilient optimism along with a willingness to compromise and let go when necessary are attributes that help the analyst deal with these difficult cases. These same healthy traits are internalized by some patients as part of their gradual therapeutic metamorphosis. Nina was able to take in and maintain these characteristics to some degree, yet she continued to struggle with the vicissitudes of greed, loss, and persecution.

# Chapter 9

# Setting the bar too high*

Melanie Klein's basic tenets of normal development (Schneider 1988) include the idea that every infant is constitutionally endowed with life and death instincts, in a relative balance. This is paired with an innate expectation of an object that can contain, understand, and satisfy these basic instincts and help to keep them in balance. This good object is expected to be omnipotently satisfying and uniquely gratifying. Klein also assumed the infant's early environment assured a reasonably positive, nurturing caretaker and family. Indeed, Klein felt the infantile ego naturally made the best out of the good experiences available with immediate and important objects.

As proposed in the last few chapters, I believe that greed, when of pathological proportion, can erode these basic building blocks of psychological health. Likewise, if the infant's early environment is more violent and neglectful than loving, the life and death instincts are tilted out of balance and greed becomes paramount in the psychic landscape.

Schneider (1988) states:

> if the life instinct prevails, there is an idealization of the feeding experience because of the infant's projection of its unconscious preconception of a good object. This projection strengthens whatever good experience is actually available so that the smallest opportunity for gratification can be imbued with something better.
>
> (p. 323)

However, I think that if the life instinct does not prevail, then the smallest infraction or failure in the quest for the perfect breast and the ideal feeding is felt to be a disaster. This creates vicious and pathological cycles of projective identification and greed. In this way, greed becomes an outgrowth of the death instinct.

---

* This chapter was first published as 'Setting the bar too high: greed, idealization, and the loss of a safe object', in *Issues in Psychoanalytic Psychology*, 2003, 25: 1, 37–52.

## CASE MATERIAL 9.1

Joe was a man who was very demanding of those he came into contact with. He felt this was appropriate, as people "should be able to provide" what he needed, when he needed it. While this was difficult to tolerate in the countertransference, I slowly discovered, by observing his real dedication to being in treatment, that he was actually idealizing me while degrading me at the same time. Joe, in unconscious phantasy, gave me great powers. Then, he demanded I use those powers to give him whatever he wanted and to tolerate his acting out. When I didn't or couldn't, he was furious. He felt I was deliberately humiliating him, manipulating him, and betraying him. So, I was supposed to be an ideal breast to feed at, at will. When he went into a feeding frenzy, he felt I had turned off the milk faucet in retaliation.

One day, as we were exploring the ways in which he casts people as so omnipotent, yet in his control, he said, "if I allow myself to realize that people are just human, that means they could kill themselves. If they kill themselves, I will be murdered. I couldn't take that again." Having worked with this patient for a number of years, I knew that he meant he had to idealize his objects or they would perish. Idealizing them was a way to protect or rescue them. Once they were gone, he felt vulnerable to annihilation from angry, vengeful objects. This was his childhood memory of his narcissistic father and distant mother who could easily crumble from good to neglectful and cruel. He couldn't bear to feel that loss and persecution again. It was only with persistent exploration that I found out how the ideal objects would die. "They would kill themselves because I am such a burden. Because I want so much love. I am insecure and want to suck out all the goodies they have, until they suddenly wither away and die," Joe said. This primitive guilt, the feeling of hurting one's object in such a severe and permanent way, is part of a persecutory guilt and fear that predated full depressive functioning (Bicudo 1964).

So, Joe's solution was to idealize people, giving them powers to endure his murderous greed. Then, he put them to the test and was demanding. If they failed the test, he was furious and kept himself afloat by looking down on them. He became the omnipotent one. Eventually, this failed and he felt lost, betrayed, and attacked. It was during these times that he suffered incapacitating depression and brief psychotic periods.

Joe grew up with a mother who was emotionally removed. Joe felt she only loved him if he followed her rules and grew up in the mold she wanted. He felt he often failed to meet these demands and was punished with criticism and neglect. While impossible to ever know for sure, I have the impression from the transference and countertransference that Joe's recollection of his mother may be an accurate memory of a combined mother–son equation. In other words, I think his mother was probably demanding, rejecting, and attacking as Joe remembers. At the same time, my relationship with Joe leads me to think he may have also been projecting a great deal of demanding, rejecting, and attacking feelings into his mother. So, I approach his case thinking his childhood experiences were a constant frustration, hatred, and desire for an ideal mother to replace his less-than-ideal real mother.

Once entrenched, greed mutates normal character development and becomes a constant way of experiencing the world. Paranoid-schizoid dynamics fuel a perverse and desperate effort at begging forgiveness with a merciless enemy. The ego attempts to both resuscitate the dead object and somehow prevent it from returning as a murderous object seeking revenge. Normal depressive dynamics are also distorted by greed into a more paranoid fear of being attacked by an injured object that refuses atonements. Both developmental positions, paranoid and depressive, become compromised. The experience of severe loss, to the point of annihilation anxiety, couples with a conviction of persecution. While greed brings on these disastrous internal phantasies, greed also fuels them. The craving and demanding for an ideal object to rescue and protect the ego from these horrors sets up more demands and expectations that fail to materialize. This is felt as yet more loss, rejection, betrayal, and persecution.

## CASE MATERIAL 9.2

Mark grew up in a poor, working-class community in Chicago. His father was a local policeman who drank every day after he came home from work. He was a gruff, angry man who always complained about life. Mark knew to stay out of his way so as to not get yelled at. While angry and arrogant described his father, quiet, passive, and helpless described his mother. She was psychotic and unable to function outside of the home. She thought aliens communicated with her through the television set and was convinced the neighbors were plotting against her and her family. To this day, she is a reclusive, timid woman who serves as maid to her husband. Mark remembers with terrible sadness the ways his father yelled at and ridiculed his mother. He recalls with pain the days when he saw his father strike his mother and push her to the ground.

Mark has two sisters and a brother. One sister is psychotic, on psychiatric disability, and lives with her parents at their home. The other sister suffers with anorexia and works at menial jobs to support herself. The brother has distanced himself from the family by living in another country.

After completing classes at a junior college, Mark landed his first job as a camp counselor. This was the start of almost thirty years of entry-level employment. He had a pattern of taking low-paying jobs that were typically filled by highschool or college students in their summer breaks. At first, Mark felt happy and carefree with jobs such as soccer coach, life-guard, waiter, or bartender. He felt the lack of rigid structure, the flexible hours, and the absence of authority figures was proof that he was living the good life. Lack of serious responsibility or commitment felt powerful and freeing. However, this way of life meant Mark was usually in debt, without health insurance, living on someone's couch, and lacking any sort of stability.

When I met Mark he was fifty years old and seemed to be a broken man. He hadn't paid taxes in ten years, so the government was after him. A shabby roommate situation and a meager wardrobe of worn-out blue jeans now felt humiliating instead of liberating. He had been through so many temporary jobs over the years that he had trouble remembering them all. A year before coming to see me, he had been reduced to living in someone's garage. A customer of the bar he worked at offered him a regular position at a printing company. When we began meeting, Mark had been able to make enough at his new job to afford a small apartment, was paying the minimal balance on his debts, and had enough left over for therapy.

The transference/countertransference situation became noticeable very quickly. With some patients, it takes a long time for the analyst to discover the nature of the omnipresent transference. With other patients, it is strong and well-defined from the beginning.

Mark's last therapist had literally taught Mark how to use a checkbook. The therapist had gone over how to log each check and what to do when monthly statements arrived. While Mark felt positive about managing a checkbook now, overall he was not so pleased about the prior therapy experience. I commented that he probably wished for more, that he wanted to learn why he was apparently incapable of managing his own life, not just his checkbook. While Mark agreed with my interpretation, I noticed something gradually happening to our relationship that was striking.

Mark would bring me stories of how badly things were going. He laid out the problems with relationships, work, money issues, health, or family in a hopeless, bitter manner that quickly drew me in. I felt like there were always obvious things he could do to improve whatever the situation was, if only he would just do it! Then, I would find myself making suggestions on how he could do some particular thing to make things better. I was put in the service of the life instinct, battling his self-destructive pessimism. Mark would often follow my advice and, indeed, things improved, for a while. But, then he would have the next crisis to unfold at the following session.

The more this transference–countertransference relationship grew, I began to notice it and started to interpret it. I emphasized several points in my comments. First, he wanted me to take over, care for him, and give him the gift of my special advice and permission. With my permission, he was lifted from the intense fear and primitive guilt over doing something that might cause terrible trouble. My permission would magically absolve his greed and the dangerous effects his greed had on others. Secondly, he was saying, "I refuse to do it, you must do it for me." This was his greed and omnipotence, demanding an all-giving good object. Finally, I interpreted his deep fear of what would happen if he made these improvements or changes himself, without me to blame. I interpreted that he was anxious of being suddenly alone and against dangerous odds. He said, "yes, I don't want to be slapped down on the ground". I thought of his memory of his mother being struck down to the ground. When I made that connection, Mark wept. He said, "she was so helpless. I feel so bad for her." Later, I commented on his possible identification with his helpless mother and his fear of an abandoning and attacking father.

For a while, I wondered if Mark was feeling survival guilt at growing up and leaving his sick mother behind. So, I made some interpretations about how he might be worried that succeeding in life would be harmful to his mother. This is a depressive position interpretation based on theories about oedipal competition, desires to please, and an integration of whole self–object dynamics. I felt my comments didn't fit and they certainly fell flat. Mark told me, "it is much more about the frightening prospect of becoming my mother. I do feel bad that I am not around to take care of her, but what really keeps me up at night is the horrible idea that I am turning into her. I feel like I am hanging onto the edge. Each day is a desperate attempt to not lose the ability to take care of myself. She is an emotional invalid. Is it too late for me?"

So, something helpful came out of my incorrect line of investigation. While Mark did not feel guilt, as I thought, he responded to my comment about fear of success. He explained that if he were to be successful, that would mean he willingly became "part of the system". He felt most jobs, relationships, and endeavors in life were really a surrender to a manipulative, arrogant, and persecutory system in which domination of others is the end goal.

Guilt did play a role in Mark's psyche, but was in a much more severe and crippling manner, characteristic of greed. Mark said, "if I take a break to watch television at night, I feel so guilty that I literally start yelling at myself. 'Lazy motherfucker, piece of shit loser!' I really attack myself because there is so much I should be doing instead. I get furious with myself." So, Mark had a massive retaliation reaction to his desire for pleasure, some television watching. Mark's problem with greed was two-fold. He wanted pleasure, which was unacceptable. But, far worse, the part of him that wanted him to be "taking care of business" and not "wasting time" was greedy and demanding. It wanted supreme adherence to "the right way" to do things.

Theoretically, one might say that patients such as Mark have an insatiable superego. To say that, indicates a clear psychic delineation between the overly active or punitive superego and the more balanced ego. Mark was not so lucky. There was no real moment of clarity in which the ego was the prominent psychological force. Rather, his ego was populated with chaotic pairs of self and object relations that were rarely in harmony and frequently at war.

Mark exposed his greed when he said, "I am furious at not having what everyone else has. They have big homes, gorgeous girlfriends, and retirement plans. What the hell! Why shouldn't I have all that too?" I interpreted how he seemed to want me to give him and teach him these treasures, but did not want to seek them out for himself. He made it clear that he wanted me and others to do it for him. Part of this was fear of being alone and without knowledge, but the other part was a greedy sense of entitlement. I said, "you feel it is your right. You feel you are owed these things." Mark replied, "of course, doc". This greedy demand also was exposed around his chronic debt. His taxes, his credit card debt, and even his personal loans represented services he deserved and therefore it felt absurd to have to pay them back. We explored the ramifications of this phantasy on our relationship and how he chose to pay his bill with me. He had projected these feelings of power and deserving into me and therefore was prone to be very subservient about his bill. He tried to pay ahead of time to avoid conflict and to appease me.

Part of pathological greed is the refusal to give to the object. This narcissistic stance is usually the result of a phantasy of loss, rejection, and persecution. In other words, to give is to feel empty. Giving to the object brings awareness of the isolation and danger one is in. To arrogantly not give props up the illusion of being full and secure. I told Mark that to work toward bettering himself meant feeding the object and giving up the wish to be fed. Mark responded, "well, it sounds pretty selfish, but you are right. I want it done for me. I want to be taken care of and be shown how to do things. I don't want to give that up. Why should I do anything myself? Is it so wrong to want to have a special life? I don't want to work, I don't want to have to pay bills. I feel I am beyond that pathetic way of living. To do what it takes to 'take care of myself' means giving in to what I see as ugly and boring."

Mark's comments illustrate the more paranoid and vicious aspects of greed and the phantasies that embody greed. This adversarial, prey–predator quality of greed erodes any movement into the depressive world of compassion, negotiation, and trust. With the cyclical nature of projective identification, these more pathological, me-or-them ways of being become entrenched. Mark's dilemma in life was made much worse by these projective mechanisms and consequently the transference had a stubborn, tug-of-war feeling. Once Mark felt his ideal object was shattered and unobtainable, the core phantasy of loss and annihilation surfaced. So, he tried to keep up the illusion of an ideal object who was simply teasing and frustrating him by not feeding him.

I tried to put these theoretical ideas into clinical practice by making interpretations that focused on his resistance to flourish unless I prodded him, taught him, and cared for him. I suggested he wishes for his father to be encouraging and his mother to be well enough to be proud of him and encourage him. I said that perhaps he is holding out for that and will not and cannot go on without that loving acknowledgment and concern. Again, Mark sobbed. Then, he raged at his father for being so arrogant and selfish. "He just wanted it his way! We had to cater to him", Mark yelled. I interpreted that he felt his only choice in life was either to be like mother, helpless and hopeless, or to be like father, arrogant and entitled. "Ouch! The truth hurts", he replied.

Envy and greed are often found together, as they fuel each other. The greedy ego searches for the ideal object that can fill the ego's endless needs. This oral aggression is projected into the object for a variety of reasons: communication, revenge, a way to jettison anxiety, and a way to protect fragile internalized objects. Now, due to projective identification, the ego is faced with a greedy and controlling object.

Dependence is felt as a weakness others will exploit. This is why Mark refused to "join the system". He felt if he began to depend on others he would be taken advantage of and lose his freedom, power, and pride. This often triggered a manic sort of indifference. Mark would say, in a cold and casual way, "I don't think I need others and I don't really care what is going on with other people. I don't need them." This indifference eventually increases the internal isolation and separation the ego experiences. Mark would feel depressed and alone and begin to resent others for seeming to have so much of what he wanted: fulfillment. So, envy took over and Mark, in phantasy, destroyed the object he wanted so badly. Now that he erased the source of nourishment, he was caught in a terrible cycle. Greedy hunger pushed him to want even more from an object that had nothing to offer. In effect, out of rage at being so hungry, Mark poisoned the food supply and then felt starved and realized he was worse off than before. This made him even more despairing, greedy, and rageful. A cycle of greed, envy, internal destruction, loss, abandonment, increased greed and persecution intensified.

Another variation of these themes emerged when he was telling me how awful his landlord, boss, and friends were. According to Mark, all these important people in his life were not giving him the type of respect, attention, and care that he needed. He felt they were all very selfish and withholding. He wanted compliments, appreciation, and acknowledgment and he wouldn't let go of that expectation. In some cases, there was a way he was trying to get blood from a stone, in that some of the people he described did sound self-centered and withholding. In addition, he seemed to expect way more than even his kind and sensitive friends could realistically give. I also noticed how Mark used his fury and disappointment as a focus point in relating to me and completely ignored or even devalued other good experiences where he was getting fulfillment. For example, he would briefly mention having an enjoyable weekend but then quickly go on to emphasize how horrible his landlord was and how he was constantly disappointed in his friends. This pessimistic, destructive stance would intensify and he would see the remaining shred of enjoyment from the weekend and circle back to attack that. It wasn't really enjoyable, he would yell, it was pathetic. Pretty soon, everything and everybody was terrible. The weekend wasn't enjoyable after all and the other small victories he had briefly mentioned were now soured. He was looking for idealistic portraits of perfect fun and blissful fulfillment. When he pressed these greedy demands up against his actual life, things looked pathetic.

I interpreted this to Mark and also pointed out how he wanted "the old man", his fatherly distortion of his landlord, his analyst, his boss, and his friends, to hand over what Mark felt he was owed: respect, love, and care. Mark said, "yes, I see what you mean. I do want my father's love and focus. Why shouldn't I?" I said, "and you won't rest until you get it. Nothing is ever good enough compared to that prize." "You bet you!" Mark replied. I also interpreted that this greedy demand for the object's continuous, golden blessing was both an aggressive, hungry demand and an angry revenge on "the old man". Finally, I interpreted that this greedy hunger and revenge eroded any good that was available. In fact, Mark seemed to feel that if he acknowledged and internalized goodness from his objects and himself, then he would have to give up hope of being paid his proper restitution of love.

The more Mark would rail at his objects, describing how they so easily failed to live up to his expectations, his entitled rage was replaced with self-criticism, fear, and timidity. He would tell me how sorry he was to bore me with his complaints and how lucky he was to have a place to live and a job to go to. I commented that he seemed to get afraid that his greedy rage would push me to the wall and in return I would react with anger. Mark said, "of course. You or anyone can only take so much. I am a pathetic complainer and am lucky you haven't thrown me out a long time ago. I don't know how you put up with it." Here, he again was gripped by fear, not guilt, over having harmed his objects so badly that revenge was imminent.

I addressed these phantasies about me and his other objects by interpreting his greed and his anxieties. First, I addressed this fear of pushing me to retaliate. Then, I said he would rather rage at me with tales of woe and worry about my reaction than to take me in as a good, secure, and reliable object. In this way, I proposed, he was more intent on his unfinished business with the "old man" than the new business of relating to unfamiliar, non-old man objects.

When I brought these ideas up, it seemed Mark had to double his efforts at fending me off. He had to convince me of the brutality of life, a fact in his mind he could control. To take me and my ideas in as new, potentially good objects was odd, different, and not in his control. He would go on his grim rants, in which he would detail out the ultimate hopelessness of the human condition. "You are born, you suffer, you die. That is your bumper-sticker." I said. "I know that to be true. And, it doesn't depress me. I just know it to be a fact." Mark replied. I said, "you are taking a stand, trying to convince me of it. If it is a fact, then we don't have to face the sorrow of wanting it different but being disappointed." Mark was silent and rose from the couch. The session was over and he left, alone and quiet.

So, in the transference and in Mark's phantasies, he was determined to settle up all 'old business' and refused to deal with 'new business' as it seemed to ignore the intense importance of the 'old business'. He would not take in a new object until he could revise the old one and settle the score. At the same time, this last-stand-at-the-Alamo attitude left him feeling empty and hungry. By having to stay at zero and not take in new objects and new opportunities, he always felt cheated. This greed left him with high and demanding expectations of what he should have in his life, so whatever he did have was never good enough. This cycle of devaluation–idealization–disappointment–loss–rage–greed was solidified with the dynamics of splitting and projective identification.

An example of Mark's struggles with unconscious greed, loss, and oral hostility occurred during a holiday break. He left me a phone message, relating how miserable he was and how life was pointless and only a painful, impossible uphill fight. Then, he told me he was glad I was enjoying my time off. He said he wished he had the same "luxury". This was said in a semi-spiteful manner, but not in an outright, envious or attacking way. There-fore, I didn't experience any countertransference persecution or impulse to attack back. It was more a communication of overwhelming or uncon-tainable greed and loss of me as an important presence. He too had time off, but could not enjoy it because it wasn't the ideal he imagined and he was feeling separated from me and separated from the hope of filling that hungry void.

When I returned Mark's call, I left a message saying I had received his call and if he wanted to talk to me before our next meeting, he was welcome to leave me some times and I would get back to him. Later, he called back and told me he was feeling a bit better and wanted to thank me for the offer. Mark said, "It meant a great deal that you called and that you offered to talk. I really appreciate that. At the same time, I am not sure if the feelings I have are 100 percent gratitude or if I am apologizing for bothering you." I think this confusion was due to Mark's struggle with greed. His incessant hunger for more made it impossible to experience genuine gratitude. To have gratitude is to give up the demand for more; gratitude is to say one has enough. Feeling greedy, Mark was unconsciously attacking me and demanding more love and care, which made him worry about my reaction. To guard against my retaliation, he had to apologize in the disguise of a thank you.

After about a year of analytic treatment, Mark was feeling less over-whelmed by his phantasies of loss, persecution, and deprivation. While still very much consumed by the dynamics of greed and primitive loss, he was far less anxious and more able to have some hope in his life. He didn't construct nearly as many emotional catastrophes with his friends, coworkers, or boss. He was slower to see me as someone who let him down or neglected him. Indeed, his life felt fuller because he was less greedy and therefore could take in more fulfillment. Mark said, "certain friends don't call me enough and when I wonder why they don't, I am disappointed or irritated. But, I don't feel the kind of deep loss and emptiness I used too. I am able to think that there must be some reason, other than they are being mean and withholding their attention. But, I still sometimes feel like I could starve to death and no one would ever know because they don't check on me enough." Here, Mark summed up the progress he has made in taming the aggressive greed that drove his life and left him facing loss and persecution. At the same time, he shows how he still is haunted by these phantasies of deprivation and cruel rejection.

## CASE MATERIAL 9.3

Some patients who exhibit problems with unconscious greed are so con-flicted and overwhelmed by these phantasies that they have a very difficult time functioning in day-to-day reality. Relationships, careers, and simple daily life are significantly thwarted. Greed creates internal cycles of ideal-ization, deprivation, loss, persecution, and rage. These cycles impede the healthy cycles of internalization and integration necessary for basic human relating.

For some, greed is mostly characterized by oral demands creating per-secutory objects. For others, greed seems to be a state of great loss and emptiness that leads to deep resentment and envy. With many patients, greed is a complicated and confusing mixture of these and other elements. Racker (1960) thinks that psychological problems with greed begin with anxiety and pain that the ego projects aggressively into the object. Racker states that the ego initially idealizes the object as the source of all that is good and all that is needed. This puts the ego in a devalued position and, by comparison to the now great object, the ego feels barren and lost. Additionally, the ego is gifting the object with the life instinct. The ego is left with a sense of deprivation and is taken over by the death instinct. Racker felt this painful state was the start of a later more aggressive mode where the ego attacked the object for leaving it so deprived and barren. This leads to the object becoming persecutory and betraying.

While in full agreement with Racker, I believe there is another aspect of greed at play in self-destructive patients. Some patients idealize the object as well as build a pathological ego-ideal. This ego-ideal is felt to be full of perfect and nourishing traits, but is felt to be unobtainable. The ego places such demands and expectations on this idealized-self that by comparison the ego feels pathetic. There is no hope of ever measuring up to or obtaining that perfect status. Thus, the ego feels deprived by itself. There begins a cycle of internal self-to-self greed, loss, deprivation, hostility, and persecution. While this cycle could be conceptualized in ego–superego terminology, I am describing the actual experiential world of the ego and the destructive object relations of the ego.

Mary was a thirty-year-old woman from a family of six children. She describes her family as eight people existing under one roof, only connected by the same name. This lonely distance left her feeling she had to figure out life on her own. Her parents were never a source of help, inspiration, or motivation. Mary said, "I felt clueless and then one day I left home and was lost and had no idea how to be in the world." Mary had dated a few men over the years but had never really had a successful relationship with a man. She had two close friends that she had gone to highschool with and otherwise felt unable to forge new friendships. She came into treatment feeling utterly hopeless and depressed. Mary wanted help in "figuring out how to relate to people" and "not be such a turn off to others".

In the transference, Mary wanted me to advise her on all manner of things. How to date better, how to talk with her boss, how to not repel potential friends, and how to get out of her low-paying, dead-end job were all matters she thought I could give her specific answers to. I pointed out how she wanted all this from me because she felt empty and barren and saw me as full of knowledge and hope. This is what Racker (1960) was explaining. Mary projected the life instinct into me and compared herself with me and felt horribly lacking. Nearly everyone looked better compared to how she felt inside. This painful sense of failure and helplessness increased when she idealized me. Now, she felt deprived and out of touch with me. This led to hostility at times and a demanding of answers. In phantasy, and sometimes the real result of pressuring me, she felt I was irritated with her and didn't want to be in contact with her. We explored how this was a mirror to how all her other relations went, only we were hopefully catching the process midstream and could do something about it.

Sadly, Mary's internal sense of void and the deep greed that prevailed led to the pathological sequence Racker outlined. Mary was in a low-paying job with no realistic path of improvement and she was unable to climb out of her predicament. Her job paid only enough to cover her basic bills, and bare essentials. She was very close to not being able to pay her rent each month. Her therapy was paid by her health insurance. Two important issues came out of our exploration of her job predicament. First of all, she wanted my advice about it.

After we reviewed the specifics of her financial crisis, it became obvious to me that she had signed up to put an unrealistically high proportion of her monthly salary into a savings account for retirement. By herself, Mary felt anxious and lost, unable to take care of herself. This was a direct reflection of how she felt in relationship to her family growing up. So, she was always feeling a painful void and distance. This alone left her feeling hungry and greedy for something more than her experience of an internal wasteland. At the same time, Mary was idealizing me, seeing me as having special knowledge about financial planning and money issues. So, in comparison to me, she was clueless and dumb. This made her even more greedy and envious. This is what was behind the pushy, needling quality of her requests for help. I commented on this and she said she felt I had the answers so why was I not giving them to her. Here, she expressed the deprivation and sense of sadomasochism that probably infected her other relationships.

Unfortunately, I was partly caught up in all these and pointed out what seemed obvious about her putting too much money into her retirement fund. Mary was immediately relieved and thanked me. I told her that I found it interesting how she wasn't able to see it herself and how she put me in the all-knowing wizard role. "But that is what I pay you for!" she replied. I interpreted that this was what she wished for from her parents, but now she is demanding it from me by taking on the clueless role and pressuring me to rescue her. "I see what you mean. I think you are correct, but I don't know how to change that," Mary replied. Here, she started to reflect on herself and how she related to me, and then fell back into the passivity of being clueless.

With her job, for which she seemed over-qualified, she would not and could not make the moves to find a more satisfying and better paying career. Because Mary presented this job dilemma in a very sketchy, confusing way, I first asked many questions and tried to sort out what the problem might be. Here, I was again caught up in her idealizing me and therefore depleting herself of knowledge and feeling empty by comparison. So, I was interpersonally acting out the role of feeding breast to her greedy, needy ego. When I made that interpretation, it helped her reclaim some of her own strength and knowledge. She told me, "I think I can't make any moves toward a better job because I have such high expectations. I see this next job as the pivotal job of my life. It will be the career path for my life and it will define who I am. Even if it only lasts for six months, it still will be THE job of my life." I interpreted that she had projected such perfection and had set such insatiable demands on this next job that it was terrifying to approach it. She said, "it is so huge, why try?"

This was a difficult period in her treatment, as this pathological greed kept her in a harsh reality. Living with such difficulty in her internal and external life made it hard for her to want to keep trying and made my job very tedious and uphill. We were both up against the quest for the ultimate: the ultimate job, the ultimate knowledge, the perfect path to relationships, and the instant cure. Mary had shrouded us in the desolation that came with her greedy phantasies. She was reluctant to climb out of it and that left me as the spokesperson for the life instinct, debating against her greed, futility, and self-destructive fortification.

Patients like Joe, Mary, and Mark are operating within the paranoid-schizoid plane of mental functioning. This is a world of absolutes and dangers that are primitive and catastrophic. For the more neurotic, depressive patient, the quest for an idealized object and the struggle with greed is difficult, but not as overwhelming. Projection of oral aggression and destructive, greedy demands bring on a fear of hurting the object. The resulting guilt and the wish to make amends and heal the wounded object are evidence of some ego control and internal negotiation of psychological need. These ego strengths are also projected into the object and for these patients the comparison between self and object doesn't feel so stark. There is still an idealization, but in a more balanced manner that retains some sense of self-capacity.

The paranoid-schizoid patient exists in a barren world full of torment and despair. Thus, the level of idealization, greed, and oral aggression is way more severe and rigid. The object seems in danger of destruction and, rather than making amends, the ego is concerned with basic survival. Manic indifference, denial, and pathological splitting offer temporary respite but actually increase dread and annihilation anxiety. Greedy desire to command all of the object leads to phantasies of having completely wiped out the object and the ego is left to suffer isolation, abandonment, and fatal retaliation from the object, which is without forgiveness. All this increases the anxious need for an all-good rescuing object and the sense of emptiness. The greed for more grows.

Patients struggling with pathological greed and the accompanying primitive loss and persecution have a breakdown in the container function. While containment usually implies a soothing, secure experience of one's anxieties and confusions being organized and understood, greed distorts this ego capacity. To these patients, to be contained or to learn to contain oneself is perceived as negative. To be contained in the usual psychological meaning of the word means to be in a state of object-related contentment. Greedy patients do not feel content. The nature of greed ensures that they cannot feel content. Therefore, analytic containment will bring on phantasies of being constrained, trapped, and limited. Patients will talk about not wanting to "just settle" and asserting that they must "live outside of the box". Greed affects the containing aspects of interpretation and how a patient responds to the containing nature of the therapeutic relationship. Often, the greedy patient feels the soothing containment provided by interpretations is never enough and eventually they experience them as confining or persecutory as well. Another problem is that greedy patients do not want to think or feel, as they don't want to have to face the painful and frightening phantasies connected with thought and affect. Containment helps clarify thought and lessens the anxiety that distorts affect and thought. When more able to think and feel, these patients become more aware of the separateness, differences, and contrasts between self and object. To their egos, this awareness of difference implies that they are being taken away from the source of nourishment. Fear of loss and persecution are common reactions to facing the individuality of objects.

My patient Mary made progress, but it was slow going due to how she experienced my interpretations. Her unconscious greed filtered my comments into depriving, persecutory, or insufficient crumbs that she had to defend against or try and reshape into more omnipotent delicacies. We would get into difficult back-and-forth dynamics where I would say something, she would take it badly, and either I would feel pushed to explain myself in an apologetic way or she would launch into a stream of apologies. This was a manic and desperate attempt to appease the now angry and vengeful object as well as denial of her own rageful disappointment in that object. This was done from a distance with a sense of control and me-against-the-world flavor, rather than a confident negotiation with someone who might understand and tolerate the perceived misunderstanding.

Mary's greed was part of a chronic conflict. She wanted to act on her ravenous hunger for all the nourishment she imagined the object held, but she felt this greedy attack would turn the supply of all that is good into something terribly bad and dangerous. To avoid this self-imposed death sentence, she went hungry; this only made her more fragmented and greedy. This back-and-forth conflict made her very fearful and self-destructive. She couldn't make a move to search for a better job; she couldn't decide to stay with her minimally gratifying boyfriend or find someone else; she couldn't pick a hobby because it might not be the right one to put all of her energy into. These and many more predicaments looked like obsessive indecision, but they lacked the more neurotic fears of competition, hurting a parental figure's feelings, or guilt over phallic striving. Mary's being stuck was more a case of trying to avoid annihilation fears and severe ideas of loss and abandonment. One of my comments she said "rang a bell in her heart" was the picture of her huddled in a basement, starving. She wanted and needed to get out of the basement to search for food as she was so empty. But, she would have to emerge into a war zone with snipers all around. To starve to death or risk death by sniper fire and maybe find a source of food was her plight. So, her indecision and reluctance to try something different was based on a much more primitive set of phantasies and anxieties.

## Comments

Several patients have been profiled in this chapter in order to illustrate how unconscious greed can play a prominent role in severe character pathology.

This greed arises from a deep sense of deprivation and oral neediness. The object is seen as innately possessing more and as being the source of the nourishment the ego so desperately lacks. A process of idealization occurs, in which the ego admires this plentiful object. However, this admiration is short-lived and turns into more of a slave–master relationship. Projection of greed and oral rage turns the object into a menacing traitor who cannot be disturbed. A cycle of loss of the ideal object, betrayal, persecution, and fear of annihilation follows.

Stein (1990) has pointed out how Melanie Klein views anxiety as the result of sadism, projection, and a vicious cycle of an anxious, hostile ego attacking an object that attacks back. Greed is a form of sadism that is fueled by phantasies of loss and deprivation. Through projective identification, the greedy attacks on the object bring on a heightened experience of loss, abandonment, and persecution. While introjection of good objects, new and positive experiences, and understanding objects that respond in tolerant and accepting ways can help to mitigate pathological greed, there is a particular problem that remains. Greedy phantasies tend to drain the good object of its worth and overlook its goodness in search of even more goodness. In other words, the grass is always green so the grass at home looks brown. To the greedy ego, good is not good enough. Like a drug addict, the ego needs a bigger, stronger dose each time and it becomes numb to the pleasures already available.

# Part III

# Interruptions to the process of change: loss, envy, and the death instinct

# Chapter 10

# The clinical advantage of the death instinct*

Bianchedi (Bianchedi, Antar, Fernandez *et al.* 1984) has outlined five areas that define Kleinian metapsychology: a theory of an object-related ego present at birth; the use of projective identification and introjective identification as basic mental functions; the theory of unconscious phantasy producing an internal dynamic world; a lifelong struggle between two intrapsychic experiences, the paranoid-schizoid and the depressive; and a unique conception of the death instinct.

In this chapter, I will describe some of the Kleinian thinking about the death instinct and explore the theoretical and clinical advantages to the Kleinian use of the death instinct. I will illustrate, through case material, how the death instinct is often part of the transference struggle with patients who experience change as dangerous.

Freud (1930; 1937) introduced the concept of the death instinct as the result of his clinical observation. He noted certain patients who seemed determined to maintain their illness and continue their course of self-destruction. The idea of a death instinct was never fully embraced by the analytic community. In fact, some analytic schools have seen Freud's theory as his misunderstanding of patients' defensive masochism and other defensive compromises.

Without tracing the historical sequence of this concept, it is clear that the death instinct has been a vague and controversial issue in the history of psychoanalysis. When referred to at all, it is often mixed together with other references to the superego, to anger turned inwards, and to blaming the patient for the analyst's countertransference problems.

Melanie Klein and her followers stand alone in taking Freud's discovery seriously. Klein felt the clinical evidence for the death instinct was overwhelming. Specifically, she believed envy was the direct manifestation of the death instinct and, as such, envy sought to spoil and devalue whatever

* This chapter was first published as 'The clinical advantage of the death instinct', in *Psychoanalytic Social Work*, 2001, 8: 2, 23–40.

seemed valuable or connected to life. Some analytic schools have debated whether the death instinct is simply another name for sadism or masochism. Klein felt the death instinct was an entirely different phenomenon. While patients often express sadistic glee at squashing the object of their envy, the sadism is secondary to the goal of the death instinct rather than primary.

Many borderline, narcissistic, or psychotic patients face a dual struggle. Their internal world is torn apart by the forces of the death instinct and a pathological superego. Theoretically and technically, it is important to make a distinction between these phenomena. At times this is difficult. The patient's paranoid-schizoid or depressive states of perception color and complicate each.

According to Freud and Melanie Klein, the life and death instincts are innate and constitutional, but are manifested as emotional id-based urges. Developmentally, these are transformed by the ego into intra-psychic, psychological phantasies that interface with reality.

Klein emphasized the psychological rather than biological nature of instincts and the resulting phantasies. These are internal dramas that involve dynamic relationships between the self and its unconscious objects. The superego functions as an independent agent of the ego, a collection of particular parental functions. It consists of the projection onto reality, the introjection of that distorted reality, and the intrapsychic reactions to that distortion. This is layered with the internalization of actual reality. Through the interplay of projection, introjection, external reality, and phantasy, the force and dynamics of the death instinct and the superego are constantly changing. All these internal situations are played out interpersonally via the dynamics of projective identification and thus lead to further mutation.

Normal development brings psychological integration and balance. As the result of ongoing internalization of good, forgiving, and supportive objects in balance with a normal level of competitive and envious aggression, the superego emerges as an understanding, confidence-building, contemplative agency. With ample containment from external objects, the superego becomes fortified with an internalized containing structure of its own. The superego then has a stop, wait-and-see, look-before-you-leap capacity. However, if the superego is a vicious, punitive force that fails as a guiding and flexible container, the death instinct may begin to function defensively.

During normal development, the death instinct and the superego operate in conjunction, with the superego representing the life instincts. If the superego takes on pathological properties, with exaggerated use of guilt and self-threat, the death instinct will try to eliminate this threat.

The superego seeks knowledge, challenge, clarity, success, and autonomy. Curiosity, direction, and motivation come from the superego. When combating the sadistic, inflated, and pathological superego, the death instinct tries to eliminate thinking, dependency, differences, and need. Differences and awareness of separateness from the object are attacked. The superego demands unrealistic states of agreement and acceptance between self and object, so the death instinct tries to eliminate the connection and relationship altogether.

With patients operating mostly within the paranoid-schizoid position, this constant internal battle leaves the ego overwhelmed and in a state of collapse. Many of these difficult patients are testing the waters of the depressive position, but experience their depressive phantasies through a paranoid lens. The paranoid-schizoid ego tries, mostly out of self-preservation, not to hurt its objects. Since the primitive ego is still struggling with strong levels of hostility, envy, and persecutory fears (based on excessive reliance on projective identification), the object seems easily enraged and prone to revenge. So, when these patients are overly nice in the transference, it is not so much out of love for the object, but fear of rejection and attack.

In this situation, reparation feels impossible on several levels. The hurt to the object feels permanent, the ego's own hostility feels too strong to contain, and the object seems too weak to survive any hurt. Precocious attempts at reparation lead to manic acting-out. These patients project paranoid-schizoid anxiety into the object and then feel unable to rescue or heal that object. This creates new superego guilt and fear, along with unrealistic demands to make it all better. The death instinct must war against this and destroy these demands. Often this creates a vicious cycle where the superego is demanding a perfect ultra-life and the death instinct must eliminate all signs of life to counterbalance this.

Ultimately, I think the concept of the death instinct serves as a useful way to understand and treat certain clinical situations. I will discuss a group of difficult patients who would be classified as paranoid-schizoid (Klein 1946). They show a self-destructive quality that seems to illustrate the notion of a death instinct. With ongoing interpersonal and intra-psychic containment, specific analysis of self-destructive intra-psychic and interpersonal patterns, and interpretation of primitive states of loss and persecution, these patients show improvement. I will use case material to illustrate some of these points.

Some of the confusing issues around the death instinct relate to whether or not it is a biological, inborn characteristic of mental functioning. Grotstein (1977) feels the death instinct is an inborn, hardwired, early-warning system. The death instinct serves to help the ego be aware of potential prey–predator situations and how to best survive within them. In this sense, the death instinct protects the ego and stands on the side of life. However, if the predator/prey phantasies are too intense and the ego is unable to manage them or incorporate them into a larger internal object relations system, the death instinct brings on a cruel and destructive battle between parts of the intra-psychic world. The ego begins to attack itself.

When the ego's death phantasies are too intense and unmanageable, the presence or absence of a containing, managing object plays a crucial role. Bion's (1962) ideas on the containing function of the object and how projective identification material is held and modified by that object are also important. Grotstein feels that while some of the death instinct is deflected from the ego outwards through projective identification, most of it remains as the basis for self-destructive personality formation.

While I agree with Grotstein that there is an inborn aspect to the death instinct, I would emphasize the psychological nature of it rather than its biological roots. However, his formulation of the prey–predator matrix is intriguing. I will add my own metaphor to this. The shell of an egg protects a bird and provides nutrition until it is ready to hatch. If the bird is too weak or the shell too thick, what normally provides safety becomes a deadly tomb. Grotstein provides a model of a built-in internal predator that pushes the ego to turn toward and introject good objects, taking a protective, pro-life stance. The death instinct and the annihilation anxiety it produces are the paranoid-schizoid equivalent of castration anxiety in the depressive position.

Segal (1993) states:

> I contend that the death instinct from the beginning is directed at both the perceived object and the perceiving self, resulting in such phenomena as pathological projective identification, described by Bion . . . One could formulate the conflict between the life and death instinct in purely psychological terms. Birth confronts us with the experience of needs. In relation to that experience there can be two reactions, and both, I think, are invariably present in all of us, though in varying proportions. One, to seek satisfaction for the needs: that is life-promoting and leads to object seeking, love, and eventually object concern. The other is the drive to annihilate the need, to annihilate the perceiving experiencing self, as well as anything that is perceived . . . The organism defends itself against the death drive by deflecting it so that it becomes aggression.
>
> (pp. 55–56)

In summarizing Hana Segal's view of the death instinct, Steiner points out how the death instinct's presence is known through chronic intolerance and hatred of reality (Bronstein, 1999). This motivates a reliance on splitting and projective identification. The ego moves away from any evidence of life, such as difference, need, and imperfection, by omnipotent and manic phantasies. As a result, the death instinct is the part of the ego that attacks the needy, struggling, anxious, or confused parts of the ego. Here, we see the dynamic conflict of life and death forces.

I think this is a view that accurately brings together clinical and theoretical perspectives on the death instinct. Whether or not it is a biological given, the death instinct can be tracked within the clinical situation. It is a viable and dynamic characteristic of the mind that is more prominent in certain patients and more silent in others. The death instinct is an intrapsychic process in which certain aspects of the patient's ego set out to attack other aspects of the patient's ego. These are usually parts of the ego that are identified with reality, with certain maternal or paternal objects, and certainly with the analyst.

Heimann (1956) stated:

> it is the life instinct that aims at union and contact, in contrast to the death instinct which aims at avoiding or breaking up contact and union. It is, of course, true that an expression of destructive impulses also needs contact with an object, but this does not invalidate the proposition that contact primarily and ultimately serves the life instinct.
>
> (p. 304)

In a more general sense, I think there is always a drive for contact with the object and that drive always embodies both aggressive and libidinal aims. Through projective identification, a part of the ego can become identified with a certain aspect of an object. Thus, the ego may begin to attack both itself and its hated object. It follows that one has to have some significant investment of love, envy, or spite in an object to wish to destroy it.

By viewing the death instinct as a psychological, object-related phenomenon, we can better understand particular transference–countertransference configurations. This is in line with Feldman's (1999) ideas about lifting the death instinct out of the realm of a biological or physiological concept. He feels the death instinct is best used as a clinical method of understanding the negative forces in patients who set out to destroy clarity, meaning, difference, and growth. The goal of the death instinct is not always to kill the self or object and is not something that brings libidinal stimulation or gratification. Rather, the goal is often to drain the life out of the self and object, reducing the ego's capacity and rendering the ego or object weak and unable to function. Therefore, thinking and the capacity to think are often the primary targets of the death instinct.

Feldman makes several valuable contributions. He is pointing out how the death instinct is really the best way to conceptualize the destructive process one sees in so many patients. These patients seem dedicated to eradicating any shred of dependence, vulnerability, and lack of control. They want to prevent change because change is seen as persecutory. Any link to the analyst is denied or erased to preserve an omnipotent, monolithic stature.

The death instinct is useful in the clinical situation as it helps explain the multifaceted ways patients are so self-destructive. At times, this vengeance on the self is defensive and at other times it seems primary. It follows that narcissism and envy are at times defensive and other times aggressive. The epistomophilic function of the ego, the desire for knowledge, is often the most hated area for these patients. They seem to have to rid themselves of any evidence that this existed, as if faced with a terrible liability. With analysis, it often turns out that they see the need to know or learn as a sign of gross weakness and as a confession to being both greedy and needy.

## CASE MATERIAL 10.1

When she entered treatment, S wanted to stop drinking, using drugs, and "ending up with the biggest losers in town". She was in her thirties and had been married four times. Each of these were to men she met in bars, had a "one-night stand" with, and married within three or four months. After several years of fighting, drinking, and financial chaos, she would leave each one.

S had tried to kill herself several times. She had overdosed, slashed her wrists, and been pulled off a bridge. I was her ninth outpatient therapist. Six months before seeing me, she had been hospitalized for the fourth time.

She was always loyal to her husbands, but had sex with someone new nearly every week when she was single. Sometimes she slept with a man, sometimes with a woman, and sometimes with both at the same time.

Finally, she had a long history of changing jobs and moving on a whim. S said this was the result of her creativity and spontaneity.

The more I talked with S, the more I gained the impression of a very motivated yet anguished person who felt taken over by vicious, self-destructive tendencies. It wasn't that she sounded masochistic. Rather, she sounded hunted down by herself and desperately trying to run for cover. This was an outright effort of working against her own growth; it was an effort to harm herself and to prevent health. She talked about a part of her mind that was "out to get her" and "make sure she would be punished and never get anything positive". S told me she had to hold herself back from killing herself and that suicide was a "constant threat". I felt this was said not to manipulate me, but more as a response to the feeling she was held captive by some sadistic part of herself. She wanted help in breaking free of that internal threat. When we agreed to begin an analytic process and start a regular schedule of meetings, she told me with great emotion, "I hope you realize what you are in for. I need you to survive what is inside me and not bail out in the middle if you can't handle it!" Again, I didn't feel this was a case of her being overly dramatic or making not-so-subtle threats. Rather, I felt she was trying to explain to me her terrifying internal struggle.

Over the many months ahead, we dealt with these split-off, fragmented aspects of her personality. For a while, she went on even more drug and alcohol binges. S was almost raped because of one of these late-night blackouts. Then, she decided to go "cold-turkey". This was very difficult as my sense was that the drugs and alcohol served as a soothing nipple she could turn to whenever she felt lost and afraid. However, this was a nipple that served poisoned milk. S began building this idea of sobriety into an all-or-nothing dilemma. Either she would instantly become a good, sober, law-abiding citizen who never was "wild" again or she was a total failure and deserved to die. Her self-destructive ways and this persecutory, vengeful part of herself kept her at a status quo. Whenever she succeeded in staying sober for a while, she began to feel intense paranoia and loneliness. She was more vulnerable to scary phantasies of being used by men and of me having zero tolerance for her.

As we continued, S started to be more aware of how she related to others. This began in the transference and then she applied it to her external world. She had clearly been putting herself in the role of servant, whore, and victim to men for many years. When S realized how she hurt herself this way, she alternated between hating all men and hating herself. She would vow to become a nun or a lesbian, but also felt deep sorrow over never having a man to be close to or trust.

I had the countertransference feeling of being kept at a safe distance. I wondered if she was reluctant to see me as a trustworthy man because she feared I might betray her and hurt her as she hurt herself. It came out that she regarded me as a safe, unique, and professional person, not a man. By seeing me as a professional doctor to whom she came to discuss her problems, she drained off any emotion and neutralized any phantasies about me. This was short-lived. She felt that she might easily bore me and dissatisfy me, that I would criticize her and reject her. S also idealized me. I was an amazing and brilliant man who could work wonders. She was glad to be on the couch, because if our eyes met, she "would surely fall in love".

S told me several times, "I don't want to tell you what I am thinking, feeling, or doing. I think you will criticize me and then throw me away." She would break down and sob. I was touched by how strongly she felt that I would really attack her and throw her away like useless garbage. I interpreted how she would always be punctual for her sessions and be very polite to me as a way to prevent this sort of abandonment and persecution.

Generally, my interpretations were a mixture of direct transference comments, extra-transference remarks, and links between historical material and the transference. I always find it better to lay emphasis on the here-and-now transference and the projections into extra-transference situations. However, the genetic parallels are useful if they can be brought in to illustrate how the past lives on in the present and how the past can be used to defend, disguise, or distort the present.

S grew up as the only child of two violent alcoholics. Her parents were drug dealers and lived a dangerous and paranoid lifestyle. The drinking and fighting were so out of control that the parents divorced when S was five. Her mother's new boyfriend was very nice to S and S "fell in love with him". He began molesting S when she was six or seven years old. When S told a teacher about this, she was removed from the home on her tenth birthday and put into foster care. She went to live with her father when she was fifteen. S told me her mother had walked in on the molestation more than once, but never did anything about it. In fact, she told her, "this happens to all little girls". In retrospect, S thinks that her mother felt forced to stay with her boyfriend for financial reasons and had been molested as a little girl herself.

The terrible lack of trust, the constantly violent family atmosphere, her mother's abandonment of her, and what to her was the punishment of the foster home all shaped her internal experience. Since I don't know what actually happened and how much distortion is involved (it may have been not so bad, it may have been worse, it may have been simply different), I try to rely on what goes on in the clinical situation (the transference and countertransference) as the best material to comment on. However, when the patient's current phantasies and conflicts seem to be a mirror of her childhood memories, I certainly make that the focus of our exploration too.

Overall, I was struck by the degree of her internal self-destruction. Certain parts of S's personality seemed to be deliberately out to destroy, erase, or gag other parts. She would say, "one part of me is begging to be heard and helped, but another part is threatening that part and if it doesn't shut up there will be hell to pay". She would say how she "killed off" the protecting and nurturing part of herself out of "rage and disgust", but then she felt "so alone, floating at sea and devastated". S would tell me there was a committee inside her and only a few members had voting rights. The other parts had to be really quiet and go along with everything or they would be killed. She said she feared these evil, bossy parts of herself might make her commit suicide if she didn't "go along with the program".

I seemed to help S best when I addressed my interpretations to this self-destructive process. I made comments about why she tried to erase, destroy, or reshape certain feelings or thoughts. It also helped when I interpreted how she was out to destroy the link between the innocent-little-girl parts of herself and me. Finally, I interpreted how she was worried about my reaction to the destructive parts of herself. To risk closing the distance between the self-hatred and the other parts of herself, as well as the link to me, meant a massive and dangerous change.

We began to talk about her feelings of loss around letting go of the destructive status quo. S felt this spelled abandonment of a severe type and that she would be vulnerable to great harm. These sessions were extremely painful and she would silently cry for a long time. In fact, this part of the analysis ushered in the third phase of treatment. First, we worked on containment of a pathological projective identification process. This was an intra-psychic process but also was manifested interpersonally. This was a long and difficult time that tested my countertransference tolerance and pushed her to challenge her fears about trusting me. Next, we suffered the seemingly relentless aggression of the death instinct. She seemed bent on crushing certain parts of herself and, through projective identification, certain aspects of our relationship. Now, after working through a great deal of the defensive aspects of the death instinct, we began to deal with her painful and frightening phantasies of loss and persecution.

S said she felt in bits and pieces and that her mind was in fragments. Often, I had to be the one to point out how lonely and needy she felt, and that she was trying to tough it out without help. Bit by bit, we learned that she "tightened the screws" on herself whenever she felt she needed me more. She deliberately tried to destroy the part of herself that looked or felt pained, dependent, or lost. Actually, her intense paranoia and persecutory phantasies were often the result of her own attacks on the part of her that felt lost and abandoned.

I noticed how she was hoping to please me with reports of new success, and have me watch out for her much like a careful parent does when the child explores the deep end of the pool. I also noticed and commented on how the more she wished for this type of relationship and the more she let herself enjoy the phantasy, the more she worried I would turn into a criticizing, attacking, and abandoning parent. I interpreted that she was projecting the self-destructive parts of herself into me. This usually decreased her anxiety and she was able to explore those fears at length. Often, she would link them to memories and feelings of being emotionally abused and set aside or ignored by her mother.

As the treatment went along, S improved greatly. She stopped getting drunk and sleeping around. She occasionally used drugs, but with much more discretion. Her employment record was less erratic and she started to choose better friendships. Of course, the most important changes were internal. Her external shifts were symptomatic of these intra-psychic changes.

S's phantasy of me changing from a protective, loving parent to a mean and rejecting parent is a core aspect of the death instinct. The mind is bent on self-destruction because part of the self is experienced as persecutory and threatening. In other words, the death instinct works in balance with the life instinct. The defensive function of the death instinct is the mind's desperate attempt to prevent loss and persecution. This sense of loss is of a very primitive nature and the ego feels faced with annihilation. The link to the object is experienced as so threatening and unbearable that all evidence of that link is destroyed. Idealized union phantasies and manic independence are part of the death instinct, as well as the oral wish for more and more out of the object. Narcissism and envy are outgrowths of the ego's attempt to deal with the death instinct and the anxieties of loss and persecution (Rosenfeld, 1971). Projective identification instigates, maintains, and aggravates the sense of loss and persecution. The defensive aspect of the death instinct is a mummification, intensification, and fortification of the more primitive aspects of the paranoid-schizoid position. Change is considered dangerous and the mind will make sure to maintain the status quo, even at its own expense.

In discussing the Kleinian view of the mind, Segal (1977) highlights the dynamics of splitting and projection. She states:

> All pain and aggression is projected, resulting in the perception of a bad persecutory object. On the other hand, the libidinal drive creates a fantasy of an ideal, all-fulfilling object. Experiences of satisfaction merge with this fantasy ideal object. Experiences of pain and frustration are felt as an attack by persecutors. The leading anxiety is of a persecutory nature; that the persecutors will annihilate the ideal object and the self identified with it.
>
> (p. 365)

Here, Segal is clearly describing the process of splitting, projective identification, and the nature of the paranoid-schizoid position. I think it is the relationship between these parts of the ego, the ideal object, bad object, and matching aspects of the self that make up the death instinct. The primitive battle between good and evil, inside the self, is manifested clinically in many guises, but within the same theme. One part of the self attempts to actively prevent another part of the self from changing, growing, and gaining freedom. Control has to be maintained over one's entire thought system and emotions. I think that within this paranoid-schizoid world, loss, primitive guilt (Grinberg 1964), and persecution are the leading dramas. The death instinct seems to be the ego's attempt to prevent loss, guilt, and persecution, yet, in a vicious cycle, the death instinct often brings out these anxieties. Clinically, when a patient seems bent on self-destruction, it is often the result of an introjection and identification of the ego with the persecutory object and its efforts at destruction, rejection, and punishment. The ego is then faced with the destruction and loss of the longed-for union between the idealized good object and the good self. This is all the result of a pathological, projective identification process. The analytic task is the containing, detoxification, interpretation, and working through of this destructive force.

Segal (1977) states:

> A very important part of the working through of the depressive position is a gradual withdrawal of this projective identification.
>
> (p. 367)

This is important technically because the death instinct is fueled and maintained by projective identification. Therefore, the analysis of projective identification within the transference, dreams, and extra-transference material is essential to facilitate a shift from the paranoid-schizoid position to the depressive position.

The death instinct and its various manifestations are the expression of multiple mental mechanisms. Some of these are more pathological and some are more normal developmental cycles. The death instinct's dynamic expressions are numerous and each individual seems to experience them in a unique manner.

As I outlined, I think of the death instinct as both primary and defensive. Spillius (1983) writes about the notion of pathological internal organizations and how these represent the death instinct, as well as defenses against it. She states,

> [These organizations] are compromise formations, that is, that they are simultaneously expressions of death instinct and systems of defense against it.
>
> (p. 327)

Clinically, I think we see many patients who seem to live within a self-destructive internal personality organization that is a direct expression of the death instinct and a desperate defense against it. Spillius (1983) notes how Segal has a similar view:

> Segal underlines the idea that narcissism is an expression of death instinct as well as defense against it, and proceeds to illustrate both aspects clinically.
>
> (p. 328)

Steiner (1982) has made the same point. He thinks that everyone has a destructive force working against themselves as well as a healthy aspect of the self representing the life force. He thinks that the essence of psychosis is the domination of the mind by the destructive parts of the ego. In normal development, the self-destructive aspects of the ego are contained and managed by the healthier parts of the ego. Borderline patients seem to have a constant struggle between these healthy and self-destructive parts of the personality.

## CASE MATERIAL 10.2

B was a patient who always reminded me how he didn't need analysis and how he looked forward to the day I would finally let him go free, so he "could get on with his life". Over the seven years of regular work together, he became less and less paranoid and more able to see the value of relationships as opposed to seeing them as threats. His ongoing struggle was with a part of himself that could not tolerate weakness, dependency, or vulnerability. He had to know everything ahead of time. Any new or unknown situation felt extremely dangerous. Feelings were for suckers and needing help was what "infected the pathetic masses". B felt above these kinds of problems. He told me "I have never felt jealous or envious of anyone. I am not susceptible to that kind of thing because I don't need anyone or anything."

Side by side with this arrogant grandiosity, B also felt persecuted by the demands of others. This was a projection of the slave–master relationship he had within himself. If he stumbled and showed any sign of confusion, fear, or hesitation, a part of him would start to go berserk. B would literally scream at himself to get it together. He would spend many sleepless nights lecturing himself and pushing himself to clean the house or balance his checkbook. Little or mundane problems took on life-and-death proportions because of how demanding and sadistic he was. He would break down crying and tell me, "I can't take it anymore. I can't take the demands and the criticism!" The way he experienced this destructive aspect of himself was eery. It was as if he were possessed by an angry and cruel ghost.

If B showed weakness or need for others, this was felt as a total lack of independence, freedom, and choice. It was a persecutory vision of no free will. To prevent this, an aspect of B's ego took manic measures and championed ultimate independence, competition, and strength.

For patients like B, I think the natural prey–predator phantasies and internal and external factors have distorted and exaggerated normal ego strivings. Constitutional and environmental influences converge and the normal life-and-death drives are intensified. This overwhelms the ego with more distorted phantasies regarding desire, fear, and aggression. Normal mental processes of projective identification and splitting are likewise intensified and produce self-destructive standoffs between conflicting aspects of the personality.

Sadistic parts of the self methodically keep other parts of the self in a cycle of inaction, fear, and resistance to change. This is an effort to prevent the breakdown of narcissistic structures. In other words, the death instinct uses narcissism as a way to control, immobilize, and neutralize object relations. This is again both primary and defensive. It is primary in normal development as a sort of governor device that keeps the organism in check. Object relations are maintained at certain levels. This is balanced out by the life drive that strives for change, freedom, and expansion in object relations. Due to excessive internal sadism, envy, and territoriality, or to external abusive situations, or more often due to both, the death instinct becomes defensive. It is defending the ego from itself and experiences overwhelming threats of loss, primitive guilt, and persecution phantasies. These set up a vicious and destructive cycle of projective identification and splitting that is very difficult to break.

The death instinct, and particularly its defensive function against primitive guilt, loss, and persecution, is expressed in acting out, transference material, and dreams.

## CASE MATERIAL 10.3

One patient, W, brought in the following dream. W said, "in the dream, I saw a car wreck. There was lots of blood and obvious casualties. I know I had the dream as a result of reading about a car crash in the paper yesterday."

Very quickly, this patient's internal struggle between an emotional, out-of-control part of herself and a dominating, rigid, and aggressive part of herself became an externalized struggle with me. Through projective identification, W cast this intra-psychic spell on our analytic relationship. She had to be in complete control and refused to need me in any capacity. She drained off all emotions and reactions to the dream. The dream was just a "fact" and she knew what it all meant. Based on years of W's tight management of our relationship and her censorship of my comments or queries, I knew as soon as I said anything that she would react violently.

To mention the transference implication of the bloody crash, to explore the frightening image of death, to comment on the sharing of a dream as contrasted to her usual withholding attitude, to notice her concern about not knowing everything about the dream, or to comment on how she did not want help exploring the dream were all invitations to battle. I felt I was facing danger if I took the wrong step. In fact, there was no safe step to take.

W's way of immobilizing me and controlling the limits of our relationship was a reflection of how she immobilized herself. Through projective identification, I was placed in the position of her embattled self and she was trying to eliminate my efforts at creativity, thought, and growth. W always tried to prevent me from pointing out any differences between us. She felt these differences could question her autonomy, strength, or control. I made interpretations about her trying to avoid the loss of herself as an idealized object and the attack and devaluation she assumed would ensue. She said she felt I would tear apart her identity and force her to need me. W said I wanted to brainwash her with my knowledge and that I was trying to discredit her knowledge.

In my comments, I emphasized how she was so firm about there being nothing in the dream or in her mind other than what she already knew and reported. I said she needed to be very certain, with nothing unknown.

Over several sessions, we were able to discuss the dream more freely and look at how and why she needed to be so right. It was not just that she was trying to show me up or gain some kind of victory (although this was part of it). Rather than a sadomasochistic fight over who was right and wrong, she was trying hard to prevent a change in what she thought and to control what occurred in my mind. The idea of options or differences that she couldn't anticipate was the same as admitting defeat and losing her safe and superior status. It was more a fear of loss and persecution than a phallic power struggle. In the transference, she would routinely engage me in a tug-of-war, but it was more to prevent a catastrophe than to feel victorious. If there was absolutely no meaning to the dream, then W felt safe from the sudden attack of persecutors and a strong feeling of emptiness and hopelessness.

Again, these transference situations were the externalization of an internal projective identification process between various parts of her ego. One part of her tried to blot out the other and persuade herself that there were no feelings, meanings, or thought.

After several years of analysis, W was able to explore, for measured periods, painful and frightening phantasies of loss, guilt, and persecution. For her, the death instinct was mostly defensive. It served as a violent reaction to internal experiences of persecutory guilt and severe states of loss. Great anxiety and paranoia usually followed these phantasies. More and more, she could deal with this and begin to allow her mind to feel, think, and negotiate with itself.

When the life and death instincts are balanced and the ego is contained and supported by plentiful good-object relations (internal and external), the death instinct remains primary and therefore silent. When this situation is not in balance, the death instinct becomes defensive and is manifested in symptoms, acting out, and negative transference phenomena. Often, if the thrust is defensive, the death instinct manifests as cruel, sadistic power-plays by the superego.

## Comments

The clinical material in this chapter demonstrates how the death instinct often becomes a factor in the transference when it becomes an ego defense. As the result of a combination of external distress, internal aggression, and excessive reliance on projective identification to satisfy primitive oral needs, certain patients seem to be struggling with overwhelming phantasies of loss and persecution. Via projective identification, the death instinct is the mind's best effort at eradicating parts of itself that feel like part of the threat of loss and the lack of safety. A vicious cycle is created that becomes externalized in the transference.

By accepting the death instinct as not only a viable theoretical construct, but a verifiable clinical fact, the analyst is in more of a position to understand and help certain patients. In many cases, this understanding can shift a treatment from a stalemate or a negative therapeutic reaction to that of a difficult but workable intra-psychic conflict. Change becomes possible, instead of a danger to avoid.

# Chapter 11

# Acting out and the death instinct*

Some borderline and psychotic patients who experience change as threatening, exhibit a particular pattern of working through. Three levels or phases of treatment emerge and present the analyst–patient pair with different and difficult therapeutic tasks. First, there is a period of acting out. This includes acting out in the sessions, behaviors outside the sessions, and somatization. These patients also exhibit acting out in dreams (Grinberg 1968). This is a situation where the patient acts one way in the treatment, usually compliant, but their dreams reveal other strong feelings, usually aggressive or rebellious. Many disturbed patients act out in a way that is final, meaning they abort treatment altogether. Given the patient's high anxiety and their excessive reliance on primitive defenses such as splitting and projective identification, the analyst must be fairly active and willing to function as a receptive container (Bion 1962) for the patient's unconscious struggles.

Exploring this pattern, inherent in the treatment of patients with chronic and severe disturbances, provides further insight into those cases where change is avoided and resisted. Research (Friedman *et al.* 1998) shows that at least half of all patients seeing a psychoanalyst in private practice have definable personality disorders as well as major affective disorders. A recent report (Israel 1999) by the International Psychoanalytic Association's Committee on Psychoanalysis and Allied Therapies underlines the world-wide phenomenon of sicker patients being the norm for most clinicians. These character-disordered and psychotic cases present the analyst with great challenges.

When these difficult patients remain with the analyst and both parties are able to preserve the integrity of the analytic relationship, a second layer emerges. The analyst begins to see the psychological workings of the death instinct. Segal (1993) has demonstrated the clinical importance of the death

---

* This chapter was first published as 'Acting out, the death instinct, and primitive experiences of loss and guilt', in *Canadian Journal of Psychoanalysis*, 10(1, 2002): 25–44.

instinct concept. During this phase, the patient shows, via transference and associations, how they pit one aspect of their mind against others. The death instinct (DI) is an effort to erase connections to the object, to knowledge, and to life. This phase of analysis is slow and frustrating, easily becoming stalemated by the patient's externalization of the DI into the transference.

Spillius (1983) speaks of patients who are recognizable by a relatively stable and structured set of anxieties, defenses, and internal relations. She describes disturbed patients who are highly resistant to change and are dependent on primitive methods of relating such as splitting and projective identification. She states,

> [these primitive intra-psychic states] are compromise formations, that is, that they are simultaneously expressions of death instinct and systems of defense against it.
>
> (p. 328)

The borderline and psychotic patients I am exploring consistently demonstrate, within their phantasies and within the transference, this compromise formation. In other words, the instinct and the life instinct always operate together, even if against one another.

If patient and analyst make it through the resistance, counter-identification (Grinberg 1992), and the stagnation of the death instinct, a third phase unfolds.

Now, the patient shows, via transference, dreams, and extra-transference phantasies, their experience of primitive loss, guilt, and persecution. Paranoid-schizoid experiences of guilt, fears of loss and annihilation, and the transformation of an ideal object into an attacking object permeate the transference.

The prognosis for these types of borderline and psychotic patients is hopeful, but often poor. Many do not stay in treatment past the first phase. They are so overwhelmed by anxiety that acting out is fundamental to how they relate. Therefore, it is just a matter of time before they flee the analytic relationship.

Others make it past their anxiety and acting out to start exploring the way they battle themselves, via the death instinct. These patients create an unbreakable standoff with the analyst that mirrors the standoff they face intra-psychically. Then, they often leave treatment as a way to banish the analyst and the life-affirming aspects of the analysis.

Likewise, some patients manage to work through manifestations of the death instinct but also stop treatment after several years. A much smaller group actually stays in treatment long enough to set aside the defensive functions of acting out and the death instinct to face their underlying trauma of loss and persecution. This entails a gradual journey from the dual fears of losing the idealized object, bringing on feelings of annihilation, and the fears of the object's persecutory retaliation. With time and hard work from both analyst and patient, this evolves into the more manageable problems of the depressive position (Klein 1935).

## CASE MATERIAL 11.1

Jack was a patient who was always on the verge of leaving treatment, yet he stayed long enough to work through many of his anxieties.

He entered treatment for a confusing mix of symptoms and complaints. His history of drug and alcohol abuse and explosive temper did not bother him. His view of the government as out to "screw the little guy" and deliberately make it hard for people to survive was a fact, not open for discussion. Jack had chronic backaches and headaches and a sporadic work history. He never stayed with one company for very long before they fired him or he walked out without notice, feeling justifiably wronged. His finances were in disarray and he owed a considerable amount. Jack told me he felt depressed sometimes and he wanted to find a steady girlfriend who wouldn't betray him.

When I asked Jack about his upbringing, he said, "childhood is not worth remembering". He grew up with an alcoholic father and a mother who tried to provide the basics for her family, under difficult emotional and financial conditions. The details of Jack's childhood are not easily disguised, so I will omit them for reasons of confidentiality. However, it is accurate to say he constantly struggled to find a feeling of physical and emotional safety and support.

Jack was hospitalized once in his twenties for alcoholism and was married and divorced once in his thirties. Throughout the first year of analysis, Jack would bring up thoughts of suicide. He wanted to end his "futile course into nothingness". Indeed, Jack had tried killing himself before by overdosing on antidepressant medication.

Sadomasochistic acting out quickly colored our relationship and Jack tried to have me side with his paranoid view of the world. Indeed, this was an undercurrent of our relationship that waxed and waned. Analysis of my countertransference was important. I noticed how we traded places in a bully–bullied role. We were able to chip away at this but it was often a difficult thread to notice.

Jack felt most people were useless to spend time with and he felt his ideas were always right. At the same time, he felt scared of people and worried that he was a weakling and a failure. Sometimes Jack got high on drugs before his sessions and other times he would cancel the session right before we were to meet. He was furious and somewhat threatening when I billed him for those sessions. He said he would quit immediately if I did and he refused to discuss it. I let him have his way to save the treatment but I felt bullied and powerless. I think he quickly used projective identification to put his feelings of weakness and fear into me, while he tried to dominate our relationship and feel in control.

Every month, I cringed at giving Jack his billing statement. This countertransference was the result of his intense scrutiny and criticism of the bill each time I presented it. For several minutes, he would examine the bill with a serious and angry look. During the silence, I felt on edge. I felt relieved when he would grunt approval and wad the bill into his pocket. Other times, he would begin to question each charge and dispute one or two with increasing rage. I felt over a barrel and felt lucky when he finally paid the bill. I tried to talk with him about the bill but also about his feelings toward me. Jack wanted nothing to do with it at first. It made him even more angry because he thought I was blaming him and diverting his attention from the bill. Only during the second year of analysis could we talk about the bill as a way to understand his inner feelings and object relations, instead of a concrete problem to fight over.

I felt Jack was taunting and teasing me when he would go on about the marvelous spiritual healers, chiropractors, and massage therapists he went to. While he never came out and said it, the message was clear that these people were superior to me and their skill was far more advanced. I felt frustrated that he paid them more than he paid me. Again, if I brought this up, Jack saw it as me being greedy and not appreciating his need for back treatment and a special relationship to spiritual matters. All these situations were the interpersonal aspects of a sadistic projective identification process. Jack invited me, through projection, to feel humiliated, controlled, and betrayed. Those feelings made me want to lash out and tell him off. I tried to keep my analytic eye on these strong countertransference feelings and phantasies as a way to better understand what might be going on internally for Jack. I think he used projective identification to put painful feelings and anxiety into me, using me as a psychic receptacle.

This process of violent projective identification is a cornerstone of the acting out phase and continues into the second phase of treatment. It is the gradual giving up of such investment in pathological projection that begins to bring on the deeper experience of loss, pain, and guilt. Steiner (1996) has explored the ways patients cope with loss and with reality when they rely less on projective identification. I think that a gradual separation from the object that is being projected into is harder when envy and persecutory fears predominate. And, if these projections are given up too quickly, the ego feels the threat of annihilation.

Jack went to tarot card readers and psychics who channeled spirits. They told him about his past lives. Based on his belief that he was an important artist and guru in a past life, he felt he was being held back and ignored in his current management job. Part of all this was his avoidance of being dependent on me or others. His envy and contempt of others pushed him to act out. Jack felt in control by relying on metaphysical solutions because he thought of them as already "part of his spirit" and therefore something he already owned. Working with me, he felt I was asking him to give up his power and control, which left him feeling enslaved.

Ultimately, Jack's acting out was a defense against his unconscious fears of paranoid-schizoid loss and annihilation. Grinberg (1968) states:

> experience in acting out has taught me that one of its essential roots is often associated with experiences of object loss and separation that determined earlier mournings which were not worked through . . . Such experiences gave rise to extremely painful affects (frustration, anxiety, rage, guilt, depression, etc.) which the patients were unable to cope with.
>
> (p. 171)

Borderline and psychotic patients' ability to move through this defensive acting out is further compromised by their internal reliance on the DI as a defense against these fears of loss.

The early stages of treatment with these difficult patients are stressful for the analyst. Over and over again, the analyst must serve as a soothing envelope to contain, detoxify, and translate the patient's violent projections. Interpersonally, the analyst often must verbally restrain the patient from acting out. Interpretations have to be directed at inhibiting the more gross efforts at immediate gratification and frustration release. I think of this period as one where the analyst must be willing to temporarily, in some instances, restrain the immature and overwhelmed ego by restrictive and supportive measures. At some point, hopefully sooner than later, the analyst must bring these measures into the complete analysis of the transference. More often than not, the supportive efforts the analyst makes are in part a result of the manipulative and aggressive efforts the patient makes. As the result of being overwhelmed by anxiety, the infantile ego resorts to any measure available.

In other words, intra-psychic acting out and the psychological manifestations of the death instinct bring about ego deficit. These patients are so in the grip of internal conflicts, battles, and bargains with their objects that certain ego functions are unavailable, compromised, or kept in hiding. Cognitive abilities are sometimes projected into the analyst for safekeeping. Parts of the ego are actually working against the patient's efforts toward health and against the analyst's position as helper. In addition to serving as a transmuting container and auxiliary ego, the analyst must try to understand, tame, and interpret this intra-psychic warfare. In other words, the role of interpersonal and psychological container is always an active stance, never passive.

When necessary, the analyst can weave supportive and containing maneuvers into the larger psychoanalytic framework. Indeed, Wallerstein (1986) reminds us:

> The supportive aspects of all therapeutic modalities, psychoanalysis proper included, certainly deserve more respect and specification than is usual in psychoanalytic literature.
>
> (p. 730)

Is this more active approach still psychoanalysis or is it supportive psychotherapy? I think a more active approach still adheres to what Freud and Melanie Klein felt were the requirements of psychoanalysis: a rigorous attention to the transference and to the patient's unconscious phantasy state.

Providing an adequate container for disturbed patients who lack sufficient ego stability helps them develop their own capacity for symbolic thought. The analyst helps the ego shift from acting out to affect management and from emotional discharge to self-understanding. In providing such a detoxifying and translating envelope, the analyst immediately becomes aware of the patient's resistance to such self-understanding and reflection. The ego fights the increase in object-relatedness and self-relatedness. The patient's transference and extra-transference associations demonstrate the intrapsychic conflict and unconscious compromises that actually undermine psychic structure and bring on states of psychological deficit. The primary force behind this is the death instinct.

In trying to understand the concept of the death instinct, it is important to remember that it is an ego structure created from instinctual dynamics. Susan Isaacs (1948) wrote about the nature of phantasy and how phantasy is the mental representation of instinctual impulses. She felt phantasy is the psychological link to the biological nature of the human experience. In that both the life and death instincts blend in phantasy formation, the patient's associations, feelings, and transference represent the clinical and intrapsychic workings of core instinctual processes.

Setting aside this debate about the death instinct being biological or psychological, I think it is primarily useful to reflect on what the patient demonstrates in the analytic situation. In other words, I think the death instinct is best understood as a clinical phenomenon in which the psychological conflicts of unconscious destructive and aggressive forces play out in the transference. Segal (1993) states:

> one could formulate the conflict between the life and death instinct in purely psychological terms. Birth confronts us with the experience of needs. In relation to that experience there can be two reactions, and both, I think, are invariably present in all of us, though in varying

proportions. One, to seek satisfaction for the needs: that is life-promoting and leads to object seeking, love, and eventually object relations. The other is the drive to annihilate the need, to annihilate the perceiving experiencing self, as well as anything that is perceived.

(p. 55)

During the second year of analysis, Jack settled down and relied less on acting out to protect himself and communicate his feelings and phantasies. He still questioned the value of treatment and often brought up the idea of ending. He still changed his appointment times around frequently and got into trouble with alcohol and drugs, but much less than before. As the acting out faded, he started to show me the cruel and exhausting way he related to himself internally. As Segal points out, Jack's mind attempted to annihilate certain aspects of itself that had to do with object-seeking and perception.

Self-reflection and self-knowledge seemed dangerous and Jack tried to get rid of them as soon as they appeared. This intra-psychic dynamic, the workings of the DI, quickly shaped the transference. Jack told me, "endurance is better than exploration. I would rather endure all this pain and the shit I am in than try and figure it out."

A certain sadomasochistic dynamic played out between us that reflected his internal object relations. He would bring up some current problem or anxiety, inviting me to help. Then, when I tried to offer some help in the way of questions, clarifications, or interpretations, he would lash out. Jack felt I was attacking him and invading his privacy. He told me it was none of my business and he would sort it out himself. Depending on me or anyone else was simply out of the question.

Jack would tell me, after I tried to respond to something he brought up, "I am not interested in that now and I will never be. If I have something to think about, I will think about it and figure it out. You have no right taking that away from me. I hope you don't push it, because I am already feeling pissed and I don't need any more fucking pressure. Anyway, that topic is not something that interests me and it is not happening in my life at this very moment, so it is boring, useless, and a waste of time. If something isn't happening at the moment, I don't see the point of discussing it. And, if it is happening, I would rather think about it myself and not have you butt in!"

I felt utterly useless. Jack kept my analytic hands tied. My countertransference took over at times, leaving me feeling fed-up, angry, and powerless. At times, I wanted to give up on Jack out of despair and other times I felt like throwing him out of treatment.

Over the years, I continued to investigate his intolerance for my ideas and my curiosity. Slowly, through the transference and his associations, Jack revealed his dark phantasies and the way he tried to cope with them. After the third year of analysis, he told me, "I won't let myself even contemplate these things. I block them out, erase them, and eliminate them before they have a chance to grow and take over."

This dramatic description of his inner experience shows the persecutory nature of his internal objects. In this paranoid-schizoid world, one part of the mind is defending itself from another. Through projective identification, Jack projected the DI into the external world. Then, it was re-internalized with the same frightening and overwhelming flavor.

In Jack's case, his childhood was not an experience of being sheltered by helpful or supportive external objects. His oral projections, uncontained by his mother, turned the few good objects he had into bad ones. These bad objects were internalized along with the less-than-optimal external objects as new parts of the ego. Now, there existed one or several bad internal objects that his ego felt threatened by. Thus, one part of his ego had to find a way to defend itself against another part of the ego. In the transference, the analyst becomes identified with either the bad, persecutory part-ego or the persecuted, weak part-ego.

Essentially, the death instinct is a part of the ego that under normal conditions helps the ego to maintain psychic balance. It works with the life instinct to create the richness of what we call personality and mental functioning. However, when the DI becomes defensive and the ego lacks sufficient good internal and external objects, the DI is a self-defeating strategy that ultimately cripples the mind. Grotstein (1985) states:

> Klein . . . saw the death instinct as an inherent capacity of the primitive infantile ego to confront the experience of frustration. Yet she also saw the death instinct as one of the principal causes of that frustration . . . Although she hinted that the death instinct had some adaptive purpose for the infant's survival, she nevertheless concluded that the end result of its use was the creation of even more persecutory objects, thereby paradoxically transforming the death instinct into a maladaptive defense.
>
> (p. 302)

Jack's effort to erase the creative, reflective, and knowledgeable part of his mind was defensive. It was an act of the death instinct, trying to establish an inner equilibrium. By destroying one part of the self, the rest will survive. However, this turns from a rescue effort to a self-destructive process. Jack illustrated this when he said, "I am trying to keep myself at zero. I don't want to improve, that would be dangerous and besides the point. If I can avoid becoming a negative number, I am happy. I feel on the edge of losing my mind, my self, my sanity. Like I will be nothing but a pile of little broken pieces that get lost in the wind. If I can maintain myself at zero, I can prevent this. The only trouble with this is that I am all alone and can't ever reach anything or anyone." Here, he shows the workings of the

DI as a defensive reaction of the ego, trying to preserve itself. By keeping everything at zero, the ego eliminates the possible growth of bad, persecutory objects and contact with them. The ego sacrifices the ideal object and the desire for it to avoid annihilation.

The three phases of analysis I am outlining are usually mixed together and one phase may reappear after having been worked through. While helpful to separate for discussion, in clinical practice they overlap. While Jack was working through the difficulties of the DI, he would often act out, as a defense against both the death instinct and loss. When I brought up sensitive topics, he would warn me, "you are just asking for trouble, you know that! Don't go down that road, you son-of-a-bitch!"

Sometimes, Jack's struggle with his own mind and the death instinct appeared in the form of acting out. He tried to force parts of his ego to succumb to other parts of his mind. Transference acting out is often a direct clinical demonstration of the defensive force of the death instinct.

As I mentioned, in the first year of treatment, Jack would verbally attack me when I gave him his bill. It was a way of forcing me into a sadomasochistic relationship that protected him from deeper conflicts with loss and the forces of the death instinct. Now, in the third and fourth years of analysis, his reaction to the bill shifted. Each month, Jack would be puzzled or shocked over the dates and charges. He claimed to not recall meeting on some of the dates and always felt I overcharged him. "This is more than I can afford" was another complaint. If a month had an extra day in it, leading to a bigger bill that month, he would feel I wrongly overcharged him until I showed him the calender. Rather than attacking like before, he nagged me with this new lack of common sense. After months of this confusing disappearance of intelligence, things started to sort out.

Jack told me he wanted me to be responsible for times, dates, and amounts. He wanted me to remind him of how his finances were going and to monitor the details of his calender. Jack meant that quite literally. The death instinct strips meaning and symbolism from the mind and reduces relationships to black-and-white, all-or-nothing things and facts. I think of the DI as primary in normal development and offset by substantial introjection and identification with good objects. In other words, in ideal development, there is an equality between the influence of the life instinct, the death instinct, and the external environment. If certain aggressive phantasies predominate, if there are only meager and fragile good objects to cling to, or if the external world brings chronic trauma, then the death instinct turns defensive. Then, the ego relies on splitting and projective identification to survive. The fears and phantasies of the paranoid-schizoid position take over and dominate the infantile ego.

Jack felt a lack of containing or understanding internal objects to rely on; he felt surrounded by unsupportive external objects. His chaotic upbringing left him with a barren internal landscape and many overwhelming feelings and phantasies. Therefore, in the treatment he demanded I become his ideal ally. To accomplish this, he used projective identification and splitting to eliminate his own power and knowledge and instead he projected these into me. Jack had to constantly stifle and devalue his own independence and skill in order to make me his ideal object.

Over time, we realized he wanted me to be his ideal, all-caring father who watched over him and guided him through life. He felt this was a reasonable request and in fact demanded it as his right. Since he felt this was never given to him as a child, he now had the right to demand it from me. Jack said, "as my therapist, that is your job! I am mentally defective so you have to be willing to take care of me!" As we explored this wish, we discovered countless ways Jack discounted and denied his own identity. The death instinct was used to deny ownership of himself and to suffocate any trace of strength or self, in order to allocate me as a rescuing, mentor father.

Jack's desire for me to take care of him was very strong, therefore his ego's reliance on the DI was difficult to change. This transference remained in place for several years. Jack's transference was an example of what Melanie Klein (1958) discussed regarding patients who have the urge to destroy their objects as well as a wish to preserve them, even in distorted form. Gradually, Jack could look beyond this all-or-nothing wish and start to acknowledge his fear of losing me and being all alone. Here, he began to explore primitive feelings of guilt, annihilation, and hopelessness.

For some borderline and psychotic patients, the death instinct succeeds in chronically or permanently disabling the ego and manages to extinguish practically all of the mind's links to the good aspects of itself. This creates the profile I think is so often, mistakenly, described as a patient lacking in ego structure or a case of ego deficit.

Rosenfeld (1971) states:

> it is the destructive aspects of the death instinct which is active in paralyzing, or psychically killing, the libidinal parts of the self derived from the life instinct . . . the psychic structure dominated by a destructive part of the self succeeds in imprisoning and overpowering the libidinal self, which is completely unable to oppose the destructive process . . . in analyzing the omnipotent structure of the narcissistic state the infantile nature of the process has to be exposed in order to release these dependant parts which can form good object relations leading to the introjection of libidinal objects which are the basis of normal fusion.
>
> (p. 169)

As Rosenfeld describes, I think the release of dependent aspects of the ego is important. However, I also think the destructive aspects of the mind need to be analyzed because the death instinct is frequently a defensive ego function that blocks introjection of any positive object relations. The treatment of these borderline and psychotic patients must be a combination of the working through of the ego's destructive motives and the ego's inability or resistance to introjection of good objects (the life instinct).

Klein (1933) felt the superego was formed by the ego's projection of the death instinct. Just as Rosenfeld later maintained, Klein thought this primitive hatred could only be transformed through the introjection of good objects. Some analysts maintain that the hope for internal balance and a healthy ego lies in the taking in of new and supportive good objects. Again, I agree but feel there must be equal emphasis on the analysis of the ego's active cruelty. I think introjection of good objects is only possible through a reduction in the intensity of the death instinct.

Segal (1974) has described the pathological aspects of the paranoid-schizoid position and how a predominance of bad internal experiences cancels out the introjection of the ideal object and any possibility of identifying with it. I think Segal (1993) introduces a valuable technical consideration when she writes, "a confrontation with the death instinct, in favorable circumstances, mobilizes the life instinct as well" (p. 57). Here, Segal is pointing out the necessity of first analyzing the destructive aspects of the ego before the ego can start to introject good objects that will help to bring intra-psychic balance.

As Jack's acting out faded and his ego made less defensive use of the DI, issues of loss and persecutory guilt shaped the transference. He worried more about our relationship and the ways it might end.

Jack wanted to know my age and had questions about my health. He even wanted to know what type of exercise regime I was on, if any. At first, he said these were mere curiosities and that I should not think there was any "underlying meaning". I was reading too much into his questions, he said. However, Jack slowly revealed the true nature of his anxious phantasies.

My patient was worried his problems were so grave that we would still be meeting in thirty years. He thought of it as an interminable but necessary relationship in which one of us would surely die of old age. He was terrified I would go first and leave him alone, helpless and without direction. In talking with Jack about this fear, I explored his worry and guilt about destroying me or wearing me down with his problems. I interpreted that he felt his oral demands, his neediness, and his aggression hurt me and might even destroy me. He feared this would leave him alone forever, hopelessly in pieces.

Jack's phantasies contained anxieties about both loss and guilt, both of a primitive, paranoid-schizoid type. I agree with Grinberg (1964) when he outlines the developmental differences in the experience of guilt. He states:

> After Klein, probably Winnicott more than anyone else has stressed that guilt, although unconscious and apparently irrational, involves a

certain amount of emotional maturity, hope, and health on the part of the ego. In my opinion, however, there is still another kind of guilt which appears at an earlier period with a weak and immature ego. This guilt increases in intensity parallel with the anxieties of the paranoid-schizoid phase, or in the case of frustrations or failures during the evolution towards the depressive phase . . . I think that there is a close relationship between persecutory guilt and the death instinct, and between depressive guilt and the life instinct . . . in persecutory guilt the main elements are: resentment, despair, fear, pain, self-reproaches, etc. Its extreme manifestation is melancholia (pathological mourning). In depressive guilt the dominant elements are sorrow, concern for the object and the self, nostalgia, and responsibility. This is what we ordinarily see in normal mourning, in which we find sublimatory activities, discrimination, and reparation.

(pp. 366–368)

I think this early, paranoid-schizoid guilt is indeed persecutory in nature and the ego feels hunted down by the object. Eye-for-an-eye revenge becomes the fear. The object is experienced as having no capacity for understanding or forgiveness.

During this third phase of the analysis, Jack still questioned his bill and wondered about the monthly charges. However, he quickly felt frightened that his need for control and his desires to not give to me were destroying me. He felt he was "pushing me over the edge". Not only was he hurting me, but I would seek revenge. He thought I might just "lose it" and throw him out or that I might start screaming at him and become violent.

This sense of primitive guilt is part of a fear of loss. The paranoid-schizoid ego fears a permanent loss of the object and a subsequent loss of the self. The nature of the paranoid-schizoid position, highlighted by splitting and projective identification, brings with it phantasies of ideal objects and persecutory, attacking objects. When the ego feels its oral needs and demands have overpowered the object or taxed it, the guilt does not bring on the desire to make reparation. Instead, it is suddenly a question of survival. When envy and projective identification are excessive (Klein 1957), the ego is unable to process guilt in a reparative manner. Instead, the ego perceives the object to be overwhelmed and bent on revenge.

Sometimes, when Jack felt too fragmented and trapped by these phantasies of guilt and loss, he reverted to acting out. Fortunately, we would both recognize this and were able to work through it fairly easily. This resurgence of the ego's reliance on acting out and repetition of pathological object relations is typical of the third phase of analysis with these disturbed patients. Lipshitz-Phillips (1999) states, "resorting to repetition is more likely when there is less trust in 'good' objects and their capacity to survive" (p. 46). The paranoid-schizoid experience of loss is that of not having any good objects to trust in and having to contend with good objects gone bad.

Now six years into the analysis, Jack started to share other concerns. He was constantly trying to control his objects and his own desires. He had to do things "right" or he felt like a loser and was very hard on himself. He could not decide if buying a new shirt was OK because he already owned shirts, so why did he need more? Jack would obsess about how his relationships ought to be and all the ways they fell short. Everything became an overwhelming decision. How much to spend on dinner, where to go on vacation, or when to get his car washed were all quandaries that immobilized Jack. He was furious at how I fell short of his ideal analyst/father, how his family members fell short in being wonderful brothers and loving sisters, and how his employer fell short in caring about everyone in the office. Jack tried to exact almost total control over his internal and external objects. This was a reflection of the intra-psychic struggle between parts of himself. His ego and superego fought it out, trying to find some type of compromise. This was impossible because of the all-or-nothing battle conditions his paranoid-schizoid mind operated in.

Jack was having endless problems with choices, decision, and simple planning. It looked like a sudden shift into neurotic and obsessive ruminating, caused by an overly strict and judgmental superego. It seemed like a move into the depressive position and neurotic conflicts. On one hand, this was true in terms of better object relatedness, less paranoia, and some trust in finding love that would not turn into hate. However, issues of primitive loss and guilt still plagued him. Hess (1999) states,

> the cruel superego can exploit the depressive suffering of the patient and convert depressive guilt (responsibility) into persecutory guilt (sadistic accusation).
>
> (p. 127)

Jack certainly seemed to be haunted by a vicious superego that constantly tried to negate his connections to the object and to life. As Freud pointed out, this type of sadistic superego is representative of the death instinct. Jack's battle for control was a desperate measure to prevent a perceived rejection or abandonment. Equally, he was trying to stave off persecution and annihilation from his superego and the internal objects that had turned from ideal to dangerous.

This type of paranoid-schizoid struggle for control is spurred by the desire for an ideal object. However, the ego's strong oral demands for perfection and ultimate feeding shatter the ideal object. Then, the ego is left feeling disappointed, angry, wanting revenge, envious, and lost. This is projected into the object and the ego now feels persecuted and attacked.

Working with these patients requires the analyst to be especially aware of countertransference. Just as the patient struggles for the ideal object, the analyst may be seduced into wanting an ideal patient. Research studies show that termination is rarely as we hope for. Indeed, most patients stop treatment before we want them to. This is particularly true for patients such as Jack. The borderline or psychotic patient who is able to work through their acting out, the strong-arm of the death instinct, and the truly painful and frightening phantasies of loss and guilt is rare. Schachter (1992) points out that analysts probably see only 25–50 mutually agreed terminations in their entire career and most see far less. He goes on to point out research that shows at least 50 percent of all cases end without mutual consent. Taking on patients such as Jack raises these figures much higher.

In his seventh year of analysis, Jack decided to stop treatment. I felt he was doing better overall, but I felt he needed to continue. We discussed it for a month and then he left. He was thankful to know he could return if he wished to. This was an important feeling to explore as he still wondered if I might be so angry at his leaving that I would refuse to see him again. Jack clearly still struggled with issues of paranoid-schizoid loss and guilt. However, his internal and external life was very different from when he started analysis. He now had an ongoing relationship that felt satisfying and mutual. His job was a place where he felt fulfilled. He also felt he contributed to the organization and his coworkers. Jack had internalized my containing function and rarely acted out. When he felt overwhelmed, he was usually able to sort it out. He no longer attacked himself internally and could access life and new objects without negating his desires or efforts. While he still lived somewhere between the realm of the paranoid-schizoid experience of loss and guilt and the depressive state of whole-object integration, he was far more psychically consolidated. He now felt alive.

# Chapter 12

# Borderline and psychotic patients*

Because of a fragile hold on reality, some paranoid-schizoid patients and certain depressive patients easily regress into persecutory experiences of primitive guilt. As a result, these difficult patients frequently stop treatment early on. However, some are able to remain and form rocky relationships that can last years.

As outlined in Chapter 11, I have found three overlapping stages in the working through of such cases. These borderline and psychotic patients are in such intense states of anxiety and paranoia that the first stage of treatment is primarily a period of limit-setting, soothing, reassurance, and containment. I sustain and contain these patients through a combination of interpersonal and interpretive interventions. I find that ongoing attention to the here-and-now transference is critical and constant interpretation of anxieties, defenses, and extra-transference phantasies is essential for reducing the patients' near-panic condition. Overwhelming feelings and thoughts reappear throughout the analysis, but are defined enough to conceptualize it as the first stage in a particular type of analytic treatment.

Analysts are treating more patients who exhibit these disorganized and frightening ways of thinking and feelings. Ponsi (2000) states:

> Proper psychoanalytic treatments are few and decreasing in number, while treatments which for one reason or another don't fit with psychoanalytic criteria are the majority and, moreover, they are increasing in number.

(p. 1)

Jean-Michel Quinodoz (2000) adds,

> My clinical experience as a psychoanalyst confronts me more and more with patients who display a mixture of neurotic and primitive

* This chapter was first published as 'Three phases of treatment with borderline and psychotic patients', in *International Forum of Psychoanalysis*, 11(4, 2003): 286–295.

organizations in various proportions, according to each individual. During the initial interviews it very often seems to me difficult to evaluate the balance between the neurotic and the "more psychotic" parts of the patient's psychic reality. As Freud himself has pointed out in 1938, psychotic features are not restricted to the realm of psychoses proper but can also be detected within the "neurotic" and in the "normal" personality. (An acknowledgment which even today seems to be too disturbing to be widely accepted.) The presence of what we call nowadays "psychotic defense mechanisms" like denial, splitting, and pathological projective identification does not necessarily mean that the patient is a psychotic in the psychiatric sense . . . I have learned that both these levels (the neurotic and psychotic) of the patient's organization can be worked through on the couch.

(pp. 1–2)

Many of these patients act out tremendously during the first phase of treatment. In fact, many of them abort the analysis altogether. However, some work with the analyst to reduce their discomfort enough to continue. As Quinodoz stated, these cases, while involving difficult transferences and psychotic or primitive defenses, can be approached with the psychoanalytic method.

While my technique during the first phase is more of a combination of support, education, and analysis of transference and phantasy, the direction remains analytic. I follow the direction of Fenichel (1941) when he remarked,

Everything is permissible, if only one knows why. Not external measures, but the management of resistance and transference is the criteria for estimating whether the procedure is analysis or not.

(p. 24)

We strive toward many ideals for sound theoretical reasons, but never obtain them in the actual clinical work. Adhering to "the treatment frame" is an ideal, but rarely a reality. At times, to adhere to the frame, whatever that might mean, is to lose the patient. With one entitled, anxious, borderline woman, bringing up the idea that she should pay for missed hours led her to scream at me and run out the door. When I spoke with her on the phone, she demanded that I stop trying to control her life. I agreed to not charge her for missed meetings and we continued the treatment. While she now controlled me by not paying for missed sessions and she did not allow us to ever discuss it, we were still able to meet twice a week. After five years, she told me that she "could see my point" and would give me "twenty-four hour notice" if she were to miss. More importantly, we began to talk about how she organized her life around phantasies of being controlled and of controlling others. Now in treatment for seven years, she talks openly about her struggles with letting me and others get closer to her and her fears of what that might mean. Again, I think of these types of parameters or non-traditional analytic work as all part of a warming-up phase that may or may not lead to a full psychoanalytic experience. It is the building up of intra-psychic momentum in an otherwise closed mental system.

As reflection and curiosity replace fear and acting out, the second phase of treatment emerges. Here, the patients reveal strong intra-psychic struggles with the death instinct (DI). Due to excessive envy and oral aggression (fueled by pathological projective identification, splitting, and idealization), often combined with environmental trauma, the patient's ego is at war with itself. Through projective identification, the death instinct compels one aspect of the mind to do away with other aspects of the mind. This defensive function of the DI also becomes externalized via sadism and acting out in the transference.

This second treatment stage of the death instinct is defined by dynamics quite different from the first stage of containment, yet equally challenging. Patient and analyst often enter a standoff as they externally play out the patient's internal battles. The analyst is burdened with countertransference feelings of hopelessness, rage, and disinterest.

If patient and analyst can endure this second phase without becoming hopelessly stuck in mutual acting out or without the patient prematurely terminating as a way to gag certain parts of their ego, then a third phase of treatment unfolds.

The first phase of acting out and intense anxiety is the result of and the defense against the workings of the death instinct. Repetitious working through of the death instinct reveals its defensive function.

The third phase is a gradual working through of the more bedrock phantasies and feelings of primitive guilt, paranoid-schizoid loss, and per-secution. The eventual goal is ego integration and the achievement of the depressive position. However, the patient must first deal with overwhelming phantasies of loss, which generate the experience of annihilation. With this type of paranoid-schizoid loss, the good, idealized object is replaced with a bad, persecutory object wanting revenge. The ego is left without safety or control.

Not all patients are able to stay in the treatment long enough to work through all three phases. However, I have seen enough borderline and psychotic patients display these phases to think that these patients' intra-psychic struggles and the way their treatment unfolds all constitute a particular working-through pattern. This includes those fragile depressive patients who rely on pathological organizations to cope internally. My impression is that some of these difficult patients see many therapists over the years and may work out one phase with one analyst and another phase with another analyst. However, it seems there is a clear pattern of structural pathology and unconscious phantasy that unfolds in this three-prong manner.

## CASE MATERIAL 12.1

After several years of analysis, P had improved a great deal. She attended three times a week and used the analytic couch. Diagnostically, P entered treatment functioning at a primitive borderline level. Her gradual internal growth and object-relational shifts gave her a different internal and external life experience. P had stopped a lifelong pattern of binges and vomiting that had landed her in the hospital several times. She no longer banged her head against the wall or yelled at herself when frustrated. P did not get drunk anymore and she had not burned herself with a cigarette for a long time. She held a better job and now she got along with her roommates. This progress was the result of a stormy but successful period of containment. I served as a container for P's projective identifications and as the recipient of her split-off feelings and phantasies.

The way I analytically related to P was shaped by my assessment of her anxiety level, the nature of her phantasies, and her chronic feelings of rage and need. Paula Heimann (1956) pointed out this pairing of technique with the patient's intra-psychic structure:

> The essential causes of the differences in psychoanalytic technique are in my view related to the analyst's appreciation of the role played by unconscious phantasy in mental life and in the transference.
>
> (p. 305)

In my opinion, the understanding of, working through, and mastery of internal phantasies are the goals of psychoanalytic treatment.

Bit by bit, P was able to function as a container for herself and manage her own affects and thoughts. This phase of analytic containment led to the next period in the treatment, the analysis of the death instinct and its manifestations in P's internal and external experiences.

Despite her overall progress, P still felt quite depressed and stuck in life. She couldn't figure out what to do for a career, even though she enjoyed her new job, and she wasn't able to find a fulfilling romantic relationship. P felt time was running out. She saw most of her friends married and secure. P envied them and felt that kind of happiness was beyond her reach.

One day she was sobbing and told me how trapped she felt. "I don't know what direction to take and even if I knew which way to turn, I don't have the will to try. If I make a move, a part of me is on alert and ready to hunt me down. It feels so hopeless." Over time, I addressed this as a fear of me harshly judging her. She was so busy trying to appease me that she couldn't sort out what she really wanted. I use the word appease because P wasn't really trying to please me and win points. She was more trying to avoid a negative feeling between us and some type of revenge or punishment. Over time, she told me this was a lifelong fear of being abandoned, abused, or both. A phantasy of being used until being useless and then being discarded colored most of P's close relationships, including the transference.

P experienced these mental and emotional troubles as coming from others at times, but often she felt it was as if a part of herself was after another part of herself. She would routinely hear my observations, clarifications, and interpretations as critical and accusatory. She would say, "you don't have to tell me I am a fuck-up, I already know that!" The more we explored her persecutory transference phantasy, the more she was able to highlight her internal persecutory experience. As we understood the transference distortion, we could see how a part of herself was indeed after another part of herself.

P told me, "I have this feeling. Actually, it's more like a fact. I have been sentenced for something, a crime or something else very bad. But, I don't know what it is. All I know is that I have to be very careful to avoid a terrible attack on myself. My sentence is to be very still. This is also the way I stay safe. I can avoid being attacked by maintaining a zero level of growth, always keeping everything at a zero balance. If I try and gain something or rise up and achieve something beyond misery, that is when I will definitely be attacked."

Throughout her analysis, P struggled with these feelings and thoughts. The more we explored them, the more it was evident they were mostly issues of annihilation, loss, and persecution. At first, the words she used to describe the phantasies sounded like oedipal conflicts regarding competition and fears of retribution for besting the parental figure. However, the more we analyzed her feelings and how they manifested within the transference, it was evident that this was a much more primitive experience. Rather than avoidance of phallic success, P was coping with pre-oedipal fears of fatal rejection. Her ego was faced with permanent loss of self and object. Likewise, she appeared to relate in masochistic ways to me and other important figures. However, it was not a strategy to gain masochistic gratification. Zero growth was a survival strategy to avoid persecution. This feeling of being hunted down came from a sadistic, destructive, and intolerant part of herself that kept close watch for any level of defiance. This was an intrapsychic projective identification process that was anti-life and anti-growth. Here were the workings of the death instinct emerging in the treatment. The strength of the death instinct in this patient led to its appearance in the interpersonal and transferencial aspects of our relationship.

Over time, I felt like P needed to maintain this vigilant stance for her safety and also as the only way to connect to me. It became clear that she deliberately hid any growth or life-affirming thoughts from me and from this destructive part of herself. To always see things as grey and grim assured her that her relationship to the object would remain predictable and constant. When some evidence of life and success leaked out, P feared the end of our relationship. She told me, "why would you let me come in if I only had good things to report? We would be different together, things would change." Indeed, she feared positive feelings and achievements would bring on abandonment and criticism. P said, "we are not here to discuss any positive crap. That is useless for our purposes. Obviously, we are here to focus on how bad I am and to find out why I am such a fuck-up." It was only after I asked lots of questions and pulled for details that I learned P was promoted at her job and the hospital staff had presented her with an award for good service. She filtered the life out of things, so I was given a very stark and negative picture of her daily existence.

As this dynamic went on, I noticed it took two forms. I became the voice of life, pointing out P's progress and her various accomplishments in and outside the analysis. She took on the voice of the neutralizer, the naysayer, and the voice of death. She would point out how each victory was hollow or tell me we weren't paying enough attention to the "important stuff", her failures. So, through splitting and projective identification, she had me hold the desire for life while she held on to the destructive aspects of her ego. This split would routinely shift, again through projective identification, to the reverse. I noticed I was at times being overly positive and invasive with my interpretations. I realized I was being dominating and pushy with my "supportive" comments. Indeed, sometimes I felt like saying "look, you are doing fine! You need to enjoy life!" I think this type of transference–countertransference dynamic is set in motion because of internal projective identification mechanisms and because these types of patients are often both defending against the death instinct and using it to attack parts of themselves. One part of the ego is attacking another part of the ego, which tries to defend itself. Via projective maneuvers, this intra-psychic battle begins to rage interpersonally.

Patients like P make the analytic situation into a battleground with progress, growth, and knowledge pitted against immobility, ignorance, self-criticism, and denial of object-relatedness. Narcissism is a common expression of this urge to destroy the link to the other. P seemed on a mission to destroy any evidence of uncertainty, need, desire, or vulnerability. She felt no compassion for herself and thought that was a disgusting attribute to have in the first place. Therefore, any link to me based on empathy or compassion was considered ridiculous. P said, "you just say what you do because you have to. I don't want your pity!" She would get very agitated and yell at me if I commented on her tender feelings for her boyfriend or her lonely feelings for her family. And, if I brought up her transference feelings, she would become outraged and tell me in no uncertain terms how I was grossly mistaken. Technically, I always operated as I do with other patients. I interpreted the transference, the extra-transference, her desires, her anxieties, and her defenses. However, I also paid close attention to the way she was so focused on destroying parts of herself and her link to the object. At this point in the treatment, I geared most of my interpretations toward the clinical manifestations of the DI.

P considered the desire for knowledge, feelings of curiosity, and any degree of uncertainty all poison and something to eliminate from her mind. She avoided people who seemed to have these toxic qualities and she hated the quest for knowledge our relationship represented. P didn't want to be "contaminated". Her violent reactions to my interpretations also revealed a breakdown of symbolic function. She felt my questions and comments were equal to a sexual assault. Sharing her thoughts and feelings was the same as being robbed, owned, or invaded. Through projective identification, she put the destructive parts of her ego into me and experienced me as a persecutory inquisitor. During these more psychotic moments, I found it best to ask P to explain, in detail, what it was I said that made her feel so defensive. We could then slowly take a second look at it and see how she had started to distort me and our relationship with her own feelings and phantasies. This period of reflection was often bumpy and stormy and took several sessions.

After several years, P's grim and grey approach to herself and our relationship began to soften. She was less cruel and less destructive. She started to play little sadomasochistic games with me. She would start a session by saying, "OK, go ahead and see if you can get something out of me." Over time, we understood this as a complex mixture of wanting me to care for her by asking questions and her defense against this caring in case it turned sour. This process was soothing, sexual, and scary all at once.

Gradually, the workings of the death instinct diminished as we explored and analyzed it from countless angles. For patients like P, I find it important to interpret the intra-psychic projective identification process that goes on between different aspects of the ego as well as the way it manifests within the transference. Extra-transference situations are also valuable to explore, as they often are easily traced back to intra-psychic struggles. As the layers of defenses and anxiety fell off, P and I were confronted with her bedrock fear of loss. I think that when the death instinct is operating as a defense, it is often a defense against a primitive, primal form of loss and persecution. Upon analysis, this turns out to be a paranoid-schizoid experience of loss in which the ego faces annihilation of both self and object.

Now, the nature of P's analysis took on a different flavor. The ongoing self-destructive aspects of the death instinct still made a jungle out of the treatment, but more and more we dealt with P's phantasies of being attacked and rejected. This fear of abandonment was of an all-or-nothing nature, in that she felt either I would truly understand and love her or that I was uninterested and ready to get rid of her. I was either for her or against her. This was the result of excessive reliance on projection. P put her oral aggression and desires into the object and then felt hunted down and overwhelmed.

The more we worked through the clinical manifestations of the DI and P's self-destructive ways, the more her internal experience of loss and persecution came to light. She was afraid that the objects she craved for could easily turn on her. The combined phantasies of being persecuted and being left alone were very difficult for P to work with. She had avoided talking about these feelings and avoided exploring her thoughts about them. However, bit by bit she was able to deal with these anxieties in this phase of treatment.

P told me the following dream. She realized, with shock, that she hadn't ever graduated from highschool. P didn't remember anything else about the dream and felt "blank" about it. She had no associations and she didn't know what it might mean. I first commented on how she was able to give me the dream and look to me for guidance on what it might mean. This dependence was different from her usual stance.

Listening to the dream, I thought of the recent sessions/classes P had missed with me and how she might have feelings about graduating from analysis. For some months, we had been exploring the ways she hid her achievements from me and denied any evidence of success. I commented on how the dream might infer her fears of success just as she seemed to fear succeeding in our relationship.

Here, I was using my own countertransference associations to organize the dream. I believe my ideas were influenced by her projections of intolerable thoughts and feelings. Rather than being a violent projective identification process, this was more an effort at communication and safety. P was using me as a maternal envelope to take in and translate the contents of her mind.

P said she was frightened to get better and graduate. She said she was scared about being on her own and how lonely and hopeless that felt. P told me a phantasy of waking up in handcuffs on a floating iceberg in the middle of the sea. It was an incredibly stark and lonely feeling and there was no hope of ever being found. Interestingly, after I offered my association, she was able to take in my function as a container and begin to reflect on herself.

Her dream and her associations to it show the oedipal↔pre-oedipal, paranoid-schizoid↔depressive position nature of her internal world. While she felt oedipal competition, guilt, and power, the underlying threat was a pre-oedipal loss and violent persecution. P was not afraid of punishment, she was afraid of being banished to utter and total isolation. When P missed sessions at this point in the treatment, it usually meant she felt I was going to "force" her to act independently. So, she tried to leave me before I left her. She pictured me taking away my support and leaving her on the lonely iceberg. P thought I was trying to "make" her grow up and in the process abandoning her. Then, she would revolt and refuse by regressing and demanding to be parented.

Another dream during this third phase of P's analysis illuminated the ongoing struggle between destructive parts of her ego and other parts that felt threatened and lost. P was standing in her home next to a litter of puppies trying to nurse. Suddenly, a vicious pit-bull attacked the puppies. P tried to rescue them but could only grab one puppy and run. As she was running, she dropped the puppy and it broke, like glass, into hundreds of fragments.

P was able to explore this dream and engage me in understanding it. She wanted more of a team effort than the other dream where she wanted me to take care of her. With this second dream, P felt we could work together. Exercising her own intellect didn't have to mean she was all alone. We understood the dream to represent remnants of the DI, in which part of her mind was vicious and out to destroy needy and vulnerable parts of herself. The hungry puppies were her neediness and her desire for my love and knowledge. The pit-bull side of her tore this bond apart. P tried to act as a container for the puppies but was only able to accommodate one puppy and she dropped it. It broke into hundreds of pieces, much like P's mind turned on itself and shattered the more needy parts of P. We discussed the parallel of her not being able to contain and save the puppy and her early experience with a mother who clearly was too preoccupied to properly tend to P. Historically, P felt her mother had dropped her over and over, just when she needed to be saved and protected.

This fear of loss and the breakdown of a container into more of a harmful agent colored the transference. There were times when P thought I was masturbating in my chair as she lay on the couch. P's fears were twofold. She thought I was abusing her by thinking of her sexually and trapping her in a dirty, dangerous, and immoral relationship. At the same time, she feared I was ignoring her and phantasizing about someone else. Here, I think she is demonstrating pre-oedipal and oedipal struggles with loss and persecution. Still later in the analysis, she feared I would die and leave her forever. This made her very anxious and overwhelmed. With both phantasies, I interpreted her projective identification of oral aggression and desire as well as genital wishes that were put into me and felt as belonging to me. These were feelings she thought were wrong or dangerous and she tried to expel them via projection.

After five years of analysis, P had progressed a great deal. Externally, she lived a full life. She had decided to change careers and focus on her creative urges. She went back to school to become a designer. P now had a steady boyfriend whom she trusted and who treated her well. Her day-to-day life was more relaxed and grounded rather than a fight for survival. These changes were the result of internal shifts in her object relations. P no longer lived within an intra-psychic battle-zone. Now that her mind had plentiful good objects and her aggressive oral drives and phantasies had been worked through, she no longer had to attack herself internally.

At the time of this writing, P still struggles with some paranoid-schizoid feelings of loss and guilt, but has a much better ability to deal with them. Most of the time, she experiences life from a more integrated, whole-object perspective. In other words, she may feel overwhelmed or guilt-ridden at times, but she feels able to forgive herself, restore her object, and find sustaining, safe contact with her internal object relations.

## CASE MATERIAL 12.2

Randy, a young doctor, is an example of a higher-functioning patient, more oedipally secure than P, but still very much struggling with the death instinct and issues of primitive loss and persecution. He was a high-functioning borderline patient who was prone to occasional psychotic regressions. He used the analytic couch and attended four times a week. Randy, and many patients like him, have a tenuous and fluctuating hold in the depressive position and frequently experience paranoid-schizoid phantasies of persecution and primitive loss. The idealized object fades and is replaced by an attacking, revengeful bad object.

I contained Randy in the beginning by very supportive interpretations closely matching his moment-to-moment affect state and not venturing out of that immediacy too much. Interpersonally, I contained him by letting him pay an extremely low fee and let him owe me for several months. I used logic, reassurance, and interpersonal support to help him deal with overwhelming feelings of anxiety and overpowering phantasies of persecution. After the first year or two, he took over this role and managed himself most of the time. Of course, we explored the many meanings of his wanting me to be in that role and the difficulties of giving that up.

Randy had entered analysis because he felt depressed. He was sleeping on a friend's living room floor and couldn't decide what to do with his life. The indecision and anxiety prevented him from working so he was almost homeless. For several months, he was unable to work due to feeling depressed and paranoid. At one point, he slept in a homeless shelter. Sometimes, he thought I worked with a secret team of colleagues who found subtle ways of testing his sanity and evaluating his commitment to therapy. When his home phone rang and no one was on the other line, he was sure it was a "test" from me and my "team". When he went out to nightclubs, he thought that I had planted spies to watch him and report back to me. Randy also feared I was slowly brainwashing him and would eventually hypnotize him into having sex with me. All these delusions and psychotic phantasies slowed down when I used a containing and supportive approach.

At the same time, I maintained the analytic focus by always bringing us back to the transference and his phantasies as they played out in the extra-transference.

Randy now works in a hospital. This is his third job after completing his schooling. His residency and the last two jobs were marked by great turmoil. He felt unable to count on his superiors and ultimately made them angry by passively ignoring their various requests. He had a "who, me?" way of relating that eventually enraged his supervisors. At the same time, Randy felt powerless and weak in his professional and personal life.

Randy hasn't had a steady relationship in ten years and is still very attached to his mother. His mother, a devout Catholic, always wanted him to be a priest. She also felt he should stay at home and take care of her. As an adult, he feels very guilty about dating and following his interest in medicine and medical research.

In the transference, I have often been the authoritative mother he censors his dirty thoughts from. He secretly has fun on the side. He feels very guilty about this but also enjoys rebelling against me and playing out a power struggle with me internally.

These sessions were from the middle of the third year of analysis. He had just started his new job at the hospital. His parents had moved out of state to retire a month prior and the Christmas holidays were just around the corner.

## SESSION I

*Pt*   I feel so tired. I have so much trouble sleeping. My stomach is also very upset. [He talks about his physical problems for a while.] Yesterday was my first day at work. It was really difficult. They didn't issue me a desk yet and most of my supplies weren't delivered. I don't even have a computer yet! It is a big hospital so there is so much red tape, it's hard to get much done. One of my supervisors asked me for some feedback on a project they have had in place for several months. It was strange to be looked at like someone who knows what they are doing. I felt intimidated.

*A*   How?

*Pt*   Well, it all seems so new. I guess I feel out of place. I don't feel like I fit in very well.

*A*   Like you don't have the right to what you think?

*Pt*   Yes. I guess what I said was OK. They seemed to like it. I don't think they have been running the department very efficiently. One of the other department heads was there and I didn't feel comfortable. It's like I am better one-on-one, but in groups I get nervous. He wanted to know what I thought and I asked if I could have some time to think it over. I felt put on the spot.

*A*   You sound worried about having your own opinion.

*Pt*  Yes, I do. I wasn't thrilled with some of the work that had been done in that department but I can see what they are trying to do in general. I just felt uneasy. Maybe, I feel I can control one mind at a time, but not a whole group. But I need to be able to interact with groups more, it's important for my career.

*A*   You are being asked to be more of a leader. From the way you relate to me, we know you prefer to be a follower and get me to be the leader, at least on the surface. You're more comfortable being the little guy and criticizing me or whoever is in authority. If you are in charge, you will be the judge, executioner, and victim.

*Pt*  Exactly. This new position means I will have to make lots of decisions and there will be people leaning on me. But, I think I can count on X for support. I am worried how I will do. If I can do it. But, even though I try and get myself worked up into a lather and feel like quitting, this time around I don't think I will actually do that. I am getting better with this stuff, not as reactive or full of crisis. I am in the big leagues now, but I am not as freaked out.

*A*   Having to be strong and showing your own identity makes you anxious.

*Pt*  Yes. Instead of being the little boy who takes orders, I want to be more of my own man. When I try and explain that to my family, especially my mother, they have no clue. They come from such a different place, everything should be about family and religion. If I don't devote my life to my family and to God, then I am doing something bad. It's hard for me to believe in what I do too. My mother called me this week, believe it or not. Usually, she makes me be the one who always calls. She started to put me down for my lifestyle and said she was very disappointed in me. She wants me to come home and "be sensible". She says she and my father are getting old now and need help. Why is that my job? She started crying and said she has lost her son. She said I have turned my back on her and the family. Of course, God was brought up, which is always so hard too.

*A*   You feel like you are hurting your mother by having your life.

*Pt*  Yes. I am just starting my life and not ready to do all the things she wants me to do. Part of me wants to cut off all contact with her for good, just run away. Maybe if I move to another state or country it would be better. Or, maybe I should give up my life and move back home and take care of them. [He goes back and forth about this for a while.]

*A*   Somebody will end up hurt. Either you or them.

*Pt*  Yes. I feel I will have to give up everything to be loved and accepted, or at least not criticized.

*A*   I think your feelings are so strong that it colors all your relationships. You feel you could step on toes at work, that you will betray your mother, and that you will get in trouble with me if you tell me everything.

*Pt* Yes. But, do I have to give everything over to you to get insight? It is all about balance. I feel I either have to give everything up or I get into lots of trouble. So, I end up disguising what I feel and what I want. [Here, he is revealing the all-or-nothing quality of his object relations and his fear of losing contact with the object should he retain his identity. Either he gives up his sense of self and feels lost or he gives up his object and feels annihilated. I think this demonstrates the mixture of paranoid-schizoid and depressive conflicts he struggles with at this point in treatment.]

*A* Like how you tried to tell me you needed to conduct some research in Europe when really you wanted to go on vacation. You thought I would try and own you if you started to have your own ideas. You worry there is a power struggle going on.

*Pt* Exactly. I paint things a certain way. I try and look innocent and not say anything that might make you criticize me. But underneath, I am thinking something else. I was afraid to tell you because it would be considered bad and you would try and convince me to do it your way, whatever that is. It's so hard to make any decisions.

*A* Especially when you feel they impact on me or your mother.

*Pt* Oh yes! I don't know if I am abandoning her or if they are abandoning me. I don't know. I am so confused, I feel pulled in two. I have so many dreams but I tear them down and think about how I need to devote myself to therapy and my family instead. So, eventually I have to come up with secret plans to do what I want behind your back. All this makes it impossible to get involved in a relationship. [He discusses a recent relationship where he felt the woman began to pressure him. Both the woman and then him felt mistreated and abandoned. This is very much how he sees his bond with his mother and with myself.]

*A* Your feelings about your mother really affect all your relationships. You are not sure if you are hurting all of us or if we are picking on you and controlling you.

*Pt* Wow! Yes. I hadn't ever thought of it like that before.

## SESSION II

*Pt* [He discusses how expensive it is to maintain his lifestyle and how much he worries about money. He talks about his concerns as if he is almost penniless, while in fact he has a great deal of money in savings.]

*A* Since I know you actually have money in savings, I think you are really talking about how you don't want to spend your own money.

*Pt*  I told my concerns to my supervisor and they managed to get me a cash advance. It is a real relief. Today was really intense. I had to talk with the department staff about how they are operating and running things. It turns out they really have no plan at all. There is a real lack of organization. I mentioned some of my concerns, which felt really strange.

*A*  You don't feel properly taken care of by the hospital and their way of running things. But, you also feel uncomfortable to take charge and make sure you do get taken care of. [I decide to take up his response, rather than point out how he ignored my comment. From the past, I know he will try and engage me in a sadomasochistic power struggle if I reflect on his dismissal. So, I choose to contain that for the moment and see if we can use his statement as a vehicle.]

*Pt*  Good point. Yes, I can see that. It is like I don't want to do something that would assure me security. That is weird. If I do, it's in a secret, round-about way. I do it under the table.

*A*  Why?

*Pt*  Because I would have to depend on other people if I did it above board. [He discusses how he would like to save for a new car but it is hard to do. Yet, he says he refuses to ask for help from anyone because of the strings that come with depending on others, especially family.]

*A*  So, the new car that you get all by yourself is like a mixture of spite, guilt, competition, and independence.

*Pt*  You have that right. But, it is hard to hear that out loud: spite and competition. That is hard to take. Yet, you are absolutely right! Goddamn it! I guess I feel like I really need to prove a point, with my parents and everyone else.

*A*  How so?

*Pt*  Well, I am not sure. Maybe it is that other people don't see me as capable or that I have a legitimate opinion or a legitimate life for that matter. [He elaborates.]

*A*  You are worried about being judged, so you want to be seen as legitimate and get approval from myself, your parents, and work.

*Pt*  Well, I think part of me wants to conform and part of me wants to rebel. I wish I could have both and not feel so divided. But, I don't want to be boring and a part of the system, like my parents. But, I also do want to have some security like they have. I go back and forth in my mind and judge all this stuff so much. I think that if I could just live each day without picking it apart so much, and just accept myself and my decisions, then I think I could enjoy each day. I want that so badly. [Here, he describes the obsessional dilemma he weaves around himself to deflect the more anxiety-producing paranoid-schizoid phantasies of loss and guilt.]

## SESSION III

*Pt*   I am feeling more in charge of the department now, but it is frustrating. Nothing seems to be getting done. I don't even have all my equipment yet. In general, the staff seems to be very laid back. Their commitment isn't very strong. No one is around to make any decisions. [He goes on for a while.]

*A*   Sometimes you want others to take charge and take care of things for you, but then you feel they do a lousy job.

*Pt*   Yes, that is true. OK. I have been thinking about that lately. Should I take more control of things and make a few more decisions or not. But, the hospital is all split up. [He discusses how he sees all the departments working against each other.] I am also very upset because I want to go and visit my parents for the holidays but I can't afford the ticket. I could ask my father but I know he will say no. It upsets me because I would like to be with them. My father seems so tight with his money.

*A*   I am interested in how you feel hurt that your father won't pay for your ticket, but you have more than enough to buy it yourself. It is like you are denying your own abilities and instead feeling like he should buy you a ticket. Maybe you think that is the least he can do given how angry you feel.

*Pt*   Wow! I never thought of that! Wow. Now, I feel really pissed at myself for not thinking of that solution. It is so much simpler. Wow. That is sure something to think about. [He takes my comment as concrete advice on buying a ticket and ignores my confrontation on his greed and sense of entitlement.]

*A*   You feel others don't take proper care of you, so you often refuse to take proper care of yourself. I wonder if you feel that would be giving in to me?

*Pt*   [He agrees with what I have said and then elaborates a bit. Then, he starts to talk about how empty and bored he is with life and how meaningless everything seems. He sounds genuinely depressed and alone. I think he is starting to feel the pain that he hides behind his sadomasochism and obsessional judgment.]

*A*   I think you want me to take care of you and run your life sometimes, and you end up feeling powerless and aimless without me. By having no opinions and decisions, you can keep us safe and conflict-free, but then you feel controlled and dominated too.

*Pt*   That is interesting. Yes. I think that is probably on target. Ouch. Yes. I do feel better when I take charge of things, but what often happens is I start to feel overwhelmed by all the things I think I should do and accomplish. [He elaborates. I think he is revealing how he depends on my superego as a less harsh and less demanding object than his own superego. When he tries to parent himself, he becomes a tyrant.

Therefore, I look like a less cruel dictator. Eventually, however, he tires of being bullied altogether. Then, he secretly rebels.]

*A*  So, it might feel better to let me order you around a bit than to be really bullied by yourself.

*Pt*  There you go! Yes. Sometimes, I go back and forth so much with myself that I feel I really am going crazy. I do notice that I've started to try and talk with people more and reach out a bit. Even though I feel I am disturbing them, it feels good. [I notice the double message of his closeness and his satisfaction in disturbing the object.]

Randy's current progress is mixed. He continues to excel at his job and is gaining respect from his peers. He has dated a few women, but never follows through in ways to build the relationship. Overall, he is more within the depressive position and whole-object functioning as a result of treatment. However, he uses the depressive position, with its obsessional defenses, as shield against the deeper phantasies and anxieties of paranoid-schizoid guilt and loss. I think he is still very much working through his fears of being abandoned by a disapproving mother object and being attacked and persecuted for being a bad son. His oral aggression leaves him with disabled and disapproving objects and few good objects to balance out his internal experiences. Yet, given his history of steady progress in analysis and his willingness to improve, I feel he will gradually find more intra-psychic integration, inner fulfillment, and a sense of guilt-free self-identity for which he craves.

# Chapter 13

# Oral deprivation, envy, and sadism*

Melanie Klein (1957) writes,

> Greed is an impetuous and insatiable craving, exceeding what the subject needs and what the object is able and willing to give. At the unconscious level, greed aims primarily at completely scooping out, sucking dry, and devouring the breast; that is to say, its aim is destructive introjection; whereas envy not only seeks to rob in this way, but also to put badness, primarily bad excrements and bad parts of the self, into the mother, and first of all into her breast, in order to spoil and destroy her. In the deepest sense this means destroying her creativity.
>
> (p. 181)

Some patients only want to be given to and deeply resent having to give anything back to the analyst. Their whole way of relating to life seems shaped by envy and feelings of deprivation. These patients seem emotionally ravenous and determined to raid the analyst's emotional resources. At the same time, they refuse to let you treat them because they perceive analysis as submission to a controlling persecutor. They want to hold the power in the relationship and they often demand answers, pills, insight, or cure without wanting to work for it. While they typically do not know what the pills or cure would consist of, they simply want whatever the analyst has to offer. At the same time, the fear of becoming emotionally vulnerable and the worry of becoming the analyst's property drives them to erect fairly intractable defenses. There is a vicious cycle in which, as Klein described, the ego wants all and then more of what the object has. However, the rage and envy causes the ego to project poisonous bad parts of itself into the object, making the source of desire contaminated and unavailable. This increases the feelings of deprivation and rage.

* This chapter was first published as 'Oral deprivation, envy, and the sadistic aspects of the ego', in *Canadian Journal of Psychoanalysis*, 7(1, 1999): 97–110.

Riviere (Klein and Riviere 1964) writes:

> dependence is felt to be dangerous because it involves the possibility of privation . . . one situation in life where we all must feel dependent, whatever our circumstances are in love-relations . . . Our dependence on others is manifestly a condition of our life in all its aspects: self-preservative, sexual or pleasure-seeking. And this means that some degree of sharing, some degree of waiting, of giving up something for others, is necessary in life. But though this brings a gain in collective security, it can mean a loss of individual security as well. So these dependent relationships in themselves tend to rouse resistance and aggressive emotions.
>
> (pp. 7–8)

Riviere's ideas are helpful in understanding the patient who is always bitter about being denied access to what is inside the analyst. Simultaneously, this patient feels weak and pathetic for having to depend on or even desire what is inside the analyst.

Freud (1913) likened the analytic process to a chess game. Working with this group of patients is more like playing "battleship" or "hangman". It appears to be a non-relational, cold, and ruthless competition to best, beat, and destroy the opponent. They play out prey–predator phantasies and analysis becomes a bloody arena where the patient craves to incorporate the analyst's mental and emotional supplies. The analyst feels compelled to either do battle in return or run for the hills. Below the surface, the patient feels desperate and dependent, wanting to cannibalize the analyst's identity. These are all urges that are defended against with a variety of primitive protective devices.

In the infant's first months, it relates its rage, fear, hunger, love, and other confusing experiences to its object. Biological needs, emotions, and phantasies are all communicated to the internal and external mother by means of introjective and projective mechanisms. Depending on the mother's ability to stabilize and translate some of these chaotic states, the infant introjects an object that is soothing at times and persecutory at others. This early paranoid-schizoid position (Klein 1946) of either fleeing or combating internal evils, while simultaneously searching for soothing objects to cling to, fosters a primitive differentiation.

This gradual differentiation builds elementary mental constructs of the self capable of affecting the object. Countless events during the infant's early development give him a crude sense that he can make a mark on what is "other than self". These innate phantasies, colored by environmentally rooted experiences, involve not only destructive capacities but loving and altruistic urges as well. The knowledge that one's love or hate can affect the object marks a maturational step in ego development. It fortifies the ego's perceptive abilities, sense of power, and altruistic inclination.

Phantasies of destroying the object, spoiling its special supplies, and otherwise losing contact with it because of one's impulses are major developmental milestones in ego maturation. These anxieties signal more two-person, whole-object experiences than part-object egocentric perspectives. The ego now generates phantasies involving abstract and sophisticated concepts of parts of the self, with various loving and hateful wishes, causing specific ramifications within complex two- and three-person relationships. The infant now feels, "I can do something to you, I can affect you."

While promoting structural growth, this awareness is equally frightening and potentially fragmenting. Survival-based schizoid concerns enrich the emerging superego. The ego and superego start to concentrate on the well-being of the object, although in extreme ways. At this point, the concern is still an egocentric one based on survival of the self rather than any altruistic motive. The projection of aggressive and loving parts of the ego and the introjection of persecutory and soothing part-objects all foster a gradual differentiation, consolidation, and integration of self and object representations. The former narcissistic bliss of phantasy fulfillment changes to a dim awareness of conditional relations. The infant becomes aware that the food supply is not always accessible. This leads to primitive anxieties about the needed nourishment.

The ego is pushed to certain phantasies about hoarding, guarding, losing, stealing, and spoiling its object. Phantasies of the object being attacked, harmed, or destroyed start to influence the infant's internal environment. Thus, schizoid fears are the heirs to the paranoid position. The ego develops various tactics to rescue, restore, or maintain the safety of the object. Manic defenses, splitting, denial mechanisms, projective identification, and primitive reparation are but a few protective devices used to cope.

One patient, Paul, was telling me about a movie he saw concerning a psychiatrist and several patients. He told me at length about one patient who never felt he was getting enough therapy and always felt so desperate and needy that he listened in at the doctor's door, hoping to share in some of the hour before his. Paul then told me about another patient who was constantly angry with the psychiatrist and regularly hurled insults at him.

After a while, I proposed that he might have identified with the movie characters and wanted to let me know how he was both desperate to be closer to me and receive more care, but also felt very angry and dissatisfied with me at times. Paul said, "I don't know how to handle it when you say stuff like that. All my doors slam shut. Maybe I shut them. When you tell me something like that, I normally refuse to listen. I feel it's like a new challenge that you're giving me. It's a difficult, painful, bloody, obligatory mission that I should undertake. You are forcing me to do it and I don't want to."

Paul paused for five minutes. Then he said, "does it make you angry that I am so much of a loser, totally out to lunch?" I said, "I am giving you a part of me, my ideas and observations. You somehow feel threatened by my offer and you start to rebel. You refuse to let me in. After a while, you're worried that you made me angry by shutting me out." Paul replied, "Anything to do with feelings has always meant pain, so if you say something that makes me feel, I freak out. If I can't get away from it, I shut down. Yes, feelings have always been so damn painful, intolerable. I just don't want to feel."

Throughout his treatment, Paul felt he was pestering, punishing, or brutalizing me with his needy, clingy wishes to be with me. Simultaneously, he felt angry with me for not letting him feed on me whenever he pleased. He felt I coldly rationed my love while he craved to "free feed" at it.

In this chapter, I am focusing on patients who have an overwhelming need to be as close to the analyst as possible, yet they are constantly upset over feeling rejected, unfed, and not properly cared for. In addition, to "admit" that they are in such need feels fundamentally unacceptable. With analysis, this proves to be a fear of overwhelming and destroying the object and being all alone and lost forever. These phantasies often include the idea that the object will then rise from the grave to seek revenge. This is not only a regression to paranoid phantasies as a defense against the horror of having killed off the only source of needed emotional supplies, but also an extension of primary process thought where life and death exist together and nothing is mutually exclusive. This is the schizoid world of split-off portions of the self and of the object, a land where anything is possible. This makes the patient's internal experience both exciting and omnipotent as well as frightening and out of control.

The paranoid experience promotes a differentiation and awareness of a separate object. However, the warlike atmosphere of the paranoid position pushes this differentiation into a feeling of a standoff or a fragile truce, where there is a tedious and tentative agreement between two parties to not attack each other. They certainly are not supportive or helpful to each other.

Klein's depressive position can be thought of as a reconciliation between these warring internal factions. How to build and maintain a truce, how to not destroy someone you depend on, and how to trust one's impulses and those of the object all become conflicts of the maturing ego. Two different yet interdependent objects learn to negotiate and relate without destroying each other. Change is then possible, without being experienced as a sadistic invitation to pain and destruction of self and other.

## CLINICAL MATERIAL 13.1

Wanda had been seeing me for nine years in psychoanalytic treatment. At the beginning of treatment, she believed I took secret pictures of her, arranged to have people follow her and report back to me, and conducted cruel experiments on her under the guise of "psychology". Wanda would cry and yell at me, demanding more frequent sessions and telling me I was heartless and not in tune with her needs. When I would offer her additional hours, she would become intensely paranoid, afraid that I would hurt her and "do mean things to her". She was always angry, feeling that I did not emotionally feed her immediately and in the exact way she wanted, yet when I offered to give her what she wanted she felt attacked. I frequently spoke to her about how she felt she would destroy me with her insatiable needs and that I would then seek revenge. The first few years, she would respond with, "yes, can you tell me something I don't know?!" Later, she began to be more curious about these fears.

During an hour that had been rescheduled to early in the morning, she told me that she noticed I was parked in a different spot, that my eyes seemed red, and that my office fan was on. I asked her what these things meant to her. Wanda said they meant I had just started my day. Therefore, she was my "number one most favorite patient". I said she was being watchful of me and was happy to think of herself as so close to me and favored in my heart. Wanda replied that she was angry at me for bringing up such "useless, worthless, and meaningless shit" that had nothing to do with her at all. I felt dismissed and thrown away and noticed myself settling in for what seemed to be another one of our many tedious sessions together.

Wanda then began discussing how she never gets along with anyone. She gave details of various fights and broken relationships where she never seemed to be able to bond with anyone. I commented that we often did not seem to get along. Wanda shouted, "there you go again, you shit!" After her telling me off, I felt more and more that I might indeed be "a shit" and felt we had embarked on yet another slow ride through hell.

Wanda then switched to asking me if she could work for me and be my personal secretary. She said it would be a way to "be with me always". Then she asked, "if I move out of state, will you move with me?" I commented on her wish to be close to me and her fear that she might lose me in the process. Wanda said, "no way, I just need a job. There are bills to pay, you know!" I repeated my comment. Wanda paused and then began sobbing. "Yes, it's true. I am so scared!" But, she then went back to discussing her need for a job. I told her it was time to end the hour. Wanda said she didn't want to leave and that she wanted to stay with me "always". I told her I would be happy to see her more often but that I had to stop for right now. She would not move, challenging me to make her go. I said I knew it was extremely hard to leave me when she felt so in need and wanting of my safety, but that we had to end for now. She got up and said, "I wouldn't want to work for the likes of you anyway!" and stomped out into the waiting room.

Diagnostically, Wanda was a psychotic woman who had an oral craving to consume her object out of need, desire, and revenge. She was easier to work with than other such patients because she had a better capacity for insight than many patients I see. This is not simply a matter of being "more psychologically minded". Insight is a process of allowing the analyst's interpretations into the mind and giving those thoughts back in the form of a reflection or conjecture. Unfortunately, such patients feel insight is an internal experience of being pierced or raped by an intruding "thing", followed by feeling forced to sacrifice or give up a vital and irreplaceable part of the self. The analytic process feels like an attack and a demand that they refuse to give in to. After many years in treatment, Wanda started to tell me things like, "I think I get scared of you when I want your love." She was able to have insight into her core fears and phantasies.

Schizoid conflicts can erode existing ego capacities and prevent growth of new or more mature ego functions. Therefore, Wanda's insight was not structural change: it was more in the line of structure building.

These patients are taxing and hard to treat, since they tend to feel nothing is ever enough but do not want to give anything in return. They feel talking, thinking, or feeling is something the analyst is forcing them to do. In turn, they hate the analyst and seem uninterested in the analytic process. The analyst feels provoked by the assaultive oral demands and devaluation, often leading to countertransference envy of the patient's seeming ability to just throw people away without caring. Treatment, if analyst and patient can tolerate it, consists of repetitious interpretation of the patient's chronic attempts to use splitting, projection, introjection, and projective identification to get inside the analyst and take what they feel is their birthright. The oral rage, neediness, and one-sided greedy urges to take must be addressed over and over again. The analyst has to carefully monitor the potential countertransference problem of using interpretation as a way to seek revenge on the patient.

Again, Riviere (Klein and Riviere 1964) was thoughtful about these matters. She stated:

> Turning away in contempt or rejection from a desired object can be a dangerous psychological reaction, if it is not used merely as a restraint on greed, and especially if revenge and retaliations inspire it as well. The most impressive evidence of this may be seen when such a reaction leads to suicide – when disappointment and the fury of revenge engender such hatred and contempt of life and all it offers that life itself is finally rejected and destroyed. Such people spend their lives seeking, then finding, then being disappointed because their desires are inordinate and unrealizable either in quality or degree; ultimately they turn away, spurn and reject – only to start the search instantly all over again.
>
> (p. 21)

This endless search results in patients who go through many different therapists, like so many old tissues. The analyst is only useful if the patient feels full of pain and ugly internal waste. The analyst/tissue becomes unimportant garbage after the patient uses them for discharge.

Wanda was overwhelmed with envy for what she felt I denied her and she felt ashamed and frightened to admit to her need for what I represented. Therefore, she often coped with these conflicts with verbal attacks and devaluation of my worth. Klein (1957) writes, "Defense against envy often takes the form of devaluation of the object. I have suggested that spoiling and devaluing are inherent in envy . . . devaluation and ingratitude are resorted to at every level of development as defenses against envy, and in some people remain characteristic of their object relations" (p. 217). Wanda felt close to me and needed an emotional feed from me. This became distorted by her envy until she could not bear the pain. She was resentful and spiteful and tried to spoil the treasures she craved by devaluing them.

While the process of projective identification is an intra-psychic mechanism, it often includes interpersonal derivatives (Sandler 1987). The extent to which a patient can seduce the analyst into echoing their internal conflicts is a method of both communication and evacuation (Maroda 1995). On one hand, the analyst then is in an advantageous position to help the patient. On the other hand, if overwhelmed and confused by these projections, the analyst can easily begin acting out the concordant or complementary (Racker 1968) countertransferences. In the former, the analyst would identify more with the patient's ego state and phantasies about the object. In the latter, the analyst would identify more with the patient's internal objects and be prone to treat the patient accordingly.

## CLINICAL MATERIAL 13.2

Kevin spent most of his hours yelling at me about how I "gave him nothing, was worthless, and never helpful in any degree". He would regularly ask in a cutting, cold manner, "when will you ever do anything that remotely helps me? I have never experienced such a waste of time or money!" Kevin had come into treatment after five serious suicide attempts in two months. Initially, he felt very needy and wanting of my help. Very quickly, he felt dissatisfied and resentful about not being filled and cared for properly. He stopped coming, citing my incompetence. After two more suicide attempts, he returned to me in the same cycle of collapse and emotional hunger, only to again feel I was failing him. He would try and deposit his frustration, despair, and rage into me as a way to save himself from and to reek revenge on his unavailable internal objects. I told him, "one of the best clues we have so far is that you now hate me as much as you do everyone else in your life. When you first came to see me, you hated yourself and felt you were inferior to everyone else. Now you have put your self-loathing into me and are trying so hard to feel better yourself. The only problem is you feel lonely now because you can't get close to me since you see me as so useless."

Kevin would sometimes be so provocative and yell so much that I longed to yell back, "I don't like you either, you are a self-centered, demanding, difficult baby!" Using my hate and dislike as an internal communication that needed to be translated, I would instead say, "it seems so hopeless between us. Perhaps it is important for us to understand how it is that you have come to see me as so completely worthless, unable to satisfy you."

In these types of difficult treatments, one often stumbles. I would find myself regretfully saying such psychobabble as, "you must be feeling upset right now" or "you appear to be angry right now". I believe these were emotional hatchets I dug into the patient's back, thinly disguised as therapeutic empathy. It was a way to retaliate, using the tools at hand.

The oral deprivation these patients feel drives them to seek out the object of their desire with an intensity that is staggering. The craving, demanding, and unending thirst they have for love is riddled with hate and fear. They are driven by internal starvation and emptiness to try to consume the object, yet they persistently feel the object is unobtainable. This phantasy of unavailability fuels their angry, righteous outbursts. At the same time, they are sure that the object will be crippled or destroyed by their neediness. The object would then be gone and they would wither away into oblivion. Usually, they also feel the object will return to exact revenge.

Therefore, these patients constantly fear being annihilated through persecutory attacks or painful abandonment and they avoid the object as a way to save both the object and themselves. Clinically, this takes the form of a patient who screams for closeness and attention yet pushes the analyst away.

These patients are aware on various levels of their ability to destroy the object. They are so full of hatred and frustration that they usually act out the rage and only later partially reflect on their actions.

## CLINICAL MATERIAL 13.3

Doris could be extremely sadistic. This was an identification with internal objects that seemed to both refuse to feed her and purposely hurt her. She would delight in making me feel controlled and helpless, alternating between withholding parts of herself from me and attacking me in cold and vindictive ways. She also would succumb to paranoid regressions about how I was "trespassing into her mind". At the start of one hour, she told me, "I am feeling far too happy today, so hopefully I can count on you to make me pissed off and depressed. You usually come through for me with that." She was a woman who clearly longed to be fed by her objects but worried that she would become too full, happy, and excited which would somehow cause her objects to be furious and damaged.

To these ideas, Riviere (Klein and Riviere 1964) states:

> Rejection can even be a method of loving . . . aimed at the preservation of something unconsciously felt to be 'too good for me'. Desertion then 'saves' the goodness . . ., spares it and rescues it from one's own worthlessness, which could ruin it.
>
> (p. 23)

As with most of her hours over years of analytic treatment, Doris managed to bring us into a sadomasochistic battle of excruciating intensity. As I sat there feeling furious, defeated, and controlled, I asked her, "I wonder if I am feeling like you did growing up: defeated, controlled, and helpless. It's a feeling of no matter what I do, I can't win." Doris replied, "Absolutely. That was how it was every single day of my life!" Then Doris fixed her gaze on me. She said in a measured, cold way, "don't worry, you will slowly get used to it. You will realize there is no way out and that this is the way it will always be no matter how hard you try. You will slowly learn to adapt to it and live with it. Don't worry, you will learn to endure it, bit by bit." I felt washed over by hate and revenge and I felt scared.

So far, I have not surrendered to those tortured feelings that she grew up with. I find that through our ongoing fights and power struggles we are able to talk about them a bit, in the context of our relationship. This interpersonal working through, as well as the intrapsychic struggles I regularly grope my way through, make for a gradual and mutual working through of her internal conflicts. Ferro (1993) spoke to this when he said:

> it seems to me that the analyst's task is to rediscover the emotional truth of the patient's mind, through the suffering of the analyst's mind and capacity to tolerate pain and truth in his or her own psychic life.
>
> (p. 392)

Part of the suffering Ferro may be thinking of is the ability to hold many conflicting part-object relations together, even when buffeted by intense countertransference emotions. At times, we are the only one in the room able to so. Indeed, perhaps it is a sign of therapeutic progress when the analyst begins to experience more whole-object relations with the patient. That may signal a halfway point in the treatment in which both parties experience a growing gratitude and respect for the mutual as well as individual efforts being made in the relationship. This would include a gradual mourning process for the idealized aspects of the relationship that never materialized.

# Part IV

# Working toward change in the face of overwhelming odds

# Chapter 14

# A case study of borderline anxiety*

As the case material in the last two chapters shows, the analyst can help these patients to work through their projective identification-fueled acting out and self-destructive patterns. At that juncture, strong and painful phantasies of loss emerge within the transference and in extra-transference situations. This is a pre-oedipal, part-object experience of loss and persecutory guilt. While many of these patients prematurely terminate well before they begin exploring these anxieties, some are able to work through enough of their core phantasies of self-and-object annihilation anxiety to reach a foothold into the depressive position. Internal transformation is possible and the patient can reach substantial whole-object functioning in many aspects of their intra-psychic and interpersonal life. I will use one extensive case report to further illustrate these complex layers of projective identification and self–object struggles.

## CASE MATERIAL

T entered analysis in her thirties, with a tangled mixture of symptoms. She would only travel on major roads or highways, as smaller roads made her feel overwhelmed and all alone. She felt the "world suddenly vanished".

T drank excessively, mostly on the weekends when she no longer had the structure of work. Her job as a manager for a clothing firm felt boring, a way to simply fill time. She had several close friendships, but T felt guilt for wanting to spend more time with her friends. She felt she was too clingy, needy, and draining. When she tried to find emotional intimacy with a man, T was constantly disappointed. She tended to date men who were distant and who left her after a few months. Sexually, T had relations

* This chapter was first published as 'A case of borderline anxiety and the process of analytic transformation', in *American Journal of Psychoanalysis*, 65(2, 2005): 149–165.

with men who used her. She was blinded by idealism and the wish to be comforted.

When feeling depressed or lonely at work, she masturbated in the bathroom for a sense of self-soothing. This, along with drinking, prevented her from feeling scattered and hopeless. Intermittently, she would also bite her arms until they bled. Also, T tended to overeat so she was overweight by almost fifty pounds.

T was the youngest of two children. Her father was an investment banker who did well in his career but was rarely home with the family. Being an alcoholic, he was unpredictable and often hostile. T's mother was an obsessive woman who needed everything to be just so and parented according to her needs, instead of for the children. She thought T and her brother should be completely involved in culture, sports, art, and music. Therefore, at any given time in her childhood, T was shuttled to and from tennis, piano, painting, dance, soccer, French, aerobics, and girl scouts. She rarely had time to think or feel. As an adult, T created her own frantic pace to avoid her feelings. While T's older brother seemed to adapt to mother's schedule, T felt lost and rushed. What disturbed T the most was that these activities were all for mother. Her mother never asked T what she would like to do. Consequently, T felt her mother was uninterested in her abilities or desires. This left T feeling ignored and used.

As a teen, T was quiet. She put up with her father's unavailability and abusive ways as well as her mother's controlling, self-centered manner. In college, T struggled to maintain herself. She had no sense of identity and no real direction so she was not motivated to learn and barely passed her classes. When she dated, she picked men who were a combination of her parents' negative attributes, leaving her hurt and hopeless about herself and her future.

As an adult, T had a string of sales jobs and then landed her current job at a clothing firm. She excelled at this because she related to the customers as her ally. Through splitting and projective identification, she put her desire to be understood into the customers and saw her coworkers as villains. She comforted herself by allying with the customers, being bonded together against the coworkers. Because of this projective process, she often felt controlled, ignored, or abused by her company and coworkers. T felt abandoned and persecuted in her career, just as she felt with her parents, and eventually with friends, with lovers, and with her analyst. One result of this was that T longed for an ideal object to care for her and with whom she could identify.

Understanding T's early development was important to her analysis. Melanie Klein (1936) felt the individual's earliest experiences of painful and frightening situations, both internal and external, built and maintained phantasies about hostile internal and external objects. T was exposed to painful external circumstances as a child. In addition, she was left to make sense out of her internal feelings and thoughts: her phantasies. She felt her mother was unaware of and uninterested in her internal state and her father left her lonely and intimidated.

Most of what I knew about T's early development was from latency onwards. It was unclear if this was different than her experience as an infant, but my sense was that it was very much the same.

Decisive to T's childhood difficulties was the lack of proper psychological containment. Kleinians (Bion 1967; Segal 1974; Hinshelwood 1999) place importance on the internalization of a maternal container that accepts, manages, and transforms primitive anxieties and phantasies. Segal (1974) states:

> the infant's relation to his mother can be described as follows: When an infant has an intolerable anxiety, he deals with it by projecting it into the mother. The mother's response is to acknowledge the anxiety and do whatever is necessary to relieve the infant's distress. The infant's perception is that he has projected something intolerable into his object, but the object was capable of containing it and dealing with it. He can then reintroject not only his original anxiety but an anxiety modified by having been contained. He also introjects an object capable of containing and dealing with anxiety . . . the mother may be unable to bear the infant's projected anxiety and he may introject an experience of even greater terror than the one he had projected.
>
> (pp. 134–135)

T lacked adequate internalization of a containing object and therefore felt overwhelmed by her phantasies and feelings. When things (feelings, ideas, and people) didn't make sense, T felt a confusing and frightening void.

T's ability to learn in school, learn from interpersonal relationships, and learn from her own thoughts and feelings was stunted. Klein (1928) has described the epistemophilic impulse as the innate desire to know and own the contents of the mother's body. Later, this extends to wanting to know about and possess the father's penis. Normally, these driving phantasies are sublimated into a thirst for knowledge in social and educational realms. However, the ego may stop itself from this quest for knowledge out of hatred or concern for the object or out of fear or envy of the object. T's conflicts with her own desires to know, relate to, and possess her parents corrupted this yearning. She no longer was curious and instead felt stupid and lost.

This emerged within the transference in various ways. T was very anxious at the start of her analytic work. She wanted help but felt I would control her. She told me I was a "cold fish" who didn't really care. All her friends were able to understand her and "share with her", "like normal people". I was stuck up and unwilling to give her the advice she needed.

Scheduling our sessions was difficult. T did not see the point of meeting regularly. She wanted to come in "as needed" and wanted to meet on the phone to avoid the traffic. Using the analytic couch was "stupid and weird" so she demanded to remain seated. Although she went on vacations and spent a good deal of money on clothing and parties, T insisted she could only pay a modest fee.

In this first phase of treatment, acting out was prominent as a defense against frightening phantasies and transference anxieties. I tried to tailor my interpretations to her in-the-moment transference experience. Specifically, I interpreted her feelings of persecution, her conflicts over establishing a connection to me, and her anxieties over being abandoned, abused, or manipulated if she were vulnerable. Also, I interpreted her confusion and ambivalence around thinking and feeling, as it meant she would be creating more of a self-identity, which appeared to be a threat to her internal objects and therefore to herself. Rather than having immediate impact, my comments had more of a gradual and cumulative effect.

Over time, T was able to take them in, store them up, and slowly use them as a bridge to me, as a container for phantasies and fears, and as a new way of thinking. However, it was only through the gradual analysis and working through of the transference that she could truly begin internalizing and integrating my comments and our relationship.

Her excessive reliance on projective identification retarded her ability to take me in as a comforting, containing object. She experienced the same type of resentment and fear that she had around taking in her mother as a viable and trustworthy container.

Much of T's initial thinking was on a non-symbolic level, so she acted out her feelings and thoughts. She focused on debates with me about who was doing what to whom and who was right or wrong.

During the first few years of analytic work, T alternated between demanding instant emotional feeding and then spitting out my attempts to offer support and insight. She would seek instant cure for her problems and say, "tell me what is wrong with me!" and "when will I feel better?" These were said in a way that was confrontational and demanding. I commented on her aggressive way of relating to me and tried to explore the deeper meanings of this angle of transference.

Early in treatment, T would respond with, "you are here to tell me what is wrong and to fix it!" She felt nervous and uninterested in participating. When I invited her to take part in understanding herself, she said she was quite bored and felt the whole idea was a waste of time. Indeed, she told me it was useless because she was beyond hope. "Some people just don't ever make it, ever!", she exclaimed. This fatalistic and self-defeating resolve was one of many clues to her internal self-destructive cycle. There seemed to be a destructive part of her mind that was pitted against other more hopeful and curious parts of her mind. This struggle was externalized into the transference via projective identification. This acting out served as a brittle compromise, or internal bargain (Waska 1999), with her objects to deal with her fears and desires of intimacy, dependence, and aggression.

T worked out all the time at the gym and felt lost without her daily regime. Indeed, sometimes she would cancel her analytic sessions because of some workout-related event. Not only did T not see the benefit of analysis, she felt it got in the way of the rest of her life. Here, she used projective identification to give me a dose of what it must have been like being with a mother who insisted activities were all-important, to the loss of personal identity or interpersonal relating.

It was striking how when I told her it might be more painful to see me than to work out and that she might come across difficult feelings that she normally ignored, she began sobbing. However, she could not understand why she was crying and started to judge herself as "stupid and silly".

I think these types of difficult borderline patients require an analyst who is capable and willing to act as a flexible psychological container for the patient's multiple projections. Treatment, especially in the beginning, must be an ongoing process of containing, managing, and co-regulating these patients' intra-psychic and interpersonal conflicts. The analyst must provide an elastic envelope for long periods of time until the patient is able to internalize this containing function. The analyst serves to translate the patient's acting out into verbal expression and their concrete thoughts into symbolic phantasies. The desire for instant gratification must be met with the analyst's inhibiting envelope of understanding and interpretation.

Along with projective identification, countertransference and counterprojective identification (Grinberg 1992) are always an issue with these patients. When T demanded advice, guidance, and immediate cure, I felt harassed, tense, and inadequate. Only when I dealt with my feelings as the sum result of her aggressive and needy projective identification efforts did I feel more stable. When I did not deliver all that she wanted and she snapped, "well, forget it then. I am probably better off dead anyway", I felt manipulated and wanted to strike back. When T sobbed and said, "all I want is to be loved!", I felt her pull my heartstrings. I wanted to take care of her. When she related to me in these and many other ways all within the same session, I felt confused, overwhelmed, and along for a chaotic ride. Again, trying to understand and analyze these projective mechanisms as her way of acting out anxiety and aggression gradually helped to stabilize both of us. Here, it was as important for me to silently interpret to myself about my feelings as it was to verbally interpret to her about her feelings.

T was unable to find closeness with her objects and felt those objects were rejecting and cruel. This anxiety was usually hidden by her acting out. Brenman (1982) explored this phenomenon in depth:

> The patient may act out: he may indulge in loveless sexuality, stuff himself with food, drink, hatred, criticisms and grievances to comfort himself. He may become excessively intrusive or, by virtue of projection, feel excessively intruded into by others. He may be occupied with continuous activity to avoid the experience of separation.
>
> (p. 303)

T acted out her phantasies and fears of separation and loss through external and internal means. She had been through four abortions by the age of twenty-eight. This was a traumatic and painful recreation of her conflicts around intimacy and loss. She drank and smoked and put herself in violent relationships to mask her feelings.[1]

T's conflicts within the transference, as well as extra-transference situations, were the result of intra-psychic projections of her struggle with herself. T had feelings, thoughts, and phantasies that were object-related strivings geared toward knowledge, strength, intimacy, and growth. On the other hand, T strove to erase or destroy these desires.

This came out more intensely during the third year of treatment. T had a negative and cruel attitude towards life and toward the growth potential of analysis. T told me treatment was completely useless because she would never change and never get better. She told me, "I am damaged beyond repair and that is that! This is my personality and it cannot be changed!" Her gritty, aggressive negativity evoked my countertransferences. When she said for the hundredth time, "I won't get any better and I don't see the point in trying! I am fine the way I am. Why do I have to keep coming here? Why should I talk about myself?! This seems pointless!", I felt like saying, "fine! So, get out and leave me be!" In projecting her hopelessness and frustration into me, I now had to contain what she was both unable and unwilling to manage in herself. Through this type of reflective self-analysis,

---

1 As mentioned in previous chapters, Melanie Klein believed the life and death instincts were critical to consider in analytic work. The ego is strained by separation from important objects so the life instinct strives for reunion and mutual inter-dependence. The death instinct tries to rid the ego of its need for an object and any evidence of hunger, desire, or dependence. In healthy development, there is a balance between the two. If, however, the ego is violently separated or torn from its needed object, the death instinct operates as a core defense mechanism. Acting out is the external response to these feelings and phantasies of separation and loss. My patient, T, seemed to illustrate these theoretical concepts rather clearly in her transference and extra-transference ways of relating to herself and her objects.

I avoided acting out my countertransference much of the time. Nevertheless, we would have periodic standoffs and quarrels.

Over the many months and years of treatment, things did slowly shift. T expressed more of her feelings and thoughts. Eventually, she was able to confide in me as more of a trustworthy object. T said she was afraid if one of us was not in control or in authority, we would "just be like friends". She explained her fear of becoming not only too close and "merged", which felt dangerous, but that we would be rendered useless to each other. In other words, knowledge had to come with domination and power. To give up control was to give up the security of knowing. We would both be lost and confused. It was better to be a bully or feel bullied than to never find a solution to her anxiety. This dominating way of relating, a power-struggle, served to cancel out the dangerous togetherness and dependency that felt so fragmenting. While the "merging" sounded sexual, T mostly felt a sense of danger and impending takeover. If it was a sexual phantasy, it was equivalent to the threat of mental rape. Generally, I interpreted her projection of controlling mother feelings into me as a way to prevent a sense of loss, annihilation, and emptiness. A conflicted relationship was better than none at all. It felt safer to be either a rebellious slave or a slave-master than to risk the deeper, more threatening sense of nothingness.

T had made considerable progress by the fourth year. Externally, she had stable employment, regular friends, and took better care of herself. Internally, she felt less chaotic, less persecuted, and less impulsive. At the same time, this was a time in which she became more resistant and self-destructive.

T took a more dig-in-the-heels attitude. The less she acted out, the more T put herself down and eliminated her progress. Positive relations with herself and others were systematically pushed away or beaten down. T managed to place herself in a one-down role with me and many others. She would go to work wearing an "I am a bitch" T-shirt and then wonder why her coworkers teased her and didn't want to include her in their circle.

As T made clear progress in her analysis, she began to sabotage it and tear it apart. She became the queen of "yeah, but . . ." when she saw evidence of her own advancement. The transference took on a sadomasochistic quality in which T invited me to be a judgmental, controlling mother who punished and lectured her. At times, I was drawn in and we acted out these roles before I was able to point them out. Bit by bit, we both started noticing these situations and became curious. Sometimes, however, T took advantage of them and told me, "see, I knew you were disappointed" or "see, I knew you felt irritated with me. I am a shit and you obviously agree!"

Over the years, T had gone from dating very dysfunctional and abusive men to dating much healthier men. This was the result of her working through certain projective identification dynamics that were acted out interpersonally.[2] During this phase of treatment, T shifted into a more destructive type of dating that paralleled her darker transference. T now dated men who were unwilling to commit to her or emotionally give to her. Rather than be curious about this pattern of not getting her needs met, she felt she had done something wrong. At every chance, she took the blame for things not going well. In the transference, she also personalized things as her fault. T started to apologize for all sorts of offenses. She felt she was too late, too whiney, too slow to improve, and too poor to pay me adequately. This was a sadomasochistic projective identification situation in which she looked to me to be the parent who made it all better, but feared I would turn into a scolding and rejecting parent. This difficult period of the analysis ushered in the deeper, core phantasies of loss, guilt, and persecution.

T had strong opposing intra-psychic forces in how she related to herself. When these phantasies began to overwhelm her, they were often projected into the transference. She then pitted one of us against the other, creating persecutory anxiety in herself and countertransference discomfort in me. This resulted in frequent power-struggles. This affected her other relationships, causing tension at work and dysfunction in her love life. T exhibited this self-directed prejudice between the different sides of the mind in her struggles with dependence versus independence, sameness versus difference, strength versus passivity, and denial versus curiosity.

In the fifth year of treatment, T began to explore her deeper phantasies of losing her objects and simultaneously being attacked by them. This terrifying state included strong feelings of guilt over having hurt the object with her greed, neediness, and aggression. Rather than feeling the object could forgive her or that she could make it better, T felt her feelings and thoughts brought on irreparable catastrophe. She feared being persecuted and then rejected. In her part-self, part-object experience, T anticipated a state of total annihilation.

2 Projective identification is an unconscious mental mechanism in which the ego projects certain loving, fearful, curious, aggressive, and needy feelings and phantasies into the internal object (the unconscious mental image of the mother and father). This is motivated by certain primitive anxieties, feelings of love, guilt, and reparation, and the desire to communicate. The ego then relates to that internal object accordingly. If strong enough, this process "leaks out" into interpersonal relationships and influences how both parties interact. The ego begins to feel overwhelmed by this distorted object and re-introjects it, creating a new identification. Now, the ego feels it contains the properties of this former object and begins to react accordingly, with anxiety, grandiosity, and so forth. This often prompts a second projective identification cycle since the ego feels overwhelmed or "too full" of these new feelings and strands of newly created identity.

The multiple functions of projective identification include coping, defense, creativity, reparation, and communication. Being able to tell how, why, and when the patient uses projective identification is critical in the therapist's ability to form helpful and accurate interpretations.

T said, "I am afraid if I get close to you or anyone else, I will get really hurt. I will get rejected or criticized and then I will get abandoned. Then, I will be forgotten. It is easier to get into trouble or kick myself until I can't move. Fighting is familiar. I am the gun at my head, but I hold the gun. I am in control. I fuck things up first, so no one can fuck me up!" Here, she described both the self-destructive and defensive aspects of the death instinct as well as the fearful torments of loss.

T went on to tell me how she felt safer and in charge by directing all her feelings inwards. I interpreted this as a way to not only save the object but to save herself from the object's wrath. The sad outcome is she feels safe from annihilation, but hopelessly lonely and unable to make meaningful contact with her objects. We discussed her internal perception of herself as an ideal person, based on her hopes for an ideal mother. At the same time, T becomes very demanding and exacting of that ideal figure. This demanding is a combination of T's own oral aggression and an identification with her controlling mother. The resulting level of pressure and expectation creates unfulfilled, frustrated wishes and a toppled ideal.

Next, T felt contempt for herself. She attacked herself with judgment and ridicule. This was the defensive posture of the death instinct, in the service of eliminating need and hope, as well as retaining control by attacking herself before the object had a chance to. This "beat me to the punch" transference was difficult to work through, because of the painful and scary feeling of loss and persecution that it defended against. But, T was gradually able to explore these phantasies and work with them internally, in the transference, and in extra-transference situations.

In the sixth and seventh years of analysis, T's anxieties continued to shift from paranoid-schizoid phantasies to more depressive concerns. As with many borderline patients, the journey to whole-object functioning can be fragile and prone to breakdown. At times, this is a defensive regression and at other times is a psychic fragmentation due to overwhelming anxieties.

T wanted to go to a weekend music festival in another state. Her plans meant she would miss our session and she would have to back out of plans with her boyfriend. The closer the date came and the more we discussed it, the more T felt strong conflicting feelings. Instead of a black-or-white splitting, she had more of a mixture of contrasting feelings. At first, she felt guilty for missing the session and felt she would hurt my feelings. The more she explored these depressive fears, the more anxious she became. When her own internal self-attacks and judgments became overwhelming, she projected them into me. Then, she felt I was picking on her and suffocating her. T started to feel I was forcing her to stay and making her miss the fun music show. So, her ability to manage the depressive phantasies broke down and they turned into persecutory object relations. However, the more we explored these anxious phantasies, the more she could slowly integrate her projections and not see us as such adversaries.

Several months later, T came into my office and noticed the overhead light was brighter than usual. I had put in stronger bulbs. She said she hoped I would turn it down a bit, with the dimmer switch, for her sessions. After some silence, she expressed her conflict. If I turned the light down, she would feel guilty for imposing her needs on me. She would be burdening me and hurting me. It was selfish. At the same time, T felt that if I didn't honor her request, I was being rude and mean. She felt angry I would do such a thing. Here, she vacillated between depressive worries and more paranoid fears of persecution.

Melanie Klein (1926) has described the importance that reality and external deprivations have for the developing ego. The child's budding personality is greatly shaped by the maternal environment and the child's phantasies about the mother. Klein believed all persecutory anxiety and fearful phantasies, at their core, embodied the maternal object.

T experienced ongoing frustrations and fear in relationship to her mother. In T's mind, mother needed T to be the embodiment of her wishes. T felt mother needed to have her be a puppet without an identity. This was a feeling of abandonment by the ideal mother she needed and wished for combined with an attack by a bad, self-serving mother.

In the seventh year of analysis, T decided to terminate. This was a combination of factors. She was now engaged to be married and was going to be moving. While she wanted to continue seeing me, she felt it was time to try life without me and see how it went. This was not a flight into health and T felt she could return if necessary. Overall, she had made quite a successful transition into health compared to her condition some years prior.

However, the last nine months of treatment were turbulent, as T worked through her separation issues as well as her anxiety about her marriage and her move. Indeed, she seemed to play out many of her transference issues through the vehicle of her wedding concerns. This time she had chosen a man who treated her well and could put up with and contain many of her strong feelings and occasional tantrums. Their relationship mirrored our relationship in many ways. At first she acted out with him. Then, she engaged in endless self-sabotage. Finally, she was consumed with fears of rejection, loss, and judgment.

As both termination and the wedding date loomed closer, T experienced a resurgence of many of these feelings. It seemed her ego was stronger now, but she did start to cycle through all three levels of anxiety and defense we had dealt with throughout the analysis.

In this last stage of treatment, T revisited all levels of her prior conflicts, defenses, and phantasies. She acted out, attacked herself intra-psychically, and felt persecuted and abandoned.

T began to feel extremely anxious and worried. She could not sleep at night. She feared she would not be the perfect bride and would not live up to all the expectations of her new role. At the same time, she was sure she was a "crummy patient" and wasn't able to be the type of case I enjoyed or even could tolerate. This state of panic led her to act out in ways she had left behind for years. Now, she started to overeat, bounce checks, and get drunk. This acting out was a display of her internal struggle with herself and her objects, as well as an expression of the transference. T tested me by coming late, not showing up at all, and paying her bill only after I reminded her.

The more we explored this acting out, we started to understand how parts of her mind were acting against other parts. She had identified with her mother and her father in particular ways. She felt she was now equally irresponsible, demanding, disappointing, and unlikable. She pictured herself as the worst bride and future mother possible. In other words, she felt she was now a combination of her bad internal mother and father. This was a terrible conflict, as her reliance on splitting was no longer so strong and she could bring her hateful and loving feelings closer together. She wanted desperately to be close to her mother but that felt like she would become ugly and evil as her mother seemed to be. Therefore, part of her acting out was an expression of an ugly mother who couldn't contain herself or her baby. It was also an attack by another part of T's mind on itself. The death instinct acted defensively to crush the life out of this mother part of T and to expel the bad mother. When her ego had the opportunity of depending on a mother figure who could hurt and abandon the little-girl part of T, her ego tried to destroy the temptation rather than risk the danger. T's negative attitude toward herself was really an attack on her internal mother.

In this way, T developed a strong prejudice for the mother aspect of herself. She launched two unconscious strategies. First, she tried to kill off or minimize that aspect of herself by criticizing and attacking it, via the death instinct. At the same time, T used manic defenses to try and become the opposite. She tried to be the perfect bride and the perfect patient. She thought of countless ways to prove herself to me and her fiancé. This created a vicious cycle, as she demanded more and more from herself and felt she was constantly failing.

As she failed, in phantasy, to be my ideal and her fiancé's ideal, T started to be anxious that we would hate her and get rid of her. She imagined being scorned and abandoned by us both. These fears of loss and persecution were clearly a paranoid-schizoid struggle. T did not feel I could forgive her or overlook her faults. Indeed, she thought I would suddenly turn from a caring analyst to an enemy. These strong phantasies of loss and annihilation were often made real by strong projective identification forces shaping her interpersonal relationships. She so desperately and aggressively wanted to be loved and protected by me and others that she, via projective identification, choked off her object's supplies of love and care. She felt left with nothing but angry and vengeful objects that would leave her.

T became so frantic and desperate during this time that I had to widen my role as a container and psychological envelope for her anxieties. Along with interpreting her phantasies and transference fears, I had to contain, soothe, and manage her out-of-control ideas and feelings. I had to help T tame these aspects of herself until she could take over and make her own choices. We talked about how to make it through each day, even how to make it moment-to-moment. Often, we had to explore in minute detail how to survive the dangers of our relationship, as she saw them. We closely examined each phantasy to fully understand what was happening, especially her transference phantasies of losing me and feeling attacked or rejected by me. We met more often. Bit by bit, we brought the pieces back together.

T started to feel more secure about herself, our relationship, and her new life with her fiancé. She was able to see how she was seeking perfection as a way to change her mother from a rejecting and persecuting object that she hated (a vicious projective identification cycle) to a wonderful ideal. This failed, so she attacked and rejected herself as she felt her mother and father had done to her.

T stopped most of her acting out and started to feel more confident. This working-through phase ushered in a new level of sadness, loss, grief, and rage about her father's alcoholism and unavailability. We worked more on her feelings about termination as well.

Finally, her paranoid-schizoid phantasies and feelings of persecution and annihilation were now more present as depressive phantasies about her father and feeling sorry for her mother. Extremes of persecutory prejudice changed to more manageable depressive, superego problems.

T told me she could now admit her gratitude to me for my help. She talked about how she was now able to give to me, rather than have a power-struggle. She described how she felt disappointed in things not going well in life, but not devastated and not attacked and hopeless. T said she was no longer self-mutilating or punching walls and she now felt a sense of freedom at work and a new confidence with men. She thanked me and said good-bye with a genuine sense of appreciation and warmth.

Now, T had a foothold in the depressive position. However, she still caved in to her former paranoid anxieties. More and more, however, she gained a new confidence and joy in life while dealing with deep feelings of sorrow, mourning, and grief over the shortcomings of her objects and her own humanity.

# Chapter 15

# Bargains, treaties, and delusions*

Analysts are familiar with those patients who appear to have no interest in or feeling for the analyst and are highly resistant to exploring that apparent void. If these patients stay in treatment, they slowly reveal fixed delusions about themselves and their objects. Patient and analyst discover inner dramas in the form of magical phantasies by which the patient lives. These delusions form mental systems that are either paranoid or masochistic, but always grandiose. Both are a last-ditch effort to avoid a sense of annihilation. A tightly woven inner mantra gives them specific guidelines on what to expect from themselves and their objects. These borderline, schizoid, or functional psychotic patients are within the paranoid-schizoid position, yet they often exhibit intense depressive anxieties about having injured or destroyed their objects. As with the other patients profiled in this book, these patients seem to have one foot in one psychic region and the other foot in another, while barely managing to cope in either.

Close examination of their phantasies reveals the introjection of a maternal object felt to be demanding, controlling, and manipulative, yet fragile and brittle. The child takes in this object as a way to deal with its persecutory nature and to save it from the ego's hostility. The ego takes it in with the hope of patching it back together as a more ideal and nurturing object. By identifying with this threatening presence, a complex psychic reaction occurs. Certain aspects of the object feel seductively powerful and attractive. Other aspects feel frightening and toxic. The object is split into hoped-for, ideal parts and unwanted, bad portions and the bad elements are projected out. Due to a breakdown in splitting as the result of a weakened ego without sufficient good objects to rely on, the unwanted parts return.

Klein (1952c) has pointed out the inherent link between projection and introjection. She writes:

* This chapter was first published as 'Bargains, treaties, and delusions' in *Journal of the American Academy of Psychoanalysis*, 27(3, 1999): 451–469.

it seems that the processes underlying projective identification operate already in the earliest relation to the breast . . . Accordingly, projective identification would start simultaneously with the greedy oral-sadistic introjection of the breast. This hypothesis is in keeping with the view often expressed by the writer that introjection and projection interact from the beginning of life.

(p. 69)

Therefore, what is expelled always returns.

Through projective identification, the toxic elements of the expelled internal mother return. Corrupting the natural maturational processes, they turn out to be stronger than the supportive, strengthening elements. Hoped-for love is overpowered by the subjective reality of rejection and persecution. Within the paranoid-schizoid position, loss of the object is equivalent to loss of the self. Therefore, loss of the longed-for love prompts feelings of annihilation and fragmentation.

The ego uses excessive and often destructive forms of projective identification and denial to fend off this maternal intruder and the ego constructs complex delusional systems to reduce these anxieties. The presence of this internal object feels necessary for survival but also damaging to the ego. A bargain is struck. Segal (1972) described a similar process. She states:

in infancy my patient underwent a psychic catastrophe and he has survived it psychically by building a delusional system. Any breach of this defense system threatens my patient with a repetition of the catastrophic situation.

(p. 393)

External trauma plays a role in the patient's history. Klein makes clear that external reality shapes the infant's internal experiences and psychic structures. In 1957 she wrote:

external circumstances play a vital part in the initial relation to the breast . . . Furthermore, whether or not the child is adequately fed and mothered, whether the mother fully enjoys the care of the child or is anxious and has psychological difficulties over feeding – all these factors influence the infant's capacity to accept the milk with enjoyment and to internalize the good breast.

(p. 179)

Later, in 1959, she wrote of:

the importance of actual favorable and unfavorable experiences to which the infant is from the beginning subjected, first of all by his parents, and later on by other people. External experiences are of paramount importance throughout life.

(p. 256)

The patients I am presenting in this chapter usually report a mother who is conditionally loving, rigid, and self-centered. The father is often in the background or controlling in a different manner. A loss of trust in the primary object results from a provisional exchange of love. The child seems to make an internal bargain, using introjection of the object. It takes the form of "I will let you live inside me because I need you. I will become like you in exchange for power and love. If I change our bargain, one of us may be destroyed. So, the price I pay is being controlled and dependent." Projective identification, splitting, and denial are used to try to gain some distance and separation from the overpowering influence of these part objects. Part of the tradeoff with the object is that the ego sacrifices autonomy for survival and acceptance.

This is a fixed delusional system based on the reduction of anxiety. Attachment to the object becomes secondary. The ego's need for attachment is corrupted by the need to control the nature of the relationship. Proximity to the object becomes more of a "necessary evil" than a desire.

The ego becomes increasingly hostile, frustrated with a less than ideal object. This aggression is always looming but must be avoided to prevent loss. Simultaneously, these patients try to expel this troubling object by denial and projective identification. Now, introjection of an infectious psychic agent leads to pathological internal defenses, out of the need to remain attached to that same object. A bitter bargain is struck between the ego and the object to observe a fragile peace. They form a mutual parasitic relationship and the resulting delusional system usually leads to minimal social functioning and a fragile hold on reality.

Segal (1972) wrote of a similar phenomenon and described how the

catastrophe is the infantile situation in which the ego is flooded by destructive and self-destructive impulses threatening annihilation. The defensive role of the 'operation' is to restitute omnipotently a fantasy world in which dependence on objects is excluded. Destructive and libidinal impulses and fantasies are contained in the defense system: on the one hand, the sadistic control; on the other, the 'savior' elements. The destructive elements, however, predominate, and the whole system is an aggressive attack on reality.

(p. 401)

These difficult-to-reach patients pull for mutual acting out of their delusional systems and create transferential standoffs. To understand the nature of this internal bargain better, I will conceptually redefine the term compromise formation.

Using Melanie Klein's notion of object relations and internal phantasy, the concept of compromise formation can be refined to better explain certain types of hard-to-reach patients who have great difficulty in giving up pathological defensive mechanisms and who resist the working-through process.

Compromise formation is generally understood as the best mental solution to the gratification of id, ego, superego, and external reality. The emphasis is on gratification and discharge. Freud used the term as early as 1896. In his paper, 'The Defense Neuro-Psychosis', Freud discussed the compromise formation between repressed and repressing ideas. He was to later elaborate on this concept in other papers over the years (Freud 1916). Boesky (1991) restated Freud's hypothesis:

> a compromise formation is the polyphonic interaction of the components of a given conflict that achieves the maximum gratification with the least possible psychic pain.
>
> (p. 16)

Brenner (1991) adds:

> everyone, patient or not, relates to other persons in ways determined by childhood instinctual conflicts. Every object relationship is a compromise formation resulting from instinctual conflicts originating in childhood and carried over, transferred, into later life.
>
> (p. 102)

Laplanche and Pontalis (1973) write:

> [a compromise formation is the] form taken by the repressed memory so as to be admitted to consciousness when it returns in symptoms, in dreams and, more generally, in all products of the unconscious; in the process the repressed ideas are distorted by defense to the point of being unrecognizable. Thus both the unconscious wish and the demands of defense may be satisfied by the same formation – in a single compromise.
>
> (p. 76)

Brenner (1992) then expanded this definition by stating, "everything is a compromise formation; not just neurotic symptoms or neurotic character traits, but everything" (p. 373).

Vaquer (1991) writes from a more object-relations vantage:

> conflict and compromise are ubiquitous in all human mental behavior. From my perspective, the relevant question is not whether a given bit of behavior involves conflict or is a compromise, but, rather, what sort of conflict is involved, what sorts of processes result in the behavior in question.
>
> (p. 117)

While the idea of compromise formation as the outcome of equally parceled out gratifications from each mental system may hold true for many patients, I believe the notion is better understood in object-relational terms. Many patients are more involved with trying to survive internal catastrophes than trying to achieve libidinal or aggressive gratifications. Stein (1990) writes, "the object is not only an instinctually gratifying or frustrating object, but a loving and loved, or a hating and hated, or envious or envied, object" (p. 504). This is certainly not an either/or issue. However, the desire to reduce unpleasure can overshadow the need for pleasure. Gratification of libidinal or aggressive urges may indeed trigger these more primitive anxieties, but the anxieties end up being of primary concern. Stein goes on to say:

> the individual will attempt to deal with the emotional conflicts by unconsciously manipulating parts of himself and of his internal objects, in ways corresponding to one or two basic positions, the paranoid-schizoid and the depressive.
>
> (p. 500)

Internal manipulations can take the form of last-resort compromise formations.

These more drastic compromise formations are intra-psychic bargains between different aspects of the self and object designed to cope with phantasies of loss, death, and persecution. Negotiations within fragile relational ties that exist in the mind give particular character to the ego and produce specific transferences that are often overtly delusional. Isaacs (1948) stated:

> phantasy is . . . the mental corollary, the psychic representative, of instinct. There is no impulse, no instinctual urge or response which is not experienced as unconscious phantasy . . . however, phantasy soon becomes also a means of defense against anxieties, a means of inhibiting and controlling instinctual urges and an expression of reparative wishes as well . . . most phantasies (like symptoms) also serve various

other purposes as well as wish-fulfillment: e.g., denial, reassurance, omnipotent control, reparation, etc.

(pp. 81–82)

These variations of wish-fulfillment are the components of compromise formations and form lasting methods of intra-psychic negotiation within the realm of self and internalized objects.

A compromise formation is usually viewed as a complex combination of wishes, fears, defenses, and unconscious solutions. Gratification of all agencies of the mind is attempted so that a psychic equilibrium is reached. The intra-psychic bargains I am referring to are more primitive and subject to the Talon law. Fairness and equality are not involved, neither is choice. An eye-for-an-eye is the rule and prey–predator phantasies are the norm. The self and object are equally threatened and hang in a tedious balance. Denial and projective identification are used as methods of adaptation and as weapons against the persecuting objects.

I am proposing a system of internal bargains based on fixed intra-psychic beliefs, usually of some delusional form, which exist to mitigate anxiety. Again, the primary goal of these compromises, or bargains, is not to achieve gratification but to fend off anxiety.

The anxiety a patient deals with in the paranoid-schizoid position concerns self-preservation. The chief anxiety is of an untrustworthy object and persecutory feelings of being tortured, manipulated, or attacked by that object. Therefore, the internal bargain is structured around preventing these troubles.

Patients in the depressive position will create internal bargains with their objects as a way to avoid hurting their object or to prevent some type of tension with them. These are intra-psychic, relational patterns motivated by the need to prevent the ego from harming the object. Alternatively, these bargains are struck to heal or restore objects that have been hurt. Guilt, remorse, and reparation fuel these intra-psychic relational treaties. The ego's main thrust is to avoid or prevent the destruction of the loved object.

These bargains, in the depressive and the paranoid-schizoid positions, are based on lasting phantasies involving the self and a cast of various objects. The ego organizes all actions around these phantasies. The analyst's job is to translate these fixed relational bargains into oral messages. Once the patient can begin passing his unconscious beliefs about us through the medium of language instead of defensive actions, we can then better work through the distortions that fuel them. Meanwhile, we find ways of interpreting the actions patients take to carry out their internal bargains.

Denial, projective identification, and fixed delusional systems are used to avoid overwhelming anxieties, whether in the paranoid-schizoid or the depressive position. These attempts at internal safety for the self or the object result in omnipotently flavored paranoid or masochistic confusions.

The common use of denial to avoid chaotic anxieties is usually a simple looking away from the realities of a relationship. The type of denial I wish to focus on is more about a splitting off of any awareness of the impact or importance of the bad maternal object. The omnipotent notion of "you don't mean enough to me to make an impact" is what eventually gets demonstrated in the transference. This is not an absence of transference, but a denial of the presence and significance of love and hate. To admit to being impacted by the object is to unleash terrible feelings of being controlled, hurt, or rejected. Obtaining ownership of the object through identification is easier, followed by splitting off any negative aspects of that object.

For some patients, this level of denial becomes a manic and paranoid style of relating in which the patient says, "I do not need anyone, why would I ever want to be close to you when all I really need is myself?" This type of transference is hollow and the patient is clearly whistling in the dark, trying to ward off intense anxieties. On the other hand, by denying any connection to a negative object, patients project the bad parts outward and then feel persecuted. This can lead to masochistic feelings of being wrong, deficient, and damaged.

By continuously waving the white flag of surrender, the ego retains its bond with the needed but dreaded maternal object. The ego forms sado-masochistic transferences to maintain internal bargains with primary objects. Again, this is an internal compromise founded on the need to deal with overwhelming anxiety about the safety of the ego and the object. Loss of safety is the primary fear and motivator for these unconscious relational negotiations. Gratification of libidinal and aggressive drives is certainly present, but secondary. Unfortunately, the gratification of these drives can often trigger further worries and phantasies about the integrity of the self or object. It becomes a vicious cycle.

A reliance on masochistic relations is a way of secretly aggressing while always submitting, in exchange for safety and predictability. More often the outcome is the paranoid experience. This is a feeling of being cornered, manipulated, and judged. A counter-offensive must take place. The rules of the game become survival of the fittest and an eye for an eye. Pleasure through victory is possible, but destruction of the object means retaliation and subsequent destruction of the self. In the transference, the analyst quickly is projected onto and related to in these ways. Patients hope and fear that the analyst will become a new object, a helper who can withstand these internal wars. Yet, the tradeoff usually feels equally daunting. To give up these intra-psychic bargains and negotiations involves phantasies of betrayal, loss, and destruction. Therefore, the working-through process is quite difficult and therapeutic standoffs or premature terminations are common.

Identification, normally a helpful method of coping, becomes a two-edged blade. The ego identifies with the object, hoping to take in the good loving object that will mitigate the effects of the harmful object and the hostile affects in the ego. In order to have a hoped-for, loving maternal object to attach to, the ego splits off portions of the object as an idealized figure to cling to. It then becomes a union of infant and idealized mother, against the ravages of fate and the cruel external world. A masochistic, paranoid stance is formed in which the ugly, controlling, and frightening aspects of the mother are projected out and then battled against. A holy war ensues, with an omnipotent team of needy self and gratifying, rescuing mother against the combined elements of a hostile, controlling mother and the angry, demanding aspects of the self. This excessive projective identification and splitting create a brittle and artificial division of the mind, resulting in the bad aspects of self and object quickly reappearing as introjective ghosts. These patients feel haunted and hunted down by these strange foreign bodies that exist intra-psychically. This leads to more desperate measures of projective identification and denial, which leaves them even more depleted and more reliant on delusional phantasy systems where more drastic bargains must be made with their internal objects.

Some patients go through life with a delusional system of internal relations tucked into the background. The more psychotic elements of that system only become activated under external stress. George was a caring father and had worked at the local hardware store for many years. He had an ambivalent connection to his rather controlling and judgmental mother. When she became critical about George's decision to take his family away for Christmas vacation, instead of spending the holiday with her, he became ever more unsettled. George told me he had just realized, through reading certain magazine articles, that the United States would no longer exist after the year 2000 because of the computer date problem. He was going to start stockpiling medication for his children and food for the family. He planned to move to the country to start growing food since there would be no more grocery stores after the economy collapsed. I commented on the devastation he felt would occur to his mother and himself if he were to go away for Christmas. I also commented on how he was unsure if I would still be around if he went away. I added that being independent was something he wanted, yet feared. It made him feel like the world was ending. George began to feel better and seemed to move from disintegration to reintegration, at least momentarily.

A delusional system is a comprehensive internal story that has an ongoing dilemma between the subject and a host of objects. It is a delusional tale that may only last a day or a week, but it is the result of a whole system of negotiations between unstable objects. It is an ongoing internal war the patient must cope with, rather than temporary distortions in self and object relations that can be righted fairly quickly.

For more disturbed patients, this delusional system is present at all times and evokes a regular loss of reality testing. These are what I call functional psychotic patients. They can usually work and manage a few important friendships or love affairs. Even so, these connections to reality are often tenuous. More important, they are involved in a fictional internal tale where they constantly struggle against rather severe persecutory and depressive anxieties.

Overwhelming anxieties dominate these patients. Mary was a psychotic woman who stayed in treatment for more than two years before prematurely terminating. She wanted to marry me and have sex, as she claimed she did with her last therapist. She did not pay her final bill for more than fourteen months and then called and asked me out on a date. Mary said we needed to communicate with our bodies because "some things need to be experienced without words". I declined the invitation. Mary said she "respected my resolve" and that meant a great deal to her, but now she knew she would not return to treatment. During the two years I treated her, she clearly organized her mind within a delusional system. It was a series of negotiations with internal objects in which she said, "I need to have a physical connection to you so I know you love me. When you do that, I feel totally filled up with you. But after a while I realize I do not exist anymore. I feel scared and angry with you and want to make you pay. After I destroy you in revenge, I realize you are gone and I feel desperate and alone and think I might die." She had acted out this intra-psychic dilemma with many therapists and countless boyfriends, friends, and employers.

Because this delusional view of the world may persist for days or may be a lifelong method of engaging with others, the analysis of the projective and denial mechanisms is different from the usual interpretation of projective identification and splitting defenses. To be effective with these patients and their delusions, the analyst must be comfortable in staying within the limits of the patient's internal bargain for long periods of time. Rather than confronting the lack of reality testing, the analyst stays within the confines of the delusional system and lives through it with the patient. The analysis of the transference occurs within the patient's psychotic world. To try to pull the patient away from that and enlist his so-called observing ego is to invite resistance at best. The ego is organizing its experience through the lens of these internal negotiations, so it is misleading to try to strike a bargain with the part of the patient we think is still grounded in reality.

Expelling the destructive aspects of the ego or object through intensive projective identification or denial creates paranoid and masochistic ties to the object. These necessary yet unstable treaties are between certain conflictual parts of the ego or between opposing parts of the object, as well as between self and object. Whatever form these underground negotiations take, the result is an omnipotent, manic-like stance from a compromised, infantile ego. The safe aspects of the object are sectioned off to squeeze out a small portion of desirable nourishment to which to cling. This then is glorified and idealized.

The maintenance of a pathological defensive structure produces fixed and stereotypic relations with inner objects, making for a chronic hesitation in the patient's engagement with life. This is based on strong convictions about the state of the ego and the objects within it. Idiosyncratic ways of being in the world evolve, based primarily on finding a way of feeling safe and avoiding overwhelming anxieties, and secondarily on the gratification of libidinal and aggressive urges.

## CASE MATERIAL

Bob was raised in a home where both his parents worked. During the day, he and his one sister were taken care of by an older retarded brother and a grandmother. From when Bob was six to when he was fourteen years old, his brother was sexual with him. They masturbated each other and performed oral sex. When Bob was fourteen years old, two critical events took place. His parents divorced and his brother announced that the sex was over.

My impression of Bob's upbringing was that he felt lonely, confused, and spent his days daydreaming and watching television. Additionally, he was over-stimulated with his brother, felt controlled by his rigid and dominating mother, and missed his overworked father.

After barely completing highschool, Bob enrolled in the local university. He was asked to leave due to poor grades. He would get up in the morning and go to each class, but never brought any books or did any homework. He only went through the motions. He lived a rather aimless life until he was twenty and decided to be a writer. He asked his parents to finance his enrollment at a distant college specializing in literature. Bob drank and took drugs for much of the first three years, but maintained passing grades. It was during his last year at the university that he began to feel attracted to the owner of a local bookstore where he worked part-time.

Until this time, Bob had never felt attracted to either men or women, never had a date, and had never had sex with anyone after his brother. He had always thought that he must be gay because of the sexual activity with his brother, but he tried to put the whole matter aside. During the last year of college, he developed a psychotic delusion about his boss. Bob believed they were in love with each other. He was sure they would spend the rest of their lives together. The fact that this man never showed any indication of affection to Bob was dismissed as his being "ethical in the workplace". Bob became centered on his thoughts about his new love.

Simultaneously, Bob began intensely ruminating about whether he was truly gay or not. For months he had been pestering all of his friends with daily reports about his fondness for this man and how he "could tell" the man was thinking about him fondly too. Now, this shifted to calling all his friends each day asking them if they thought he was gay or not. At first, all of his friends had much advice to give and Bob collected it all and worried about every detail. He also bought various books and listened to television and radio for help in deciding whether he were gay or not.

These activities were all-consuming and drove his friends away. They told him to stop calling. During this last year of school, his grades began to decline, as he could not concentrate. He started to feel his boss no longer liked him. Now, Bob thought this man felt manipulated by him and was angry about it. Bob started to have brief hallucinations in which the person he was talking to was suddenly naked. At the end of his school year, he had one last test to take in order to graduate. The day of the test, it occurred to him that the boss might not want him to pass the test because of the ill-feelings between them. This scared Bob and he was unable to return to school to take the test. This is when I began seeing him.

When Bob came in for his first appointment, he had just cut off his hair, to try to "change his attitude". Here, I think he had lost the symbolic functions of the ego and was reduced to concrete thinking. He told me he could not stop thinking about his boss and about his sexual preference. He said he wanted help to decide which way to go with his sexual identity, which idea to choose for a book to write, and where to apply for work as a writer.

Fairly early, I commented that he might be trying to find elaborate ways of controlling his anxiety and preventing bad things from happening to him. I went on to say he was in the grip of these problems right now, but it was easier to think of them as potential problems he could control in the future. Distancing and sterilizing his bad objects and his feelings about them were ways of protecting himself. In other words, Bob tried to see his current anxieties as potential future difficulties that he could plan for and prevent. He shifted time from the present to the future and his role from participant to observer.

Bob told me that he usually went by the name of one or two famous literary figures, but if I needed to call him by his real name that was acceptable. This was my introduction to his grandiosity, which had alien-ated many of his peers and coworkers. His feelings of power were always edged with corruption. Bob worried that the other students felt inferior about their abilities since he was so brilliant. He told me that people at his job felt he was seducing the boss to get a raise. He also thought that men and women he met at parties were falling in love with him because he was so friendly and nice, but they had gotten the wrong idea and thought he was flirting. Overall, he worried he had some kind of power to make people fall in love with him and also felt falsely accused of taking advantage of people. Here, he identified with the seductive brother and the controlling aspects of his mother that he hated.

Two weeks before starting treatment, he stopped having hallucinations. I believe this was due to a phantasy of having someone to help him and to organize his disintegrated ego. When he began searching for help, I became an idealized organizing mother in his mind. Frequently, patients report they feel better right before starting therapy. Some actually do not begin treatment because they feel so good that going seems unnecessary. While this is certainly a defensive flight into health, some of these reactions, like Bob's, also are the creation of a hoped-for helper object in their mind to whom they can begin to cling. All sorts of things may occur with this new internal object before they arrive in our office. Therefore, the transference is not only immediate in a treatment, but it has already existed and permutated several times over.

Upon beginning analysis, Bob felt better being able to talk over with me all the things with which he had felt alone. He welcomed the couch as he said it allowed him to think freer and more clearly. I saw him four times a week. However, he sometimes asked for a fifth session during a particularly difficult week and he would usually call me four or five times a week as well. Bob was still functional enough to work, and go to school. Many people thought he was strange, but no one ever confronted him as having problems. I suggested a medication evaluation due to the extreme anxiety Bob constantly suffered from, but he declined.

When Bob decided to go out of town to take a break from what he felt was a boring, unexciting life, he mentioned in passing that he would see me the following week. I pointed out that he seemed to act like I did not matter. I interpreted his desire to be with me and others in a close and meaningful way, even sexual, but it was confusing and scary. He had to stay away from me for safety. To actually show his feelings for me or others would feel like too much of a risk to himself and me.

Another time, he told me he was going to write a few novels over on weekends that he could sell to pay his rent and buy a new car. He approached this the same way as he did his "love affair" with the boss. He called friends and book companies to find out how much he should market the novels for and what type of artwork should go on the covers without ever lifting a pen to paper. I commented that it seemed to be the same type of personal dilemma he felt with me and others.

Bob keenly noticed certain parts of his illness. He said he observed himself linking thoughts together that then overwhelmed him. He found that if he did not link the ideas together, he felt more stable and less frightened. An example of this was when he went to buy a pair of shoes. The salesperson bent over to take the shoes out of the box. Bob thought that because the man had bent over and was presenting him shoes, he must be falling in love with him and was bending over for sex. Bob could untangle these thoughts later and see them as random details with no necessary overlap. While this insight helped him a great deal, he still was convinced that he had an erotic influence on the salesman.

Bob's family denied the severity of his condition. They felt he was "just going through a phase" and should "just grow up". A month or two before he saw me, they started to take his suffering more seriously and told him to "get some medicine" and "stop wasting his life". Interestingly, Bob's father told him that he was supportive of Bob's attempts at working and school. He was willing to support Bob financially so he could pursue his writing career. Bob's mother, on the other hand, repeatedly told him to come back home and live with her. She felt it would be best if he just lived at home and "took it easy". He felt she treated him like an infant and was controlling his life. He was able to discuss his ambivalent feelings about her and her domineering way, but only with caution. Only when he felt certain that I was not taking either parent's side could he tell me that he wanted to be more independent than mother wished.

Bob's family was paying for his tuition and most of his bills. His part-time job covered some minor expenses. While his family paid for treatment, his mother made it clear that she did not want him to see me and instead wished that he either "stop fussing about being gay" or take medication to get better.

Bob reported one dream after about two months. He said he was walking along when a man came up to him. He thought he might know the man but was unsure. This person began fondling him and touching him sexually. Bob felt shocked and tried to run away. The man ran after him. Bob said, "at that point, I turned around and peed on him, like a little kid would". I commented that this was a direct link to how he must have felt with his brother. I then suggested that he may also feel that way with his mother and even with me at times, if I seemed to be too controlling or inattentive to his needs. He said he felt embarrassed that he was like a little kid in the dream, but he agreed he was trying to get away from someone he "didn't like".

The treatment with Bob was difficult and confusing, as he rapidly fluctuated between various elements of an internal bargain with himself and his objects. Boyer (1986) states:

> in primitive patients, traumatic infantile relationships have been split off from the main psychic current and continue to exert their pathological effects on both the patient's mental equilibrium and external adaptations. Such early 'islands' of trauma pathologically influence emotional and structural development, resulting in constriction, arrest and distortion of innate drive toward maturation. The split off infantile relationships regularly cause such patients to develop psychotic transference reactions . . . The analyst's comprehension of the extent to which projection and projective identification are involved will help him preserve his objectivity.
>
> (p. 29)

With Bob, projective identification and splitting played a large role in maintaining these islands of trauma and delusion.

I found it best to use a combination of genetic reconstruction and here-and-now transference interpretations. Also, I frequently functioned as a safe house, to contain and frame his continuous projections. The genetic reconstructions served as a buffer, to temporarily help him move away from the immediate anxiety he felt overwhelmed by and it provided a less threatening avenue into his phantasy life. Valenstein (1989) has pointed out that

> for more disturbed patients . . . who are so interactively and intersubjectively impelled, it may be necessary to introduce interpretations related to early pre-oedipal experience much sooner during the treatment to mitigate the intensity and immediacy of the overwhelming transference experience intellectualized though such interventions may be. Nevertheless, in such cases the ultimate veritability and insight value of the reconstructions may be realized during the later phase of the treatment as they are worked through, and gain in conviction and validity.
>
> (p. 435)

Listening to his material and containing his various projections, which seemed loving, hateful, and curious, was necessary to avoid assaulting him with premature return of those projections and a forced, premature re-internalization. I had to simply take in his material and wait. On the other hand, I felt there were moments in which it was vital to make here-and-now interpretations. These had to do with his fear of my not accepting him and his worry of losing my love. Also, it proved necessary and helpful to comment on his negative transference when it threatened the treatment situation.

Bob undoubtably felt confused, overstimulated, and anxious about the sexual relationship with his brother. From the nature of the transference and his phantasies about life, it seemed he felt overwhelmed by the controlling and needy state of both mother and his brother. He also seemed to have strong phantasies about being able to control his objects and yet easily damage them as well. It came out in the analysis that he was concerned people were so weak that he should go along with their needs to not hurt them. Unconsciously, Bob imagined he could hurt his objects with his needs and his aggression. He struck an internal bargain with his objects in which he said, "I must be so overwhelming and powerful to my brother and mother that I must be careful. I must have magical powers. I will save them and others by keeping my distance. If I go it alone, others will be safe." This manic denial of need for the object helped Bob cope for many years. However, it also felt like a confinement. He had to always watch out for them and be ready to do whatever they needed.

When he became attracted to his boss, he said it was because the boss was identical to him physically, emotionally, and mentally. Bob had identified with his manipulating brother and controlling mother, as well as his distant father. He projected the good aspects of these internal objects onto external objects and felt drawn to them. On the other hand, he projected the bad aspects of this identification onto others and felt persecuted. In the end, he only managed to project the openly hostile and manipulative parts of his objects and was left to identify with the corrupted and victimized aspects of the objects he believed he had wronged. Not only was there a confusion between self and object, but a mixup of part-self aspects with part-object aspects. The loving and dependable parts of his objects were meager and idealized. Therefore, the more corrupt elements he tried to project easily overran them. He tried to deny any flaw in himself or his objects as a way to avoid catastrophic anxieties, feelings of loss, and persecutory phantasies. Instead, he imagined himself in union with a carbon copy of himself, both at bliss, without any imperfections.

Clearly, Bob's early developmental history shaped his adult character. His delusional thinking was a system built out of desperate coping measures. His yearning for his father, his lack of an empathic, available mother who respected his autonomy, his sexual involvement with his brother, and his parent's divorce were but some of the external factors that pushed his ego to develop special methods of negotiating internal phantasies and overwhelming affects. Feelings of guilt around how he may have drained, hurt, or overpowered his family seemed predominant and served as a defense against loss and persecution. It seemed Bob put himself in an emotional limbo as a way to avoid hurting his objects and being hurt by them. His attraction to his boss and his looming graduation were signs of life in an identity that had been asleep for many years. With the reawakening came the overwhelming internal conflicts that he had managed to avoid for many years.

The breakthrough of aggressive and sexual desires toward the boss and his impending graduation triggered a potential loss of his internal objects. He was afraid he would damage his mother and brother again, now in the form of his boss, friends, and analyst. In the transference, he tried to ignore me, to save me from these threatening feelings. Eventually, he began to wonder what I thought of him and worried about if I accepted him or not. When he felt vulnerable and scared about my judgment, he would act superior and deny any connection to me. Therefore, in the transference and with others, he quickly switched between projecting his destructive feelings onto me, and worrying if I was in pain and wanting revenge, to projecting his own frightened self onto me, and then trying to save me by ignoring me. He felt that if he turned away from me, I would not be a victim of his magical powers.

Generally, these confusing and shifting internal states were all brought about by the projection of his frustrations and anger and later introjection and partial identification with objects that were controlling and sadistic. He then felt afraid for his objects, fearful that he would manipulate and damage them. This led to the use of denial, projection, and manic defenses. As a result, there was a psychotic cycle of persecutory and depressive anxieties that continually haunted Bob.

Stein (1990) points out that:

> The primary principle of development in Kleinian theory is infantile omnipotence (rather than infantile sexuality), which is a form of control of feelings (e.g. defensively experiencing grandiosity instead of helplessness) development is, accordingly, the necessity of phase – appropriately renouncing absolute control of feelings.
>
> (p. 508)

Bob developed a sense of infantile omnipotence through projective identifications with idealized yet frustrating objects that left him with a sense of dangerous sexual powers. This constant and intense projective identification process left Bob with a confusion about what was internal and what was external; therefore he was vaguely aware that he was talking about parts of himself, yet worried that it was something that was not him. The connection between himself and his objects was predicated on a fragile bargain to not harm one another.

Isaacs (1948) writes:

> unconscious phantasies exert a continuous influence throughout life, both in normal and neurotic people, the differences lying in the specific character of the dominant phantasies, the desire or anxiety associated with them and their interplay with each other and with external reality.
>
> (p. 96)

Most of Bob's phantasies were directed at maintaining a bond with the object. The anger he felt for the object and his desire to assume control subsequently corrupted this. Bob was then caught in a circle of depressive and persecutory fears. Analyzing his anger and disappointment with me and his objects was very difficult as he felt this would overwhelm us and cause us to retaliate. This fear of harming his objects was also reflected in the grandiosity of his delusions. He saw himself as ready for incredible power and success in which he towered over others. He managed to quickly undo these phantasies by such ideas as how he would instead be a humble mentor who would lead his students to greatness.

Freeman (1989) says:

> it has been recognized for a long time . . . that certain persecutory manifestations which arise at the onset of a psychosis are manifestly the result of an identification with an individual who was of emotional

significance to the patient prior to the attack . . . the symptoms of the psychotic attack can then be seen to arise from a 'psychotic' identification with a real or imaginary object choice.

(p. 445)

Using Klein's object relations theory we can see how the symptoms would then include an attack by the ego on parts of the object which are now located in the ego as an identification or a partial introjection.

## Comments

The case material is meant to be representative of those individuals who have typically suffered poor attachment with their maternal object and through projective identification have developed highly conflicted object ties within the ego. These relations produce cycles of intense persecutory and depressive anxieties, forcing the subject to rely on excessive splitting and other primitive defenses. As part of these protective maneuvers, the ego begins to build internal bargains and treaties with the adversarial objects. These repetitious intra-psychic negotiations lead to delusional thought systems that bring on the very anxiety the ego tried to avoid, creating vicious feedback loops with more severe delusional systems and more rigid bargains to strike.

For the price of survival, and the maintenance of an intact object, the ego builds and maintains certain relational configurations. These are attempted solutions for phantasies about destructive forces threatening the ego or the object. Self and object protection are the goals. If these intra-psychic bargains break down, phantasies about self and object destruction, loss, or annihilation overwhelm the ego. Infusing the concept of compromise formation with the ideas of object relations theory allows a better understanding of this highly defended anxiety state.

# Chapter 16

# Symbolization and the good object*

Melanie Klein began writing about symbol formation in 1930. Hanna Segal followed in 1957, exploring its place in the treatment of both neurotic and psychotic patients. Both Klein and Segal thought symbolism was achieved by the ego's displacement of aggressive feeling toward the mother's body. This displacement of aggression and anxiety created numerous sublimatory symbols. Contemporary Kleinians have continued to write about symbols, symbolization, and the symbolic process (Meltzer 1978; Money-Kyle 1968; Segal 1979, 2001; Bell 2001; Temperley 2001; Joseph 2004; Rusbridger 2004) and their place in the clinical process.

Angry attacks, in phantasy, on the mother's body or on the imagined parental intercourse generate anxieties about the destruction of one's ideal object and its possible retaliation. To deal with this tension, the ego develops the defenses of displacement, identification, sublimation, and symbolization. When one symbol becomes too closely aligned with the original ambivalent phantasy about mother or the combined parents, further displacement creates yet another symbol. In healthy development, this sequence generates a certain creativity that brings balance to an otherwise conflicted ego. Segal (1957) states:

> the symbol is needed to displace aggression from the original object, and in that way to lessen the guilt and the fear of loss . . . The symbols are also created in the internal world as a means of restoring, re-creating, recapturing and owning again the original object.
>
> (p. 42)

I would add that there are early precursors to symbolization arising in the paranoid-schizoid position which act as primitive methods of coping

* This chapter was first published as 'Symbolization and the good object', in *Bulletin of the Menninger Clinic*, 69(1, 2005): 81–97.

with the loss of the idealized object and the fear of attack from the bad object(s). Segal (1957) seemed to understand this when she stated:

> Symbol formation is an activity of the ego attempting to deal with the anxieties stirred by its relations to the object. That is primarily the fear of bad objects and the fear of the loss or inaccessibility of good objects . . . Symbol formation starts very early, probably as early as object relations, but changes its character and functions with the changes in the character of the ego and object relations.
>
> (pp. 40–41)

The paranoid-schizoid ego has not achieved whole-object relating, ambivalence, and integration of affect. Therefore, symbols mentally developed within the paranoid-schizoid experience are not steady or dependable. These brittle symbols feel risky to patients who need things and people to be in a fixed way, always predictable and rigid.

Particularly in the case of more disturbed patients, who have experienced external trauma and a history of chronic disruption of the mother–child bond, phantasies of loss and persecution prevail. So, rather than transform or creatively sublimate the ego's conflicted feelings about the mother and her body, symbols can amplify the dangers of object relations in those patients consumed by despair, oral aggression, loss, and the conviction of treacherous persecution.

Why is the early ego so full of aggression to begin with? As noted, most of these patients have experienced a combination of external and internal pressures. Goodness is an experience that is tainted and difficult to trust, in the self as well as in one's objects. The analyst knows this through the patient's narrative as well as the transference relationship.

So, while keeping in mind the filter of unconscious phantasy, most of these patients do seem to have experienced external trauma of some type early in their development. For some it was a direct assault by abusive parents, causing emotional, sexual, or physical harm. For others, it was the experience of being with parents so burdened by their own mental problems that the parenting was inconsistent. For other patients, one parent was overindulgent and another was unavailable or intrusive. Over-stimulation is often combined with under-stimulation. Finally, actual loss of a parent through death or divorce is common in the lives of many of our patients.

Melanie Klein was aware of the influence of external forces on the ego's development as well as the internal pressures that shape its character. Gammill (1989) was in supervision with Klein between 1957 and 1959. He states:

> I asked her once if she felt that the lack of gratification of libidinal desires (independently of the aggressive reactions that followed their

frustration) should be completely excluded as a possibility of creating anxiety. She remained silent for a considerable time; having in her eyes an extraordinary expression of someone who was looking deeply inside herself. Finally, she said, "I don't know. After all, anxiety is a complicated problem. Of course, I maintain my opinions concerning aggression and death instinct. However, I have never re-thought the theory of libido in relation to normal projective identification of the life instinct and of the good parts of the self. If for internal or external reasons there is no suitable object available to receive these positive projections, it may be that some sort of terrible collapse occurs in the self which would generate anxiety. Maybe there is a link with Freud's idea of withdrawal of cathexis, with a passive destruction of the external and the internal object."

(p. 13)

For many patients, all of these traumatic elements (external and internal) combine to make for a very insecure upbringing. Today, contemporary Kleinians use Bion (1957) and Rosenfeld's (1983) ideas of normal projective identification to better understand the ego's projection of love that is then unmet or under-contained, resulting in what Klein called the "terrible collapse" (Gammill 1989).

The child makes a significant contribution to the family's emotional matrix. Whether constitutionally or environmentally induced, early methods of relating that are characterized by oral aggression, lack of frustration tolerance, and lack of emotional safety make change, separation, attachment, autonomy, or dependency all quite difficult. Through projective identification, these conflicts and phantasies get played out repeatedly and become fixed ways of relating.

Normally, the infant's struggle with self-destructive urges, the death instinct, is mitigated by a build-up of internalized good objects that provide symbolic expression for both the death instinct and its derivative, the urge to destroy the breast. When there is a significant lack of good objects, due to excessive internal and external destructiveness and under- or over-stimulation, the ego's aggression toward self and object becomes overwhelming rather than controlled and modified.

When I refer to good objects, I mean something rather specific. The whole object of the depressive position is a theoretical, academic term to describe a concept. This term conveys the internal representation of an object which has developed into an integrated, full-spectrum, mature mental presence that in turn provides the ego with a matureness, an integrated manner of relating to the world, and a full spectrum of coping mechanisms.

The good object of the depressive position is the subjective, experiential reality of the whole object, as taken in by the ego. The infant does not experience a whole object. They experience the goodness that comes out of the resilience, understanding, and love of the wholeness of that object. The symbolizing object, or the symbolizing function of the object, is one of the many aspects of goodness within the whole object. In other words, the wholeness of the depressive object, experienced relationally as a good object, provides many functions to the ego including the symbolizing function. The infant can attack or hate a specific aspect of the good object, a specific area of goodness. So, the infantile ego can come to hate the containing function, the symbolizing function, or the supportive, growth-oriented actions of the good object.

The containing function of the internal and external parent is a vital element of the paranoid-schizoid position, when there is a need for a basic management, tolerance, and holding of primitive affect and acting out. It would also be a function of the whole, good object within the depressive position. The experience of being contained, under optimal conditions, would be internalized and personalized as the ability for frustration tolerance, patience, and tolerance of others.

Developmentally, the symbolizing function of the internal and external parent would take place more within the depressive position and would be internalized as the ability to conceptualize, create, think, and develop insight. There is a natural coexistence of the containing and symbolizing functions, being internalized and experienced as a good object that in turn could be identified with to create the experience of an integrated, good self.

The good object, in its stable and multifaceted state, fosters the ego's relational and intra-psychic experience of compassion, caring, understanding, and tolerance. In addition, the process of containing and symbolizing is in a sense taught and transmitted to the ego as part of the goodness of the object. Healthy splitting is part of symbolizing and mental creativity, so the ego develops the ability to hate parts of the object, love other parts, and still feel supported and loved by other parts. This is the meaning of the "I love you, but I hate your actions". Guilt and reparation are part of this healthy developmental cycle.

These patients are difficult to treat. Aborted treatments, long and stormy *impasses*, and chronic acting out are common. Countertransference confusion and anguish are frequent. For this type of patient, cure feels equal to the problem with which they already live. In treatment, these patients infuse the transference relationship with phantasies of idealization, devaluation, loss, and persecution. Overall, there is a denial of abstraction. The patient starts to pressure the analyst with feelings that are experienced as concrete and absolute, eventually feeling pressured by the analyst as a result of projective identification.

Creativity, symbolic thought, and insight (all intimate elements of psychoanalytic therapy) bring on the painful awareness of the ideal object's inherent flaws and therefore the potential loss of that object. This in turn feels as though one were inviting not only rejection, but attack and annihilation. To create, via symbolization, is to destroy the idealized self or object. Therefore, both symbols and the symbolizing, containing maternal object must be destroyed in order to maintain the ideal state of self↔object union. The ego becomes bent on killing off its beloved object and thereby itself in the process.

In normal development, the ego constantly tries to avoid its conflicted feelings toward the maternal object by switching to yet another symbol. If the levels of aggression, guilt, and fear are not overwhelming and the internal relations between self and object are increasingly integrated within the depressive position, this switching is relatively smooth.

However, the growth from fragile and threatening paranoid-schizoid experiences with symbolic objects to more stable and integrating symbolization within the depressive position is quite problematic. If the ego is struggling with exaggerated oral aggression, destructive projective identification mechanisms, feelings of loss and persecution, and the lack of proper container objects to rely on, then this period becomes a grave challenge.

Clinically, we often see patients who have mastered some aspects of symbol formation and the depressive position but are so threatened by the goodness of the object that they strive to destroy the symbolic function altogether. Defensively, the patient either idealizes or, more commonly, devalues the analyst's translating and insight function. In other words, the ego strips the symbol created by analytic interpretation of its ability to hold a spectrum of affect. It is reduced to one exaggerated feeling or just meaningless verbiage.

So, some of these patients will argue that treatment is useless because it is "just talk". Whittling down the treatment into a safer non-symbolic relationship is a typical transference resistance. These patients will echo facts and lists of events. They often demand cognitive and behavioral techniques as a way to avoid contact with their feelings and fears. All this prevents any insight or symbolic tie from occurring between patient and analyst and eliminates the risk of contact with the good object.

Since symbols and the act of symbolizing represent one aspect of the goodness of the object, which is threatening to some patients, those patients will defensively attack symbols and the symbolizing object as a way to erase or hide from contact with the good object.

The good object is considered too uncertain and open to change. The traumatized ego prefers to be forced to coexist with an easily controlled, concrete, bad object or to coexist with the image of an idealized, perfect object. In the effort to stay away from good objects that could turn into bad ones, the ego must constantly evacuate goodness and cling to the anger and despair that it is left with when denied, by the self, the nurturing, support, and love it craves. One way to do this is to avoid the symbolizing function of the analyst and of the self.

As a result, the ego can feel so much loss, aggression, and persecution that the normally healthy process of symbol formation becomes part of a pathological cycle. An example of this was a patient who saw a lawn that was brown from under-watering or disease. She felt overcome with feelings for the lawn. She projected neglect, abandonment, and loss into the lawn and then felt depressed and angry with the world for days. In the transference, she would be very insistent that I give her concrete tasks to perform and "cognitive exercises" in order to be cured. She dismissed the idea of exploring her mind and told me that finding meaning in her feelings or actions "was useless". Her excessive projective identification filled the symbol of a brown lawn with such raw affect and phantasy material that it became a persecutory object that trapped her. Simultaneously, she attacked me and her treatment, stripping both of any value.

Free association is a precursor to relational symbolization and analytic intimacy. Patients can feel this is a demand to sacrifice their identity and give up their hold on the idealized object. Their resulting anxiety produces a narcissistic and controlling transference resistance that is difficult to interpret without causing the patient to feel even more anxious. This in turn can cause the analyst countertransference impotence. In some cases, the analyst acts out by providing supportive measures to relieve this countertransference tension.

These patients create a difficult analytic *impasse*. The detoxifying, containing, and symbolizing aspects of the good object which the analyst personifies are savagely attacked. As the symbolizing function becomes more and more a part of the analytic couple, part of a shared goodness, these patients increase their resistance to it and double their efforts to devalue and destroy it. The symbolizing component of analytic work represents dangerous evidence of possible loss, persecution, and annihilation because it is equivalent to the good object. For these patients, the good object is fragile, prone to betrayal, and a reminder of past trauma.

For some, their early environment and their mother's failure to be a containing and symbolizing object seems to be the major factor in these feelings about the good object and the defensive, repetitious cycles we see in the treatment setting. For others, excessive envy and destructive projective identification have been the primary factor that spoiled the normal self↔good object experience. I think most patients are dealing with a combination. Segal elaborated on these ideas in an interview (Hunter 1993) by stating:

> there is this whole work of Bion, container and contained, in which he says that when the child has favorable development he projects into the mother and she lifts it from what he calls Beta to Alpha. The child reintrojects a container capable of the containing functions of alpha elements, of symbolism.

(p. 25)

Here, Segal is making the important link between the containing function of the object and the creation of symbols. The interviewer then asks if Segal feels the patient she had been discussing had a mother who was unable to contain the infant's projections. Segal answers, "either that or he was too envious to bear containment" (Hunter 1993: 25). This points to my previous proposal that, under pathological conditions, the ego will enviously destroy or denude the symbol and the containing-symbolizing, good object.

As Segal points out, the object also may be unable to contain the infant's projections. This can be the result of a mother who is depressed, resentful, or otherwise unreceptive. Therefore, multiple factors may prevent the maternal container and symbolizing object from purifying the infantile ego's phantasy material and affect states.

One patient, a borderline psychotic man, was thinking of having a vasectomy. He was flooded with anxiety because the symbolic meaning of the operation had become distorted and fragmented. He started to think of how he might have the operation and then a nuclear war would devastate the world. He would be the only man left and then meet the last woman. Because of his operation, he would then be responsible for not repopulating the planet and humanity would end due to his bad judgment. This phantasy left him quite nervous. This was similar to many other terrible phantasies he had over the years. They all related to his autonomy or identity causing the loss of all good objects and the sudden appearance of countless bad and attacking objects. My interpretations were focused on how the combination of doing something for himself and his idea of increasing the intimacy with his wife (his good object) had triggered a catastrophic anxiety.

While it appeared that he suffered from guilt about hurting his objects and then felt punished (a more depressive phantasy), his anxiety was actually much more primitive. He felt his separateness and his desire for intimacy in this new way caused the complete destruction of others which in turn caused his own annihilation. It was a paranoid-schizoid phantasy of loss and persecution (Waska 2002). Generally, this related to his ideas about his mother, who seemed as angry and judgmental over any move he made away from her. His projections of enormous aggression and fear strained the symbolic meaning of the vasectomy. The containing function of his mind was unable to maintain the symbolization in a helpful manner.

These patients are often struggling and suffering with how to control knowledge in themselves and in their objects. Knowledge can be conceptualized as a collection of mental symbols that contain core affects and phantasies woven together with cognitive information. Wisdom, understanding, and a sense of truth are the symbolic outcome of knowledge. Knowledge provides the important internal reassurance that there exists some type of meaning and order to things. This is a sublimation of the desire to know and control the mother's body. Therefore, knowledge represents union with the good object. The gain in self-knowledge that is the essence of analytic progress can be experienced as a threat. Establishing an intimacy and connection with analyst as the good object is the same sort of threat. Therefore, the knowledge gained through contact with the analyst must be fought off.

In this way, one sign of progress is when these patients begin allowing the analyst some degree of autonomy and capacity to think and interpret. One man would become angry and physically threatening whenever I made interpretations that were about the deeper meanings of his feelings or actions. In other words, if I proposed there being more than just the facts and various crises he related, he became very agitated. We slowly understood that for him, if he let himself contemplate anything, he felt he was "talking to himself". "Talking to himself" meant he was insane. Therefore, he always tried to eliminate any inner dialogue. The fact that I encouraged it, through free association, was especially threatening. After several years, he now will say, "I've been thinking about X, Y, or Z." Also, he will clarify what was said with me instead of feeling attacked and overwhelmed. He will say, "when you said X, what exactly did you mean?" This is done without the former verbal or physical threats to me and my office.

## CASE MATERIAL

When I first met Nancy, a middle-aged borderline patient, she seemed to have no grasp of common knowledge. While very bright and at times quite insightful, she could not allow herself to know certain things. These were usually facts about herself that pointed out her being regular and human and needing intimacy. After a routine dental checkup, she was shocked at finding out she had a cavity in her tooth. She was amazed, after we talked about it, to hear that adults ever have problems with their teeth. Her belief was that small children have cavities and then "grow out of it".

When Nancy discussed her mother and father, she would only use their first names. When I called attention to this, she claimed she had never called them anything else and wondered why I brought it up. I made the interpretation that she didn't want to use the words "mother" and "father" as it was too painful to realize she needed them. In response, she became highly agitated and paranoid. She threatened to leave. Nancy said I was attacking her and making her have thoughts she didn't want and never had to begin with.

Over the course of several years, we explored the idea that she felt her parents had never given her important and basic lessons in relating and never gave her any indication of understanding or warmth. This combined with her own refusal to take in any clues from them, as she felt her parents were threatening and hurtful.

Nancy was also threatened and perplexed by the concept that we might have feelings for each other. When we explored her bewilderment about this, it came out that there could be only two possibilities. We were either total strangers involved in a relatively safe and meaningless business transaction or I was a bad man trying to seduce her and brainwash her.

Nancy acted as if she was without need. She believed she did not need close relationships and certainly not with her analyst. She claimed to be a self-sufficient island and the idea that others are important was an insult. The experience of a good object was intolerable, let alone the risk of making contact and interacting with it.

Nancy grew up as the oldest of three children, with two younger brothers. Both her parents were alcoholics and her father overcame a cocaine addiction when Nancy was six years old. Nancy's father was in the Navy and out at sea for months at a time. When he was home, he would keep to himself, secluded in his home office, drinking and watching television. Nancy sees him as an ineffectual man who never cared about much in life and still is unavailable to her in her adult life. Nancy's mother would drink throughout the day, always maintaining a mild intoxication. This left her mother anxious, confused, and not sure how to conduct daily affairs or parenting.

As Nancy recalls her upbringing, her parents were a twosome of "plodding, indecisive, pathetic weaklings". Throughout her childhood, Nancy felt elected by her parents to make major decisions on their behalf and stand up for issues that were beyond her abilities as a child. Her mother would ask her to plan the dinner menu, choose new wallpaper, and figure out which car mechanic to use. Much of this adult responsibility was handed to her when her father was out to sea. However, it also occurred when he was home and seemed to not want to be bothered with such things.

The emotional result of this power imbalance was profound. Nancy felt extremely important, smart, and powerful. At a very young age, she saw herself as the family savior, the guide, and the sage. This was usually short-lived. Once Nancy made a big decision for her parents, they would discard her until the next time they needed her wisdom. She was only as good as her last great decision. To make matters worse, she felt blamed if the choice didn't work out, but not rewarded if it did.

Most of her childhood, Nancy was in a power-struggle with her parents, usually with her mother. To this day, she will get into very picky, tit-for-tat standoffs with both her parents. Her father, now retired, continues to drink in his office, not offering much to the whole family picture except as an inebriated shadow. As Nancy grew up, she felt her parents also gave her alternating views on her own life decisions and achievements. When she won awards in school or piano recital contests, she recalled her parents always choosing sides. One of them would praise her for her great skill and the other would play it down as nothing of real significance. More often than not, it was her father who would tell her to not make such a big deal out of everything. He told her in so many words, "that is certainly nothing to be so proud about".

As Nancy grew up, her life became punctuated by the same back-and-forth style, only now it was self-induced. In highschool, she would win more music awards. At college, she was on the dean's list. Medical school seemed simple and easy to grasp. Her internship at a respected hospital felt like destiny. All these victories, signs of true skill and intelligence, were met with sharply contrasting emotions. Nancy thought she was the only one who could really do the job at these appointments. Other contenders looked weak, simple, and limited. She felt superior and strong.

At the same time, she pulled herself down by imagining how others would question her views, find fault with her skill, and attack her decisions. So, it was an erratic ride that left her anxious and depressed. A new position would open up at the hospital. She would get excited that she was "the" candidate for it. She would put her application in and wait. Then, she started to think of all the mistakes she made on her application. There were all the other people who would envy and hate her if she was chosen. Nancy envisioned getting the job only to have the whole hospital despise her. Soon, she couldn't sleep at night, picturing herself trapped in a job where no one respected her and where she would probably be performing in a substandard way. She would deliberate over withdrawing her application. Finally, she was given the job and she accepted it, but was overwhelmed with fear and dread. Now, to avoid the ridicule of others, she felt she had to excel and prove them wrong. So, she would put in countless hours of overtime and feel angry and exhausted. Every step of the way, each portion of the job search, and then the job itself took on enormous symbolic meaning. But, this meaning was part of a primitive black or white, paranoid-schizoid world. First, she was the star. Then, her fans turned on her and she was ignored or attacked. This was a new version of the painful cycle of power, loss, and persecution she experienced with her family.

In the transference relationship, these same types of problems occurred. First, the very idea of needing help was something that enraged Nancy. Not being able to solve her own problems made her furious. To need me felt humiliating at best. Over the years, this softened a bit and she would tease me by saying, "you know this is a huge concession so don't make a big deal out of it, but I don't know how I could have done it without you. Don't press me on that though, be happy with what you've got or I might take it back." I pointed out to her how she was now being her controlling parents and I was her, having my fragile victory.

Throughout most of the treatment, she would become visibly upset and cry when discussing her childhood or her fears of other people hating her in her adult life. However, never would she use the box of tissues in front of her. I would offer her a tissue on occasion, only to have her wave it away with an angry look. Over time, I came to understand that the tissues took the form of a symbol. To Nancy, using a tissue to wipe her tears meant she was submitting to my control, being weak and humiliated, and in a dangerous intimacy with a good, supportive object. The piece of tissue meant so many threatening things that it had to be fought off. To believe in a good object who offered genuine care and a tissue was inviting disaster.

Making interpretations with Nancy was very difficult. She wanted to come to any insight all on her own. Nothing counted unless she thought of it first. For me to create mental symbols, thoughts, and images was both frightening and irritating to Nancy. I felt like we were in competition and if I came up with an idea first, she felt I had bested her. I noticed that she would refuse to hear what I had to say, only to mention my idea weeks or months later as if she had just discovered it. I made the mistake of pointing this out once or twice, only to have her become very defensive and angry.

This sort of "exclusive rights to new thoughts" approach also included bringing up topics that she didn't feel ready to discuss. I could bring up almost anything and if Nancy felt she had not gained emotional control over that issue, she refused to talk about it. Because of this process, it was hard to find out much about it. But, slowly it came out that Nancy felt she ought to be able to fully resolve any problem on her own. If she wasn't finished resolving it or had been unable to solve it at all, my bringing it up felt like salt in a wound. If I persisted, Nancy would threaten to leave the room or stop treatment altogether. My interest became a persecution and an inquiry that she felt she could not control. So, the symbolic process of free association and mutual exploration took on a cruel and frightening shape.

Just as symbolizing and containment are aspects of the good object and part of what the self experiences from its relationship with the good object, so is benign and caring interest. These difficult patients resist and undo all these qualities of the good object as they feel uncertain and dangerous. Better to create and control a bad object than to trust a good one and be exposed to betrayal, attack, and abandonment.

All this made my job as emotional translator and interpreter quite difficult. I, in the countertransference, felt bullied to abandon the symbolic and stick with the concrete. Only then did I feel safe from causing trouble and conflict. This was a taste of Nancy's past and current object relations experience. For Nancy, looking at things from a psychological perspective, searching for the symbolic meaning, was, as she put it, "a horrible surprise attack, out of the blue" or "a cruel thing, rubbing my face in it".

Part of how I worked with this was to interpret through my countertransference. I told Nancy that I often felt I was in a minefield with her. Things might seem OK or even quite good, but then I took the wrong step and disaster fell. I told her this might be how she felt growing up, where things went well and she was captain of the ship. But, then she hit the iceberg of her parents' shifting moods and the boat sank. This approach helped and a few years into the treatment, Nancy would apologize for causing me grief with her moods. Or, she would start a session by saying, "I want to warn you up-front, I am about to be a bitch." It took a while for her to allow me to explore this new way of relating, but gradually she could talk about how she felt out of control and bad for "bleeding all over" me.

I consider Nancy's analysis to be successful, yet her life remains punctuated on occasion by these sharp personality states. Over the course of treatment, she made many internal and external changes. Yet, she had to go through the same frightening phantasies each time. However, she kept trying to improve herself and understand how she perceived things, so the phantasies became less intense and less devastating. An example of this bumpy success was in her finding a boyfriend, becoming engaged, and getting married. It was a real show of progress that she allowed herself to become involved and dependent on this man. Nancy would be vulnerable for a while and then invariably start a fight with him to gain distance and control back. But, bit by bit, their relationship grew. When they decided to get married, the prospect of a wedding ceremony became a twisted symbol of sickly love, mushy dependency, and public humiliation. Therefore, Nancy insisted on a bland, safe, civil ceremony. She saw a public wedding with family, friends, and expressions of love and commitment to mean oppression and persecution.

The treatment ended in this same mixed way. Because of her hard work in analysis, she was now married and had earned a new position in the surgery department of a respected hospital on the East coast. She was to move and start a new life as a married woman and possibly start a family. She told me she truly appreciated me and what we had done together. This was very heartfelt and genuine. When I told her she could call me in the future if she ever needed to and I would welcome any news from her if she wished to tell me how her new life was turning out, Nancy stiffened. She said, "thanks, but I wouldn't be able to do that. That would mean I was falling backwards, failing. Even if I needed to, I wouldn't because then it would be a confirmation that I wasn't able to do it on my own. But, thanks. I know you mean well." So, in the end Nancy was still in the clutches of symbols that became persecutory and relationships that were fragile. The good object was tolerable, but still a possible threat. But, she could also move slightly beyond that enough to believe that I meant well. The good object was in sight. It was blurred by the bad, but still visible and reachable.

In Kleinian theory, the infant normally introjects the external caretaker as a helper and good object who will mitigate toxic, bad internal objects. When the external object, in particular the mother, is more of a hindrance than a helper, the introjection process compounds the natural harshness of the internal world. This results in a projection onto the external object of these now poisonous conditions. As a result, the ego views the external object as a threat, leading to further introjection as a defense. Continuous projection, denial, and hostile degrading of the object's importance leads to an unconscious fear of retaliation by a damaged and enraged object. These are magical and mystical delusions of a killed-off good object resurfacing from the grave and regaining a foothold as a dangerous bad object. This is actually what does occur, through over-identification and excessive projective identification. The ego's pathological splitting and projective identification cycles create a demand of loyalty to certain idealized aspects of the self and object relationship, which are in direct opposition to other aspects of that same relationship. The good object is lost in the shuffle. In fact, it is actively fought off and treated as dangerous.

In normal development, the ego communicates the innate life and death instincts in both loving and hateful ways to the mother through the process of projective identification. The mother functions as a basic container, translator, and modifier of these infantile drives. Together, this represents the alpha function (Bion 1962) which is a precursor to the symbolization process. All these important maternal functions are part of what is experienced as a good object. These functions are internalized and identified with for normal ego maturation. However, these basic elements of early life experience can go quite wrong.

Symbolization begins in the paranoid-schizoid position as elementary, unconscious phantasies with brittle constellations of positive and negative affect. Splitting is again the major mechanism that bolsters early symbolic organization. Therefore, when symbols emerge within the paranoid-schizoid position, the symbolizing maternal-container is a one-sided, idealized object.

Loss within the paranoid-schizoid position, due to the eventual failure of idealization, is a destabilizing failure of an ideal, meaningful object who translates and modifies elements of the death instinct into safer more tolerable aspects of the self. This type of loss is by definition a loss of self due to the self–object blur caused by strong reliance on projective identification. The ideal object is lost and replaced by a non-symbolic persecutory object and the self is left to the mercy of the death instinct.

Symbols only become completely formed psychic structures when the ego becomes fully integrated within the depressive position. Depressive symbols represent whole and complex objects and are an amalgam of the love and hate felt toward those objects. The good object is the relational other of the depressive position, that presence which can be depended on, identified with, and trusted. Segal (1978) notes that depressive symbols are part of healthy integration of loss, disappointment, and fear. I would rephrase that slightly to emphasize how symbols are an important part of the good object experience in which the ego learns creative solutions to loss and anxiety. The good object can be scary or disappointing at times. But, the depressive ego has integrated enough positive aspects of love and support from the good object to mitigate these less than ideal experiences, thus making them tolerable, acceptable, and understandable.

The more fragile the bond between ego and object, the more the good object is felt to be a threat to the ego. When destructive forms of projective identification and excessive oral aggression erode the splitting process, the ego begins to lose hold of its idealized objects. These objects then easily shift into persecutory objects. This creates a cycle in which the ego desperately tries to maintain idealistic visions of the world to ward off a sense of loss and attack. Manic and omnipotent styles of relating and narcissistic delusional states are common in building back the lost object and preventing attack. These primitive paranoid-schizoid methods of coping are then brought to bear in the ego's gradual shift into depressive functioning. This creates more distorted experiences of the self and the object, leading to a corruption or derailing of the internalized good object.

The patients I am highlighting in this chapter, as well as all the case examples in this book, are individuals who experience intimate relationships as an impossible task. They can attach to an object that is a constant reminder and constant threat of loss and persecution or be without a protecting maternal object that translates, modifies, and symbolizes otherwise disturbing inner conflicts. Specifically, they can align themselves with the mental image of a good object with all the important complexities of the wholeness found in depressive objects, but feel a looming loss and betrayal to be imminent. Or, the ego can deliberately detach from the experience of a good object and feel in control, but lost and alone. Either way, the ego feels lost in a frightening world with no safe haven.

A symbol is inherently healing to the psychic system, restoring ties to the object and resolving unconscious relational conflicts. To these difficult patients, however, their internal hostility is so great and the projective identification process so destructive, that symbols, and in turn the symbolizer (the good object), become corrupted. In other words, oral aggression, transported through projective identification, reduces meaningful symbols to concrete threats. The healing potential of the good object is replaced by hate, despair, and fear, leaving the ego unable to benefit from the safety and stability of the good object.

In seeing the symbolizing function of the good object/analyst as a threat, these patients retaliate or defend themselves. The analyst can not be good, can not be helpful, and can not stimulate growth. Insight, the analyst's containing and symbolizing activity, is experienced as something that catches the ego off guard. It reveals something that was previously unknown and therefore unpredictable and frightening. In response, the patient will try to keep the treatment very safe, predictable, and narrow. Everything must be already understood or known. New knowledge or change is dangerous.

# Summary

Psychoanalytic treatment, conducted from a Kleinian framework, links the patient's current psychological experience to early infantile and childhood interactions with the internal and external world (Steiner 2004). As a result of greed, envy, frustration, and desire, the immature ego feels hatred toward the object, resulting in phantasies of an injured or dying object. As a result of identification, to ward off loss and guilt, the entire world seems to collapse and annihilation seems imminent. At that point, the history of contact with good objects is crucial to bring balance to this internal catastrophe. With ample good object experiences, the ego is able to approach and transition to the depressive position. There, mitigating factors such as guilt, integration of love and hate, reparation, restoration and forgiveness, compassion, and acceptance make it possible to make it through those overwhelming anxieties. There is a happy ending to the story. The self and the object are whole, good, and able to tolerate the inconsistences, disappointments, and flaws that life, self, and others bring.

However, if there has been a lack of good object experience, or if the good object has been tainted with abusive and painful experiences, the ego may not be able to tolerate the natural pain, despair, fear, and rage of living. This causes a breakdown of the internal world in which the very qualities that were potentially growth-enhancing become disabling. Guilt feels very persecutory, reparation seems impossible, hate overcomes love, and compassion seems like a lie. Mutuality or dependence is deadly. The regressive qualities of the paranoid-schizoid position take over, making it feel worse, more ominous. So, the ego tries to block off both methods of relating and simply hides out or sets up a last-ditch standoff against the good object.

From a theoretical perspective, the patients profiled in this book can be conceptualized as emotionally forced by early childhood experiences (both internal and external) to defensively engage in quasi-depressive methods of relating while still dealing with undue paranoid-schizoid difficulties. These experiences include traumatic self–object stressors in which aggression, guilt, betrayal, abandonment, and loss were too prominent for the infantile ego to process. The lack of fallible yet wholesome and adequate good objects providing a secure base makes it treacherous to move forward in psychic development. As a result, there is a pathological mixture of paranoid-schizoid problems, primitive methods of navigating the depressive position, and an ongoing breakdown of these immature and brittle depressive abilities into more paranoid experiences.

From a clinical perspective, these patients present as very difficult individuals who seem to go out of their way to avoid a connection with the good object, and thereby create therapeutic stalemates. Technical approaches that exemplify the author's Kleinian stance have been presented. These techniques include close monitoring of the transference and interpretation of the moment-to-moment phantasies which clinically unfold interpersonally, by direct associations, and by various defensive maneuvers, including acting out.

The complicated cases presented throughout the book are typical of the patients analysts see in private practice. They don't have one glaring behavioral symptom to focus on. However, they all have the central psychological theme of avoiding the good object at all costs. Therefore, the analyst may feel excluded, misrepresented, or ignored in favor of a very distorted transference image. As Brenner (1970) suggests, treatment should proceed as it does with any other case of transference analysis. Yet, I think that focusing on interpretations that address the tangled mixture of paranoid-schizoid features and immature depressive functioning can offer the analyst a more advanced sense of clinical direction. And, bringing the patient's transference fight against the good object into the very center of the analytic exploration and working-through process is critical in these difficult cases. Similar to Steiner's (1993) ideas of psychic retreats in which the ego finds systems of defense to avoid the unbearable feelings of both the paranoid-schizoid and depressive states, these patients seem to be simultaneously suffering the anxieties of both psychological positions but without any workable respite, pathological or otherwise. There is no clearing, no hiding, no retreat for them. The best they can do is to refuse entrance to goodness, growth, or love while under the sway of their phantasies about the treacherous nature of the good object.

Melanie Klein (1957) stated that greed is an insatiable craving that goes beyond what is needed or what is available. She thought the unconscious essence of greed lay in the ego's attempt to aggressively rob the maternal object of all of its valuable love and nutrition. Envy, Klein wrote, is the destructive taking of what is good and replacing it with bad, a projection of poisonous elements. Greed is the constant introjection of everything good the object possesses.

While some patients are ruthless about carrying out these greedy, selfish urges, other patients are alarmed and panicked by these phantasies. I think this occurs in two ways. Some patients are scared of the consequence to the self. The paranoid-schizoid phantasy of greedy takeover includes a destroyed object that rises from the dead to exact revenge. Therefore, the ego is faced with a dual threat: complete loss of the object and annihilation at the hands of the object.

Other patients struggle more with the consequences, in phantasy, of their greed to the health of the object. These patients fear they have damaged, burdened, or stolen from the object and feel enormous guilt and remorse. These patients often use a strategy of not having any needs to prevent any possible hurt to the object.

When greed is the cornerstone of a patient's internal world, they often struggle enormously with all of these concerns. The guilt can take on a persecutory flavor and the desire to make reparation can take on a do-or-die paranoia. This can be confusing for the analyst, who may feel the treatment is lurching between progress and failure. Therefore, countertransference is important to notice and utilize. Projective identification, splitting, and denial are common defenses in these cases and produce difficult transference–countertransference dynamics. Gradual analysis of greed and the accompanying paranoia and hopeless feelings can bring about a better balance between these otherwise frightening and immobilizing phantasies.

Good object experiences and a solid internal connection to the life force are two prerequisites for sound mental functioning. The life force strives for change, difference, and emotional mobility. The death force seeks predictability, stability, and safety. Ideally, these dual drives operate in balance to offer the ego phantasies of an internal world where self-and-object connections are rich, flexible, enduring, and fulfilling.

Depending on the nature of unconscious phantasy, the degree of balance within intra-psychic conflicts, and the adequate quantity of good internal object relations, this life-and-death balance will result in a variety of unconscious dynamics. It may be that the ego experiences coexisting forces of challenge and change side-by-side with the desire to maintain unity and peace. Or, the ego may experience a great deal of envy and greed that outweighs any feeling of contentment and satisfaction. In other words, the death instinct is silent when there is an adequate balance between the life and death forces and when an adequate supply of good objects fortifies the ego. In more pathological situations, the ego is taken over by the death instinct and its dynamic struggles to control the self and its object relations.

In normal psychological development, the maternal containing function manages the ego's chaotic and intense oral striving. Through a healthy process of projective identification, the mother acts as a translating receptacle for the phantasies of the infant's life and death instincts.

With proper containment, understanding, and detoxification, the ego is stabilized and fortified with good objects. The ego internalizes this container function and is able to deal with its own frustrations and disappointments. While the phantasy for an ideal object remains, the ego better tolerates its unavailability.

However, multiple factors can prevent this optimal outcome. The external environment may prove traumatic or overly frustrating. The ego may be too aggressive or disabled by envy and conflict. The necessary container-envelope that a mother hopefully provides may not be available for identification and internalization or the ego may resist taking that function in as it is associated with a hated or envied object. In other words, many environmental, intra-psychic, and biological factors work together to facilitate or hinder the normal growth of the ego.

The search for the ideal object, its shattering loss, and its return as a cruel and dangerous persecutor are hallmarks of these difficult patients. The cycles of acting out and the death instinct usually keep this more basic anxiety in the shadows. However, if patient and analyst manage to stay with it, the vicissitudes of paranoid-schizoid loss and guilt permeate the treatment. Segal (1974) sums up much of what I have stated:

> if early envy is very intense, it interferes with the normal operation of schizoid mechanisms. The process of splitting into an ideal and a persecutory object, so important in the paranoid-schizoid position, cannot be maintained, since it is the ideal object which gives rise to envy and is attacked and spoiled. This leads to confusion between the good and the bad interfering with splitting. As splitting cannot be maintained and an ideal object cannot be preserved, introjection of an ideal object and identification with it is severely interfered with. And with it the development of the ego must necessarily suffer. An ideal object cannot be found, therefore there is no hope of love or help from anywhere. The destroyed objects are the source of endless persecution and later guilt.
>
> (pp. 41–42)

I would simply add that guilt does not come later. Primitive phantasies of loss and guilt work hand-in-hand to bring on the experience of losing the ideal object and simultaneously being attacked by that now spoiled and bad object.

Translation and containment of intense anxiety and paranoia reveal the destructive and defensive workings of the death instinct. Gradually, this turns out to be a large-scale intra-psychic defense against fears of loss, annihilation, and persecution. Projection identification of oral rage, splitting and idealization, and manic defenses permeate all three stages of treatment. If both analyst and patient can tolerate these three lengthy and stressful parts of treatment, the results are startling. Significant character change is possible and these patients emerge with much greater ego capacity and internal resources. Object relations become whole and integrated and internal experiences begin to more closely reflect and match external reality.

The analytic situation is an intimate study of the evolving intra-psychic and interpersonal relationship between analyst and patient. The patients profiled in this book find the idea of such a back-and-forth exchange fundamentally intolerable. These are patients who are enraged and pained by the concept of giving in any capacity. Careful analysis reveals phantasies of wanting to control, own, or feed on the emotional nutrients the patient feels the mother/analyst has denied him or her. The feeling of starving and the phantasy of being blocked from the analyst/mother's breast create resentment and desires for revenge. Envy of what the analyst has and doesn't provide shapes a transference reaction in which the patient is always demanding and simultaneously being careful to never be dependent or forthcoming.

Klein (1957) writes, "greed, envy, and persecutory anxiety, which are bound up with each other, inevitably increase each other" (p. 187). I have explored some of the difficulties with patients suffering from these oral anxieties and chronic envy. These patients use projective identification and devaluation to ward off the introjection of the good object as they see it as giving in to a dominating and humiliating experience. They feel ashamed of feeling dependent and in turn refuse to give to the analyst. Rather than feeling hopeful and grateful, they demand praise and feeding as their right. This omnipotence is a negation of intense feelings of deprivation and loss and an expression of rage, revenge, and a cry for restitution. Such a patient wants, and demands, an undoing of past hurt, revenge for ongoing feelings of disappointment, and the handing over of never-obtained idealized goods from a hoped-for object that never was. Careful analysis of both projective identification processes and countertransference reactions are crucial in this type of treatment. Hopefully, a gradual understanding and mourning of these lost objects and persecutory deprivations is possible in the context of the transference. This leads to a move into the depressive position and the acquisition of whole objects, gratitude, and trust.

The patients presented in this book have an unsteady foothold in both the paranoid-schizoid position and the depressive position. Their experience of the depressive world is immature and distorted, leading back to regressive methods of operating within its parameters. So, sooner rather than later, new symbols and new experiences with good objects shift from being integrative and healing, losing their safety and containing potential, and become chaotic and threatening. Unless this process is repeatedly interrupted by the understanding, containing, and interpreting function of analysis, the ego's fight, flight, and standoff with the good object never ends.

# Bibliography

Asch, S. (1976) Varieties of negative therapeutic reaction and problems of technique, *Journal of the American Psychoanalytic Association*, 24: 383–407.

Bell, D. (2001) Projective identification, in Catalina Bronstein (ed.), *Kleinian Theory: A Contemporary Perspective*. London: Whurr Publishers.

Bianchedi, E., Antar, R., Fernandez, M., Podetti, B., De Piccolo, E., Miranvent, I., De Cortinas, L., De Boschan, L. and Waseman, M. (1984) Beyond Freudian metapsychology: the metapsychological points of view of the Kleinian school, *International Journal of Psychoanalysis*, 65: 389–398.

Bicudo, V. (1964) Persecutory guilt and ego restrictions of a pre-depressive position, *International Journal of Psychoanalysis*, 45: 358–363.

Bion, W. (1957) Differentiation of the psychotic from more psychotic personalities, *International Journal of Psychoanalysis*, 38: 266–275.

Bion, W. (1962) *Learning from Experience*. London: William Heinemann.

Bion, W.R. (1967) *Second Thoughts*, ch. 8. London: Heinemann.

Boesky, D. (1991) Conflict, compromise formation, and structural theory, in Scott Dowling (ed.), *Conflict and Compromise: Therapeutic Implications*. Madison, Conn.: International Universities Press.

Boris, H. (1986) The "other" breast: greed, envy, spite, and revenge, *Contemporary Psychoanalysis*, 22: 45–59.

Boyer, B. (1986) Technical aspects of treating the regressed patient, *Contemporary Psychoanalysis*, 22: 25.

Brenman, E. (1982) Separation: a clinical problem, *International Journal of Psychoanalysis*, 63: 303–310.

Brenner, C. (1970) Panel: negative therapeutic reaction, reported S. Olinick, *Journal of the American Psychoanalytic Association*, 18: 655–672.

Brenner, C. (1991) Conflict and compromise: therapeutic strategies for clinicians, in Scott Dowling (ed.), *Conflict and Compromise: Therapeutic Implications*. Madison, Conn.: International Universities Press.

Brenner, C. (1992) The structural theory and clinical practice, *Journal of Clinical Psychoanalysis*, 1(3): 369–380.

Bronstein, C. (1999) *A Day of Psychoanalytic Papers to Celebrate Hana Segal's Eightieth Birthday*, IPA Internet Website, posted 7/13/1999.

Caper, R. (1992) Does psychoanalysis heal? A contribution to the theory of psychoanalytic technique, *International Journal of Psychoanalysis*, 73: 283–292.

Ellman, C.S., Grand, S., Silvan, M. and Ellman, S.J. (1998) *The Modern Freudians: Contemporary Psychoanalytic Technique*. Northvale, NJ: Aronson.

Etchegoyen, H., Lopez, B. and Rabih, M. (1987) Envy and how to interpret it, *International Journal of Psychoanalysis*, 68: 49–61.

Feldman, M. (2000) Some views on the manifestation of the death instinct in clinical work, *International Journal of Psychoanalysis*, 81: 53–65.

Fenichel, O. (1941) *Problems of Psychoanalytic Technique*. New York: Psychoanalytic Quarterly.

Ferro, A. (1993) From hallucination to dream, *The Psychoanalytic Review*, 80(3, Fall): 389–404.

Frankiel, R., Harris, A. and Spillius, E. (2001) To have and have not: clinical uses of envy, *Journal of the American Psychoanalytic Association*, 49(4): 1391–1404.

Freeman, T. (1989) Schizophrenic delusions and their pre-psychotic antecedents, *International Journal of Psychoanalysis*, 63: 445.

Friedman, R. *et al.* (1998) Private psychotherapy patients of psychiatrist psychoanalysts, *American Journal of Psychiatry*, 155: 1772–1774.

Freud, S. (1896) The Defense Neuro-Psychosis, *Collected Papers*, vol. I. New York: Basic Books, 1959, p. 163.

Freud, S. (1913) *Beginning Treatment*, Standard Edition, vol. 12. London: Hogarth Press, p. 123a.

Freud, S. (1916) *Introductory Lectures on Psychoanalysis*, Standard Edition, XV–XVI, 358–359.

Freud, S. (1918) *An Infantile Neurosis*, Standard Edition, London: Hogarth Press, 1957.

Freud, S. (1923) *The Ego and the Id*, Standard Edition, 19: 3–66. Hogarth Press, 1961.

Freud, S. (1930) *Civilization and its Discontents*, Standard Edition, 21.

Freud, S. (1937) *Analysis Terminable and Interminable*, Standard Edition, 23.

Gabbard, G. (1997) Case histories and confidentiality, *International Journal of Psychoanalysis*, 78: 820–821.

Gammill, J. (1989) Some personal reflections of Melanie Klein, *Journal of Melanie Klein and Object Relations*, 7(2): 1–16.

Gorney, J. (1979) The negative therapeutic interaction, *Contemporary Psychoanalysis*, 15: 288–336.

Grinberg, L. (1964) Two kinds of guilt: their relations with normal and pathological aspects of mourning, *International Journal of Psychoanalysis*, 45: 366–371.

Grinberg, L. (1968) On acting out and its role in the psychoanalytic process, *International Journal of Psychoanalysis*, 49: 171–178.

Grinberg, L. (1979) Countertransference and projective counteridentification. *Contemporary Psychoanalysis*, 15: 226–247.

Grinberg, L. (1990) *The Goals of Psychoanalysis: Identification, Identity, and Supervision*. London: Karnac Books.

Grinberg, L. (1992) Countertransference and projective counteridentification, *Contemporary Psychoanalysis*, 15: 226–247.

Grotstein, J. (1977) The psychoanalytic concept of schizophrenia: 1. the dilemma, *International Journal of Psychoanalysis*, 58: 403–425.

Grotstein, J. (1985) A proposed revision of the psychoanalytic concept of the death instinct, in the *Yearbook of Psychoanalysis and Psychotherapy*, vol. 1.

Heimann, P. (1956) Dynamics of transference interpretations, *International Journal of Psychoanalysis*, 37: 303–310.

Hess, N. (1999) Psychoanalytic psychotherapy for chronic depression, in S. Ruszczynski and S. Johnson (eds), *Psychoanalytic Psychotherapy in the Kleinian Tradition*. London: Karnac Books.

Hinshelwood, R.D. (1994) *Dictionary of Kleinian Thought*. London: Free Association Books.

Hinshelwood, R.D. (1999) Transference and countertransference, in B. Burgoyne and M. Sullivan (eds), *Klein–Lacan Dialogues*. New York: Other Press, p. 135.

Horney, K. (1936) The problem of negative therapeutic reaction, *Psychoanalytic Quarterly*, 5: 29–44.

Hunter, V. (1993) An interview with Hanna Segal, *Psychoanalytic Review*, 80(1): 1–28.

Isaacs, S. (1948) The nature and function of phantasy, *International Journal of Psychoanalysis*, 29: 73–97.

Israel, P., Dispaux, M., Jimenz-de La Jara, J., Kirshner, L. and Mellman, L. (1999) IPA report of the Committee on Psychoanalysis and Allied Therapies, *Winter Newsletter of the International Psychoanalytic Association*, IPA Website.

Joseph, B. (1960) Some characteristics of psychopathic personalities, *International Journal of Psychoanalysis*, 41: 526–531.

Joseph, B. (2004) *In Pursuit of Psychic Change*, in Edith Hargreaves and Arturo Varchevker (eds), Hove and New York: Brunner-Routledge.

Kaplan, H. (1991) Greed: a psychoanalytic perspective, *Psychoanalytic Review*, 78(4): 505–523.

Kernberg, O. (1984) *Severe Personality Disorders*. New Haven, Conn.: Yale University Press.

Klein, M. (1926) The psychological principles of early analysis, in *The Writings of Melanie Klein*, vol. 1. *Love, Guilt, and Reparation and Other Works, 1921–1945*. New York: Free Press, p. 128.

Klein, M. (1928) Early stages of the oedipus conflict, in *The Writings of Melanie Klein*, vol. 1, *Love, Guilt, and Reparation and Other Works, 1921–1945*. New York: Free Press, p. 188.

Klein, M. (1930) The importance of symbol-formation in the development of the ego, *International Journal of Psychoanalysis*, 11: 24–39.

Klein, M. (1933) The early development of consciousness in the child, in *The Writings of Melanie Klein*, vol. 1, *Love, Guilt, and Reparation and Other Works, 1921–1945*. New York: Free Press, pp. 248–257.

Klein, M. (1935) A contribution to the psychogenesis of manic-depressive states, in *The Writings of Melanie Klein*, vol. 1, *Love, Guilt, and Reparation and Other Works, 1921–1945*. New York: Free Press, p. 262.

Klein, M. (1936) Weaning, in *Love, Guilt, and Reparation and Other Works, 1921–1945, The Writings of Melanie Klein*, vol. 1. New York: Free Press, p. 290.

Klein, M. (1940) Mourning and its relation to manic-depressive states, *International Journal of Psychoanalysis*, 21: 125–153.

Klein, M. (1945) The Oedipus complex in the light of early anxieties, *International Journal of Psychoanalysis*, 26: 11–33.

Klein, M. (1946) Notes on some schizoid mechanisms, *The Writings of Melanie Klein*, vol. 3. New York: Free Press.

Klein, M. (1948) On the theory of anxiety and guilt, in *The Writings of Melanie Klein*, vol. 3, *Envy and Gratitude and Other Works, 1946–1963*. New York: Free Press.

Klein, M. (1952a) The behavior of young infants, in *The Writings of Melanie Klein*, vol. 3, *Envy and Gratitude and Other Works, 1946–1963*. New York: Free Press.

Klein, M. (1952b) The mutual influences in the development of ego and id – discussants, *Psychoanalytic Study of the Child*, 7: 51–53.

Klein, M. (1952c) The origins of transference, *The Writings of Melanie Klein*, vol. 3, *Envy and Gratitude and Other Works, 1946–1963*. New York: Free Press.

Klein, M. (1952d) Some theoretical conclusions regarding the emotional life of the infant, *The Writings of Melanie Klein*, vol. 3, *Envy and Gratitude and Other Works, 1946–1963*. New York: Free Press.

Klein, M. (1955) On identification, in *The Writings of Melanie Klein*, vol. 3, *Envy and Gratitude and Other Works, 1946–1963*. New York: Free Press, p. 154.

Klein, M. (1957) Envy and gratitude, in *The Writings of Melanie Klein*, vol. 3, *Envy and Gratitude and Other Works, 1946–1963*. New York: Free Press, pp. 176–235.

Klein, M. (1958) On the development of mental functioning, *International Journal of Psychoanalysis*, 39: 84–90.

Klein, M. (1959) Our adult world and its roots in infancy, in *The Writings of Melanie Klein*, vol. 3, *Envy and Gratitude and Other Works, 1946–1963*. New York: Free Press, pp. 247–263.

Klein, M. (1963) On the sense of loneliness, in *The Writings of Melanie Klein*, vol. 3, *Envy and Gratitude and Other Works, 1946–1963*. London: Hogarth Press, p. 300.

Klein, M. and Riviere, J. (1964) *Love, Hate, and Reparation*. New York: W.W. Norton and Company.

Laplanche, J. and Pontalis, J.-B. (1973) *The Language of Psychoanalysis*. New York: W.W. Norton and Company.

Limentani, A. (1981) On some positive aspects of the negative therapeutic reaction, *International Journal of Psychoanalysis*, 62: 379–390.

Lipshitz-Phillips, S. (1999) Early loss and unresolved mourning, in S. Ruszczynski and S. Johnson (eds), *Psychoanalytic Psychotherapy in the Kleinian Tradition*. London: Karnac Books.

Loewald, H. (1972) Freud's conception of negative therapeutic reaction with comment on instinct theory, *Journal of the American Psychoanalytic Association*, 20: 235–245.

Maroda, K. (1995) Projective identification and countertransference intervention: since feelings are first, *The Psychoanalytic Review*, 82(2): 229–247.

Meltzer, D. (1978) A note on Bion's concept 'reversal of alpha-function', in *The Kleinian Development*. Perth: Clunie.

Money-Kyle, R. (1968) Cognitive development, *International Journal of Psychoanalysis*, 49: 691–698.

Moser-Ha, H. (2001) Working through envy, some technical issues, *International Journal of Psychoanalysis*, 82: 713–725.

Olinick, S. (1964) The negative therapeutic reaction, *International Journal of Psychoanalysis*, 45: 540–548.

Olinick, S. (1970) Panel: negative therapeutic reaction, reported S. Olinick, *Journal of the American Psychoanalytic Association*, 18: 655–672.

O'Shaughnessy, E. (1964) The absent object, *Journal of Child Psychotherapy*, 1(2): 34–43.

Ponsi, M. (2000) *IJPA Discussion Group*, Bulletin 264, Feb. 8th.

Quinodoz, J. (1996) The sense of solitude in the psychoanalytic encounter, *International Journal of Psychoanalysis*, 77: 481–496.

Quinodoz, J. (2000) *IJPA Discussion Group*, Bulletin 262, Feb. 4th.

Racker, H. (1960) A study of some early conflicts through their return in the patient's relation with the interpretation, *International Journal of Psychoanalysis*, 41: 1, 47–58.

Racker, H. (1968) *Transference and Countertransference*. Madison, Conn.: International Universities Press, pp. 135–137.

Riviere, J. (1936) A contribution to the analysis of the negative therapeutic reaction, *International Journal of Psychoanalysis*, 17: 304–320.

Rosenfeld, H. (1964) On the psychopathology of narcissism: a clinical approach, *International Journal of Psychoanalysis*, 45: 332–337.

Rosenfeld, H. (1971) A clinical approach to the psychoanalytic theory of the life and death instincts: an investigation into the aggressive aspects of narcissism, *International Journal of Psychoanalysis*, 52: 169–178.

Rosenfeld, H. (1975) The negative therapeutic reaction, in P. Giovacchini (ed.), *Tactics and Techniques in Psychoanalytic Therapy*, vol. 2. New York: Jason Aronson, pp. 217–228.

Rosenfeld, H. (1978) Notes on the psychopathology and psychoanalytic treatment of some borderline patients, *International Journal of Psychoanalysis*, 59: 215–221.

Rosenfeld, H. (1979) Difficulties in the psychoanalysis of borderline patients, in J. LeBoit and A. Capponi (eds), *Advances in Psychotherapy of the Borderline Patient*. New York: Jason Aronson, pp. 203–204.

Rosenfeld, H. (1983) Primitive object relations and mechanisms, *International Journal of Psychoanalysis*, 64: 261–267.

Rosenfeld, H. (1987) *Impasse and Interpretation*. London: New Library of Psychoanalysis.

Rusbridger, R. (2004) Elements of the Oedipus complex: a Kleinian account, *International Journal of Psychoanalysis*, 85(3): 731–747.

Sandler, J. (1987) The concept of projective identification, in J. Sandler (ed.), *Projection, Identification, and Projective Identification*. Madison, Conn.: International Universities Press, pp. 13–26.

Schachter, J. (1992) Concepts of termination and post-termination patient-analyst contact, *International Journal of Psychoanalysis*, 73: 137–154.

Schneider, M. (1988) Primary envy and the creation of the ego ideal, *International Journal of Psychoanalysis*, 15: 319–329.

Segal, H. (1957) Notes on symbol formation, *International Journal of Psychoanalysis*, 38: 39–45.

Segal, H. (1972) A delusional system as a defence against the re-emergence of a catastrophic situation, *International Journal of Psychoanalysis*, 53: 393.

Segal, H. (1974) *Introduction to the Work of Melanie Klein*, 2nd ed. New York: Basic Books, 37–38.

Segal, H. (1977) Psychoanalytic dialogue: Kleinian theory today, *Journal of the American Psychoanalytic Association*, 25: 363–370.

Segal, H. (1978) On symbolism, *International Journal of Psychoanalysis*, 59: 315–319.

Segal, H. (1979) Postscript to notes on symbol-formation, in (1981) *The Work of Hanna Segal*. New York: Jason Aronson.

Segal, H. (1983) Some clinical implications of Melanie Klein's work, *International Journal of Psychoanalysis*, 64: 269–276.

Segal, H. (1993) On the clinical usefulness of the concept of death instinct, *International Journal of Psychoanalysis*, 74: 55–61.

Segal, H. (1997) *Psychoanalysis, Literature and War: Papers 1972–1995 Hanna Segal*, ed. John Steiner. London: Routledge, pp. 17–26.

Segal, H. (2001) Symbolization, in Catalina Bronstein (ed.), *Kleinian Theory: A Contemporary Perspective*. London: Whurr Publishers.

Spillius, E. (1983) Some developments from the work of Melanie Klein, *International Journal of Psychoanalysis*, 64: 321–331.

Spillius, E. (1993) Varieties of envious experience, *International Journal of Psychoanalysis*, 74: 1199–1212.

Stein, R. (1990) A new look at the theory of Melanie Klein, *International Journal of Psychoanalysis*, 71: 499–511.

Steiner, J. (1982) Perverse relationships between parts of the self: a clinical illustration, *International Journal of Psychoanalysis*, 63: 241–251.

Steiner, J. (1985) The interplay between pathological organizations and the paranoid-schizoid position and the depressive position, *International Journal of Psychoanalysis*, 66: 201–213.

Steiner, J. (1987) The interplay between pathological organizations and the paranoid-schizoid and depressive position, *International Journal of Psychoanalysis*, 68: 69–80.

Steiner, J. (1993) *Psychic Retreats: Pathological Organizations in Psychotic, Neurotic, and Borderline Patients*. London and New York: Routledge.

Steiner, J. (1996) The aim of psychoanalysis in theory and in practice, *International Journal of Psychoanalysis*, 77: 1073–1083.

Steiner, J. (2000) Containment, enactment, and communication, *International Journal of Psychoanalysis*, 81(2): 245–255.

Steiner, J. (2004) Gaze, dominance, and humiliation in the Schreber case, *International Journal of Psychoanalysis*, 85: 269–284.

Stephen, K. (1934) Introjection and projection: guilt and rage, *British Journal of Medical Psychology*, 14: 317–331.

Symington, N. (2004) Two sessions with Lawrence, *International Journal of Psychoanalysis*, 85(2): 253–268.

Temperley, J. (2001) The Depressive Position, in Catalina Bronstein (ed.), *Kleinian Theory: A Contemporary Perspective*. London: Whurr Publications, p. 50.

Thorner, H. (1952) The criteria of progress in a patient during analysis, *International Journal of Psychoanalysis*, 33: 479–484.

Valenstein, A. (1973) On attachment to painful feelings and the negative therapeutic reaction, *Psychoanalytic Study of the Child*, 28: 365–392, New Haven, Conn.: Yale University Press.

Valenstein, A. (1989) Pre-Oedipal reconstructions in psychoanalysis, *International Journal of Psychoanalysis*, 70: 433.

Vaquer, F. (1991) An object relations approach to conflict and compromise formation, in Scott Dowling (ed.), *Conflict and Compromise: Therapeutic Implications*. Madison, Conn.: International Universities Press.

Wallerstein, R. (1986) *Forty-Two Lives in Treatment*. New York: Guilford Press.

Waska, R. (1999) Bargains, treaties, and delusions, *Journal of the American Academy of Psychoanalysis*, 27(3): 451–469.

Waska, R. (2002) *Primitive Experiences of Loss: Working with the Paranoid-Schizoid Patient*. London: Karnac.

Waska, R. (2004) *Projective Identification: The Kleinian Interpretation*. London: Brunner/Routledge.

Waska, R. (2005) *Real People, Real Problems, Real Solutions: The Kleinian Approach to Difficult Patients*. London: Brunner/Routledge.

Williams, G. (1997) Reflections on some dynamics of eating disorders: 'no entry' defenses and foreign bodies, *International Journal of Psychoanalysis*, 78: 927–941.

# Index

abandonment 3, 5, 33, 58, 93
acceptance 18
acting out xi, 107, 154, 163; anxiety 200;
    borderline patients xii, 51, 152; death
    instinct 160; defense 156, 198; dreams
    152; internal bargain 199; panic 205;
    projective identification 155;
    psychotic patients 152
aggression x, 67, 73–4, 76
aimless 25
Alex 59–61, 62
alone x, 20, 21, 25, 33, 70, 75, 84
alpha function 229, 236
ambition 83
anger 23, 24, 28, 29, 97
Ann 83–9
annihilation xi, 7, 170
anorexia 81, 82
anti-good object transference 46–7
anti-growth 3, 4, 5, 6, 42
anti-relating 11
anxiety: acting out 200; denial 212–13;
    future difficulties 217; greed 129;
    inferiority 36, 37; loss 33; self-
    preservation 212
Asch, S. 3
attachment 209, 223
attack 11

B 147–8
bad object ix
bad self ix
bargains xii, 199, 211–12, 219, 220
behavior 3
Bell, D. 224
beta function 229
Betty 22–8
Bianchedi, E. 137

Bicudo, V. 18, 121
Bion, W. 140, 152, 197, 226, 229,
    236
Bob 216–23
Boesky, D. 210
borderline anxiety 195–206
borderline patients xii, 51; three phases
    of treatment 152–4, 167–8
Boris, H. 101, 118
Boyer, B. 219
Brenman, E. 80, 200
Brenner, C. 32, 210, 239
Bronstein, C. 140
bullying 43, 44, 154, 201

Caper, R. 77
change 3, 21, 62, 141
childhood experiences 16, 33, 51, 106,
    117, 120, 144, 196–7, 221, 232, 238
choice 29
Christy 81–3
commitment 29, 89–90
competition 3
compromise formation xii, 210–12
confidentiality 107
conflict 9
containment xi, 145, 169, 175, 220;
    active 156–7; detoxification 95;
    flexible 199, 206; greed 132–3;
    maternal 197; symbols 229–30
control 26, 27, 84
coping 33, 35
counter-projective identification 43,
    199
countertransference 19, 25, 27, 30, 35,
    43, 56, 59, 68, 84, 90, 110, 111, 116,
    123, 143, 165, 199
• creative outlet 56–7

death instinct 3; acting out 160; biological characteristic 139–40; clinical importance 152–3; defensive xi, 146, 147, 148–9, 150, 159–60, 172, 200, 205; destructive aspects 161–2; ego deficit 161; envy 88–9, 137–8, 146; greed 120; ideal development 160; innate and constitutional 138; introducing concept 137; life instinct and 120, 153; masochism 138; multiple mental mechanisms 147; narcissism 79, 146, 148; projective identification 146–7; psychological nature 138, 140–1, 157–8; reality 140; sadism 138; self-destruction 142, 145, 146, 147, 172; separation 93; superego 138–9, 162, 164; thinking 141

delusions 175, 207, 208, 209, 212, 214–15, 216, 219, 222

denial xii, 8, 17, 212–13

dependence 89, 126, 183

depression 56, 108

depressive altruism 20

depressive anxieties 6, 9

depressive guilt 164

depressive phantasies 4, 6

depressive position ix, 4–5, 70, 101; dynamics 63; internal bargains 212; primitive form 87–8; psychosis 33; reconciliation between warring factions 185; symbols 236; working through 18

desertion 190

despair 34, 60

destructive cycle 68

detachment 8

devaluation 188, 242

difference 28, 93

discontentment 7

distancing 34, 69, 93

Doris 189–90

dreams 13, 101–2, 149–50, 152, 173–4, 219

eating 70–1, 72, 81, 82, 196

Ed 89–90

ego: good objects 33, 47; greed 90, 91, 92; hunger 38; toxic 22

ego-ideal 129

emotional starvation 92

empty x

entitlement 29

envy x, xi, xii, 3, 4, 32, 79, 80, 109, 239; death instinct 88–9, 137–8, 146; devaluation 188; ego 91, 92; greed 89–90, 126

epistemophilic impulse 197

Etchegoyen, H. 59

evacuative character 95

expectations xi, 106, 118, 126–7, 128

external experiences 204, 208–9, 225

extra-transference 143, 172

failure 52

family environment 67–8, 73, 81, 93; see also fathers; mothers; siblings

fathers 7–8, 10, 19, 22, 23, 28, 35, 36, 50, 55, 68, 83–4, 94, 107, 121, 122, 126, 127, 154, 196, 197, 209, 216, 219, 231, 232, 233

fear 96–7; pseudo-depressive 75

Feldman, M. 118, 141

Fenichel, O. 167

Ferro, A. 190

food 70–1, 72, 81

forgiveness 9, 18, 92

Fran 19–22

Frankiel, R. 118

free association 229

freedom 29

Freeman, T. 222

Freud, S. 3, 32, 137, 138, 164, 183, 210

Friedman, R. 152

fulfillment 92, 126–7

functional psychotic patients 214–15

Gabbard, G. 107

Gammill, J. 225, 226

genetic reconstructions 220

George 214

giving xii

good 10–11

good objects ix, x, xii, 17, 21, 117; avoidance 21; change 62; ego 33, 47; letting in 12; mental health 18; progress 62; reluctance to accept 7, 11, 16, 18–19; specificity 226–7; symbolization 227

good self 16

goodness phantasy 50

Gorney, J. 32

grandiosity 148, 217, 222

gratitude 128

greed xi, 45, 67–78, 96–7, 182, 239–40;
  ambition 83; analytical relationship
  99–100; anxiety 129; containment
  132–3; death instinct 120; debt 125;
  denying 110; difference 93; ego 90, 91,
  92; elusiveness 91; envy 89–90, 126;
  expelling in concrete way 82; genuine
  80; gratitude 128; guilt 124; hunger x;
  introjective processes 79; masochism
  80, 97, 98, 113, 114; mutating normal
  character development 122;
  narcissism 79, 117, 118, 125; normal
  growth 86; oral 71, 72, 116; oral
  aggression 76; pain 129; perfection 99;
  predatory 113; prey–predator 125;
  projective identification 92, 101, 116;
  protecting objects from 71–2;
  sadism 134; separation 80, 88; social
  relations 70; trust 86–7; unleashing
  71, 73; unrealistic demand 113;
  unrelenting and unstable internal
  experience 92
Grinberg, L. 43, 88, 95, 98, 102, 110,
  146, 152, 153, 156, 162, 199
Grotstein, J. 139, 140, 159
growth 3, 170
guilt 25, 32; analytic progress 59;
  depressive 164; developmental
  differences in experience 162–3; greed
  124; persecutory 110, 121, 164;
  primitive xi, 88, 146, 153; sorrow 4, 5;
  survival 124

hallucinations 217
Harris, A. 118
Heimann, P. 141, 169
here-and-now 220
Hess, N. 164
Hinshelwood, R.D. 79, 118, 197
hope 24, 86
hopelessness 92
Horney, K. 3
hunger x, 7, 38, 76, 82, 83, 85, 88, 91,
  96–7
Hunter, V. 229, 230

ideal object x–xi, 7
ideal self xi, 7
idealization 121
idealized relationships x
identification 213–14
imperfection 69

independence 42
indifference 126
individuation 21
infantile ego: emotional starvation 92;
  pathological object relations 101
infantile omnipotence 222
insight 187
intellectualization 17, 56–7
internal bargains xii, 199, 211–12, 219,
  220
intimacy 92
introjection 79, 207–8, 235–6
Isaacs, S. 157, 211, 222
Israel, P. 152

Jack 154–65
Jim 35–42, 47–8
Joe 121–2
Joseph, B. 224
Judy 28–30

Kaplan, H. 113
Kernberg, O. 4
Kevin 188–9
Klein, M. ix, x, xi, 3, 18, 32, 59, 67–8,
  70, 75, 76, 77, 79, 83, 92, 93, 94–5,
  100, 101, 116, 117, 120, 137–8, 139,
  154, 161, 162, 163, 182, 183, 187, 188,
  190, 196, 197, 200, 204, 207, 208, 224,
  225, 239, 242
knowledge 230–1

Laplanche, J. 210
libido 76
life instinct 93, 123, 138, 200; death
  instinct and 120, 153
Limentani, A. 32
Lipshitz-Phillips, S. 163
Loewald, H. 4
loneliness 100
Lopez, B. 59
loss xi, 5–7, 75, 78, 88, 93, 96, 153, 170,
  230; anxiety 33; primitive 6–7, 34, 43;
  self 236
love 4, 9, 18, 57, 76, 77, 89, 90, 113, 115,
  121

M 10–15, 94–105
Mark 122–9
Maroda, K. 188
Marti 42–6, 48
Mary 130–3, 215

masochism 4, 55–6, 95, 213, 214; death instinct 138; greed 80, 97, 98, 113, 114; paranoid-schizoid prevention strategy 77
masturbation 196
Meltzer, D. 224
mental health 18
metaphysics 156
migraine 108
Money-Kyle, R. 224
mood fluctuations 56
Moser-Ha, H. 118
mothers 7, 8, 9, 10, 15, 17, 19, 22, 28, 34, 36, 40, 50, 55, 60–1, 73, 83, 87, 93, 94, 107, 121–2, 124, 144, 154, 174, 176, 177–8, 183, 196, 197, 204, 205, 209, 214, 216, 219, 230, 231, 232
mourning 18

Nancy 231–5
narcissism 4, 51, 91, 92, 96, 171; death instinct 79, 146, 148; greed 79, 117, 118, 125
needs 97, 186
negative relating 11
negative therapeutic reaction 4
negotiation 92
Nina 107–19
"no-entry" 11

O 7–10
object, confusion with self 93
Olinick, S. 3, 32
opinions 87
oral aggression x, 76
oral deprivation 187, 189
oral greed 71, 72, 116
O'Shaughnessy, E. 21
overweight 70

P 169–75
pain 32, 129
panic 205
paranoid experience 213
paranoid fears 60
paranoid phantasies 4, 6, 20
paranoid-schizoid phantasies 20
paranoid-schizoid position 5–6, 18, 75, 132; internal bargains 212; symbolization 236
paranoid state 70

parents x, 8, 17, 22, 29, 34, 41, 43, 51, 53, 69, 81, 93, 94, 107, 130, 144, 225, 231, 232; see also fathers; mothers
Paul 16–18, 19, 68–78, 184–5
perfection 80, 81, 99, 106
persecution xi, 4, 6–7, 23, 25, 33, 58, 88, 96, 146, 153, 170, 230
persecutory guilt 110, 121, 164
phantasy 157, 211–12
pleasure-avoidance 42
Ponsi, M. 166
Pontalis, J.-B. 210
power struggle 60
pre-depressive position 18
prey–predator 38, 125, 148, 183
progress 62
projective identification x, xii, 5, 11, 17, 30, 38, 43, 71, 95, 171, 172, 198, 199, 212, 214, 242; acting out 155; death instinct 146–7; delusion 219; dynamics 146; greed 92, 101, 116; ideal self xi, 7; interpersonal and intra-psychic 43–4; interpersonal derivatives 188; introjection 207–8; medication request 69–70; multiple functions 202; pathological 21, 40; patient demands 35; self-diagnosis and treatment 103
pseudo-depressive fear 75
psychic barricade 34
psychic retreat 34, 49, 239
psychoanalytic theory 3
psychoanalytic therapy 3; healing 77
psychosis 33, 51
psychotic patients, three phases of treatment 152–4, 167–8

Quinodoz, J. 88, 100, 166

Rabih, M. 59
Racker, H. 111, 129, 130, 188
Randy 175–81
reality 140, 204
rebellion 3
rejection 93, 190
reparation 18, 32, 77
resistance ix, xii, 21
responsibility 23, 25
retaliation 189
revenge xii
Riviere, J. 4–7, 15, 183, 187, 190

romantic relationships 7, 8, 11–12, 84,
   112–14, 115, 142, 195–6, 201–2, 235
Rosenfeld, H. 4, 32, 51, 79, 117, 146,
   161–2, 226
rumination 8, 216
Rusbridger, R. 224

S 142–5
sadism 134, 138, 148, 189
sadness 56
sadomasochism 32, 201, 202, 213
Sandler, J. 188
satisfaction 106
Schachter, J. 165
Schneider, M. 92, 120
Segal, H. 33, 117, 118, 140, 146–7,
   152–3, 157, 162, 197, 208, 209, 224,
   225, 229, 230, 236, 241
self: confusion with object 93; loss 236
self-attack 11
self-destruction xii, 88–9, 143, 144, 148,
   198–9; death instinct 142, 145, 146,
   147, 172
self-harm 88, 95, 196; see also suicide
self-help tapes 103
self-incrimination 69
self-psychology 97
selfish 45
separation 28, 80, 88, 93
sexual abuse 53, 54–5, 83, 87, 94, 107,
   144, 216
sharing 24–5
showdown 51–2
siblings 22–3, 29, 44, 53, 94, 107, 122,
   216
solitude 100
sorrow 4, 5
Spillius, E. 80, 118, 147, 153
splitting x, xi, xii, 11, 17, 25, 40, 111,
   146, 171, 214, 219; symbolization 227,
   236
spokesperson 43, 44, 45–6, 110
standoff ix, xii, 3, 13, 14, 16, 30, 50
Stein, R. 134, 211, 222
Steiner, J. 34, 49, 63, 70, 95, 110, 147,
   155, 238, 239
Stephen, K. 22
story-telling 56–9

success, fear of 3
Sue 52–5, 62
suffering 57
suicide 142, 154, 187, 188
superego 32, 124; death instinct 138–9,
   162, 164; pathological 138
survival guilt 124
survival phantasy 21
symbolization 233, 234, 235; brittle 225;
   containment 229–30; denial xii–xiii;
   depressive 236; destruction 228–30;
   displacement of aggression 224; early
   precursors 224–5; external trauma
   225; free association 229; good object
   227; knowledge 230; paranoid-
   schizoid position 236; splitting 227,
   236, threat 237
Symington, N. 18
symptoms 3

T 195–206
Talon law 212
Temperley, J. 18, 224
Thorner, H. 11
Tony 55–9, 62
transference x, 3, 7, 8, 18, 19, 23, 36, 53,
   57, 58, 60, 71, 81, 85, 107, 109, 123,
   130, 143, 150, 197; all-or-nothing 32;
   anti-growth 4, 6; combative 27;
   coping 35; psychosis 51; standoff ix,
   50
treatment frame 167
trust 86–7, 92

understanding 92

Valenstein, A. 3, 32, 220
Vaquer, F. 211
victims 29, 44, 55, 111

W 149–50
Wallerstein, R. 157
Wanda 185–8
Waska, R. 5, 21, 28, 34, 43, 62, 199,
   230
Williams, G. 11

zombie 109